MW00658305

Life Jacket

A Memoir of a Float Camp Teacher

For Connie -
I hope you enjoy
this book.
Biz Robbins

Biz Robbins

Book Publishers Network

Book Publishers Network
P.O. Box 2256
Bothell • WA • 98041
PH • 425-483-3040
www.bookpublishersnetwork.com

10 9 8 7 6 5 4 3 2 1

Printed in the United States of America

LCCN 2014939255
ISBN 978-1-940598-37-6

This is a true story. The dialog and description of events has been reconstructed as best as possible from my notes, my letters, and my memory, and in some cases has been altered slightly to more dramatically portray the personalities of the individuals involved in the story and the atmosphere surrounding the events depicted in this book. This book contains my perspective of the events that took place and does not necessarily represent the views or opinions of the persons named in the book.

Editor: Julie Scandora
Cover design: Laura Zugzda
Interior design: Leigh Faulkner

Table of Contents

Preface

My husband Don had been dead for two weeks when I returned to Polk Inlet and the floating logging camp that had been our home for the previous six months.

It had been Don's dream to live in Alaska, something I found out three years into our marriage. I thought we were happy, living and working in Colorado Springs. We both had been teaching school, Don in high school and I in elementary, when he said to me one evening, "I'm moving to Alaska. Do you want to come with?" He said he had always wanted to move, but when we fell in love, I kept him in the big city. Our marriage was good, and I wanted to keep it, so I followed him.

We found jobs in logging camps, nestled in various outlying areas in Southeast Alaska, and moved from place to place, ending up in a floating logging camp that required only two teachers. Don fished, he boated, he jet skied, he fixed the pipes when the water froze, he was the principal teacher, and he took the lead in much of our lifestyle.

We were doing just fine when his colon cancer invaded our lives. Don fought it but lost, and I was left alone. I thought I was ready to live my life without him, but in reality, I needed a lot of help.

Polk Inlet School and the floating logging camp that supported it became a place to grieve and a place to heal, the best place I could have been at that time in my life. I found the people in the community to be sympathetic, protective, and helpful as I tried to survive the day-to-day living challenges: getting a new propane tank, thawing frozen water pipes, getting rid of mice, clearing clogged sewer connections, fixing a faulty furnace, and in a way, taking the place of my husband.

In the classroom, the children became my teachers. Day by day, they helped me see the world without sorrow and regret, they valued my efforts to teach, and they offered hope for the future.

And the sense of God's majesty was ever present in the power of the sea, the tides, and the storms, as well as the beauty of the forests and the wild creatures that shared the area with us.

The people and lifestyle of Southeast Alaska's logging communities provided what I needed to grieve, recover, and grow. After Don's death, the float camp became my Life Jacket, keeping my head above water until I learned again to swim on my own.

Beginning the Book

Although I've learned to adapt to whatever role I play in this world ... I can't shake the truth of just wanting to go home ... To a tiny little camp of the biggest people I have ever known ... resting in the palm of the Creator in some quiet bay or inlet ... deep in my memories and untouched by time.

—John Gildersleeve

As I flew high above the water of Southeast Alaska, my mind churned. I had caught a ride with a mail plane, a de Havilland Beaver, as it made its journey from Ketchikan to Thorne Bay. What would I find, I wondered, as I returned to a place where I had lived many years before.

The forested coastline rose sharply from the depths of Clarence Strait. We crossed the deep water to follow Prince of Wales Island northward until we reached our turnoff. Perhaps a bear was lumbering toward a rare spot of grassy shoreline, or dozens of seals were gathered on a sun-heated rock to bathe. A pod of killer whales might be swimming up the strait, their fins gleaming above the water's surface as their spume powdered the air with rainbows. Or maybe eagles were watching from high trees, their white heads visible against the shadows, waiting for the flash of scales to catch their eye. On this beautiful day, the waters sparkling with sunlight, I noticed none of these wonders.

Reassured by the constant rumble of the engine, I stared out the window. I was happy the air held no turbulence; my mind held enough. I was going to Polk Inlet School, where I'd taught for six years—aboard a float camp.

Now the camp was closing down. Living and logging in the ways of the past had become economically and environmentally unsound. Only Marilyn and Richard and their kids were left on board. Richard Gildersleeve, camp manager, Marilyn, his wife, and their children, my former students, Telitha and Josh, were left on board. They stayed behind to make sure closing the camp was done the way its owner, Richard's cousin Keaton Gildersleeve, wanted it to be done.

The camp had moved from one remote location to another many times after I had left, to out-of-the-way places, named Dora Bay, Grace Harbor, and Tolstoi Bay. As I journeyed toward where it was now moored, I knew I had come to say a final goodbye.

We circled above the camp, preparing to land, and I noticed the layout of the buildings was much the same as I'd remembered. On one end was the beautiful cedar home of the Gildersleeves, and on the other, my double-wide trailer next to the school float.

When we taxied up to the airplane float, I half expected Maggie, in charge of the camp commissary, to throw open its door and take the rope on the plane's wing, to pull it in to safety. But instead, Marilyn and Richard walked from their home, down the walkway, to the plane to greet me.

"Hi there," Marilyn smiled. We hugged.

"Are you ready for one last look?" Richard inquired.

I nodded.

We ambled down the walkway, past the camp generator float, still roaring with life, past the empty propane cylinders, past the "apartments," and then past the school.

"Watch your step," Richard warned me as we stepped onto my trailer's float, making a slight dent in the water. A claw-footed bathtub, which served as a planter, was still in place, although its strawberries were long gone, and we carefully scooted around back, avoiding the piles of otter droppings that littered the float.

"Where's the greenhouse?" I asked. I remembered when Sheri (my aide and friend) and I shared its fall harvest: tomatoes, peppers, squash, onions, and other vegetables.

I was told that it had been sold long ago to Sheri, and she continued to use it to grow her own garden. But then she too left, and Marilyn used it.

Richard opened the back door of my former home, which was framed between two stained-glass windows. Inside lay total abandonment. Gone were the green-and-white plastic lawn chairs. No wooden benches or warm fire in the little red woodstove. Into the trailer we went, where only the imprints of the furniture on the carpet remained. No kitchen table, no inviting couch. Only an empty nest—a double-wide trailer with an attached wanigan, a mud room, filled with unseen memories.

"Let's go over to the school," I suggested.

We exited the way we'd arrived, again avoiding the signs of otter, and climbed a set of stairs to the school. As we entered the coatroom, I remembered the life jackets that had once hung there and the rubber boots that had stood underneath them, and I was eager to enter the classroom.

Sadness enveloped me as I walked inside—it was a desolate place. Nowhere was a desk visible. No chairs, no computers. Only maps, lying on the floor, their pages pulled from the rollers and folded untidily.

And books.

They dotted the floor, helter-skelter, punctuated by larger maps and smaller construction-paper piles. A museum of throwaways.

As I shook my head at the waste, my eyes fell upon an old history book. It was one of the high school texts—US history—from the first year that I taught high school students. I remembered having to read like crazy to learn the concepts before presenting them to my students. It was one of the hardest subjects for me, my mind not remembering dates and events very well. Melissa, Evan, Cindy, Brian, and I would sit on the beanbag chairs upstairs and discuss what we had each understood of the readings. Many times, their historical knowledge was much more complete than mine.

I smiled as I thought of Brian … big and tall, a gentle giant among all the smaller and younger students, he was quite the special kid. He had a small green boat, called the Green Weenie, and would frequently give the little kids rides in it after school. He struggled with academics, and his assignments were sometimes surprising to read.

During the early stages of our study, we had reviewed Columbus's trip to the New World and his efforts to get the king and queen to finance his voyage. In answer to the test question asking how Columbus was successful, Brian had written, "He bedded Queen Isabella for six years."

"Are you sure?" I chuckled as we reviewed the test answers the next day. We knew that Columbus had "begged" the queen. All of us got a good laugh—Brian probably the loudest.

That same kid who reversed his ds and gs had a gift for writing. He placed second in the teen division of the Ketchikan Daily News's Christmas story competition that same year. He tried to accomplish whatever he was faced with, and his actions were filled with earnest efforts and good humor.

All those high school kids were special. They were truly my cohorts in the learning process, our discussions going far beyond the textbooks. They were my helpers with the younger children, too. When I was otherwise occupied and a second grader was stumped, one would come to his rescue … quietly, kindly, amazingly.

I think I must have had a wistful smile on my face as Richard's voice broke through my reverie. "Biz, the plane is coming back."

Yes, I could hear it landing and collected my thoughts. I cast another look back on the room before I abandoned the building. Somehow, it seemed warmer than when I'd first arrived.

Richard and I were exiting the school as the pilot strode toward us.

"We're ready to leave." He had his schedule to keep.

So I thanked Richard, walked back down the walkway to the plane, and got aboard. We rose from the water, and I looked back for one last view.

As memories tumbled into my mind, I seized them, clutched them, and couldn't let them go. I found myself needing to record

Polk Inlet Float Camp
Courtesy of Telitha Gildersleeve

them, to let others know of this lifestyle, this community that was my home for six years. A friend called it "an island of humanity in a sea of wilderness," and it was indeed.

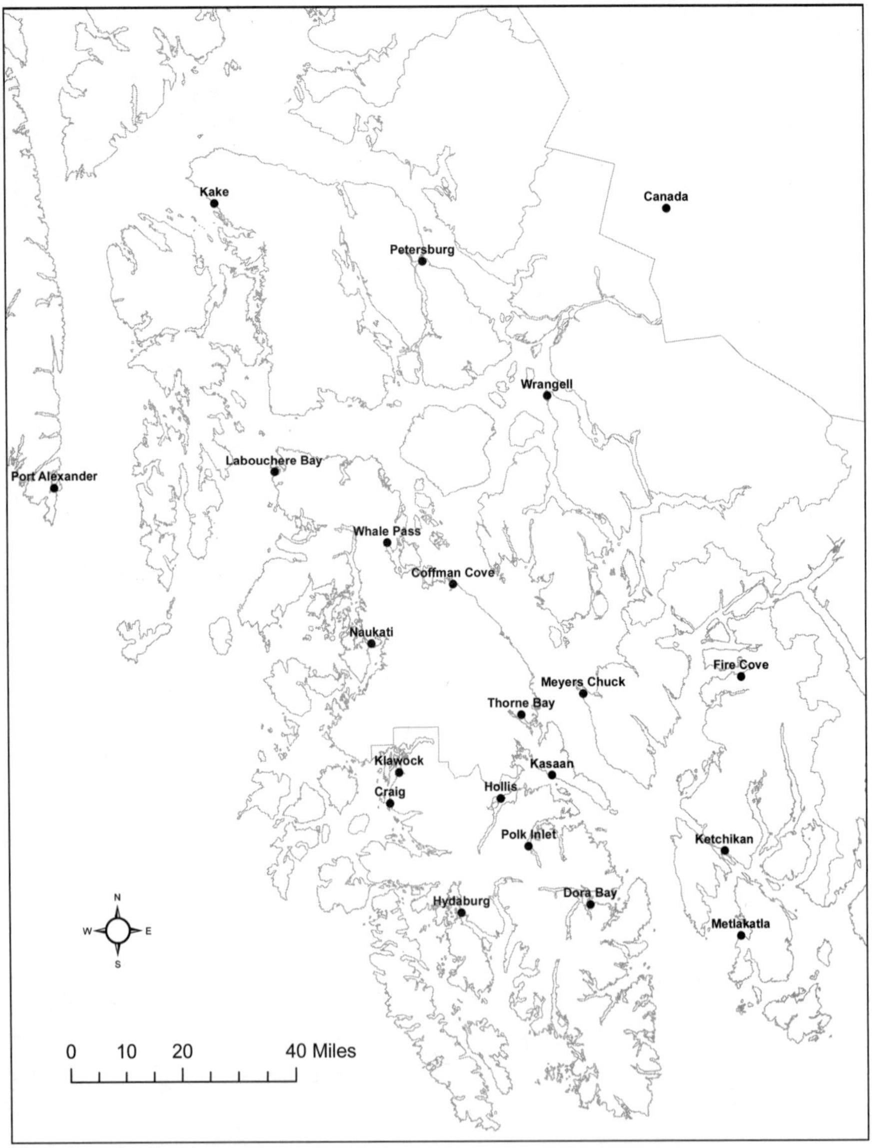

Southeast Alaska

Laurell's Letters

One of the most unexpected gifts I received from my mother-in-law, Laurell, after her death was a box of letters. When my husband, Don, and I moved from Colorado Springs, she lost the Sunday brunch connection with us. We moved to Southeast Alaska, driving north through Wyoming, Idaho, Washington, and British Columbia, finally taking the ferry from Prince Rupert, British Columbia, to Ketchikan, Alaska.

Don was the youngest of Laurell's boys, and she and I had bonded. I was Don's second wife, and she called me her "daughter in love." I thought she was going to miss us, and I vowed to keep cards and letters going her way after our move. I never thought they'd be returned to me, though. But they were. Every letter Don and I had written and every card we had sent were mailed to me after her death.

As I began reading through the letters, I was drawn back to the time we began our residence in this beautiful and sometimes wild state. We were relatively naïve, although we were also relatively old (late thirties, early forties), and some of the thoughts in the letters surprised me. Others brought back reflections of the life we chose to lead, far removed from the schoolteacher jobs we'd held in the big city.

We arrived in Ketchikan on the afternoon of our fifth anniversary, July 31, 1978, and began looking for a home to buy. Available property that we could afford was mighty scarce. We settled on a small forty feet by eight-feet-wide trailer, attached to a living room.

As we were closing the sale of the home, a floatplane, a Grumman Goose, crashed on the north end of Prince of Wales Island, killing all on board. One of those killed was the high school teacher of a logging camp in Labouchere Bay, a place neither of us had ever heard of. However, Don had previously transferred his teaching certificate from Colorado to Alaska and was interviewed for the job to replace that high school teacher shortly after the accident.

The earliest letter Laurell had saved was not from me, but from Don, written from our little trailer.

> *Dear Mom,*
>
> *Enclosed are a few pictures of our house. They make it look a lot better than it is, but it is fairly comfortable and not in need of any drastic immediate repairs (I hope). I am supposed to leave this morning with the superintendent or asst. or both for Labouchere Bay and my new job. Haven't heard from them yet. They really said little about what to take, so am throwing together a little of this and a little of that. Biz is planning to buy some groceries and send them over on the supply boat Friday. Until then, I have soup, peanut butter, and cheese. We have decided to buy some inexpensive dishes and pots and pans, etc. to take over rather than haul a lot of things (particularly breakable things) back and forth. I will have a break from Dec. 16 until Jan. 21. Wrote Dick and suggested we all get together at Friday Harbor sometime during the Christmas holiday. Hope we can do so … The superintendent here called Edison for references. I don't know who he talked to, but he came back quite impressed wondering why I ever left there. Will keep you informed as things develop.*
>
> *Love,*
>
> *Don*

Dick was Don's older brother, at this time living in Friday Harbor, Washington. He and his wife had bought a 104-foot tugboat, the Island Champion, at auction after it had been seized in Alaskan waters, probably with illegal drugs. Although they lived aboard, we had traveled with them the previous summer from Friday Harbor to Namu, British Columbia, up the eastern coast of Vancouver Island. The month-long trip probably confirmed Don's earlier decision to move to Alaska. He enjoyed the water, the fishing, the beauty and grandeur of the outdoors.

However, when we arrived in Ketchikan, all the beauty and grandeur were overrun by people. The summer streets were crowded with fishermen, loggers, and tourists—not the small town he envisioned. Don had told me he was leaving Colorado Springs because it was growing too fast, and he had visited Ketchikan the previous January. Not too much activity goes on in the city in the winter months. However, during August and September, it was all a-bustle.

Don interviewed at the school district's Ketchikan office. When he came home to tell me about the job he'd been offered at Labouchere Bay, he was ecstatic.

"Biz, let me get you a map. Here we are in Ketchikan. Now look to the west—do you see that water? That's Clarence Strait, and on the other side is Prince of Wales Island. If you go across the island and north to the tip, that's where we'll be. There's no road, so we'll have to fly until I can get my boat."

I had a few questions. Like, how do we get our things? Can we shop? What will we live in? How far away is it?

"Well, the superintendent told me it's about a hundred miles away by air, and the school plane takes about an hour to get there."

The school district had its own pilot, Jim Webster, who flew a Cessna 185 floatplane, called The Bug Eye. We wouldn't be able to use the school plane, though, as it was for the itinerants. They, music teachers, a kindergarten teacher, and special ed. teachers, were based in Ketchikan as were the administrators and the support personnel.

Another reason Don had wanted to leave Colorado Springs was that he often didn't agree with his previous administration's decisions. A big draw to this new job was that the superintendent was a hundred miles away—available only through marine radio or a floatplane visit. "Biz, I can do my own thing there. The high school programs are just developing, and I can help design them. That's what I was told.

"Although I may fly in on the school plane for an occasional high school meeting, you won't be able to use it. We'll have to fly in and out of Ketchikan commercially, and we'll order our groceries from the stores in town. They will put our order on a boat that'll arrive on Friday nights where we are."

His voice quivered with enthusiasm and excitement as he answered every question I asked. He reinforced the belief I held. He would be happy here, and thus far in our marriage, whenever he was happy, so was I.

So Don left, full of optimism with his new job, and I stayed behind to close on the house and to order him some groceries.

The next letter that Laurell saved, Don had also written. I wasn't out there yet, and he'd been in his new job a week and a half. He told his mom much of what he thought she'd want to know.

9-17-78

Dear Mom,

I've been in Labouchere Bay 1½ weeks now. Things are beginning to fall into place nicely. I'm anxious for Biz to arrive. Hope it will be soon. We have a nice little house to live in—two rooms and a bath. One large room is the living room, kitchen, and utility room. It has a washer and dryer furnished, which is nice.

This is a typical lumber camp. (I guess.) It's not very attractive, but was not intended to be. Almost all the living quarters are trailers. Ours and several others have a patch of grass and some flowers. The rest of the place is rocks—big and little. The people next door call it Alcatraz for that reason. Everyone is very friendly. The students are nice kids—I have 12 in the high school. The camp usually closes down in October and reopens in the spring. Some of the families stay here, but a lot leave.

During this time, the school population may go down quite a bit. Received a note from Dick. School is out on Dec. 15, so we will be there? We will probably spend a few days in Ketchikan and go to Seattle on the ferry. Will see you there whenever.

The weather here, so far, has been much like Ketchikan. Fall is in the air. It's beginning to get quite nippy at night. The big deal here is Friday evening when the supply boat arrives and Saturday when there is a movie in the company recreation room. Last night they showed a Walt Disney film. Not many of the logging crew showed. Last week the film was Magnum Force with Clint Eastwood, and the place was packed.

It's quiet here in camp. The logging is done 20-25 miles away. The basic activity right here is when the trucks arrive with a load. They are banded together and dumped in the bay where they are collected into a large raft that will eventually be towed to the pulp mill in Ketchikan.

I ordered my first groceries by mail this week. Had to estimate prices a lot. I send the order with a check to a grocery in Ketchikan. They pack the order and deliver it to the transportation company for delivery here on Friday. The store charges a 7% service charge and freight is about $5.00 per 100 pounds, so the higher prices in Ketchikan are even higher out here. This is our only real expense though. The school district pays the rent on our house (which includes utilities). The only place to spend a little money here is at the company commissary which stocks a few items—soap, candy, detergent, soda pop, etc.

There is no phone and no television. We can call out if we can get to Point Baker, about 15 minutes away by boat. If I get over there, I will call you—collect. I will apparently be going into Ketchikan about one day a month at school district expense for small high school conferences. That will be a nice change of pace. The school district takes in half of southeastern Alaska except for the larger towns. It operates schools at 14 locations with 32 teachers and about 10 administrative staff including a special ed and music teacher that travel around to all the schools. Flying here and there is a way of life here. Float planes fly in and out of here 5–10 times a day. There is regular service by one small airline. The rest are charter operations. The school district has its own plane and pilot.

The school district has tickets to see the King Tut exhibit in Seattle on Oct. 21, but we are not going. It had been planned, but too many problems arose. The logistics and cost of flying 21 kids and three adults out of here were huge—cost for trip $5000–6000. The evening I arrived, there was a bake sale to raise money for the trip that netted over $2300. It was the wildest thing I ever saw. The camp manager spent $500–$600. One plate of fudge went for $105. I got into it, but bought several of the cheaper items—two dozen chocolate chip cookies and a cake for $41. A lot of the bidders were having fun bidding against one another. They all make big money, so guess they could afford it.

This is the first year for the high school program in these remote camps. The students are still using correspondence courses, but have access now to reference materials and a teacher. They also have the vocational courses. Next year, the idea is to phase in a regular curriculum with correspondence as a supplement. I will be teaching a required course later this year on Alaska history. Received the materials this week and have started to read. This is something I had wanted to do eventually, so it worked out fine.

The history of Alaska is quite fascinating. From the reading and some contacts with people so far, I have discovered an interesting thing. Some people that work here don't maintain an official residence in Alaska. Many more say they will go back home when they retire. Alaska has many problems—perhaps part of the problem is the people themselves. Anyway, I'm sure glad we came. The southeastern part is immense and quite wild and, yet, this part of Alaska is tiny compared to all that lies north. It may be that the sheer size and remoteness cause some discomfort for people and will not allow them to identify with this state.

Biz is buying plates and pots and pans through Sears to use here. One of these days I'm going to buy a larger boat—one with sleeping space, head, and galley that we can do a lot of traveling with—and the dishes, etc. we can use in the boat. Our plan at Christmas time is to head back to Colorado from Seattle. School here doesn't take up again until Jan. 22, so we will have time to arrange shipment of our things and haul the Model A up. We will probably sell the washer, dryer, freezer, and perhaps, one of the beds in Colorado Springs. We don't have room for the bed, we have the other appliances already in the house, and shipping costs are enormous. All our moving expenses are tax deductible, so that will help some.

Salaries are something else in Alaska. When the pipeline was being built, wages of $1000-1500 per week were common. I heard one logger here say his deductions for one month were $1200 so his gross had to be high. My work year is 185 days which figures out to approximately $144 per day in wages I'm receiving.

A lot of the costs here are not much higher—others are huge. The taxes on the house we are buying are $135 per year—fire insurance is $365. This is almost the reverse of costs in Colorado Springs. A great deal of cost is involved in shipping charges.

There is really very little industry in Alaska. Most ships go back to Seattle empty or nearly so—therefore, we pay essentially round trip cost for everything brought in.

There is something to be said for government subsidies, especially when one benefits directly. When we order from Sears, they mail everything that can be mailed. This cuts down a lot on cost with the lower cost of mailing over private transport.

Will fill you in more at Christmas. The day to day routine is much like anywhere else, but there is something here that makes the atmosphere pretty special and exciting.

Love,

Don

While Don spent September and the first part of October in Labouchere Bay, I was alone with our two miniature poodles, living in the small trailer that we'd bought. Every day I'd drive Don's huge International Travelall down the highway to the town post office, praying that somebody had sent us some mail. I hated driving that rig as it was so large, especially compared to the small Fiat Spider convertible that we'd sold before moving, and Ketchikan's roads were much narrower than those we'd left. My trips to town were short but predictable. After I gathered whatever catalogs had been in our box, I drove back to our home, unless it was a Wednesday.

That was the day that the new grocery ads were in the paper. I'd scour them closely and make a list of what I might need, which was very little now that I lived alone. Then, after the post office, I'd drive a few blocks more to Seamart grocery, parking where I could drive forward when leaving, and wander through their aisles picking up the few items I'd marked. Meat that cost under two dollars a pound usually headed the list, but I picked up a few veggies and milk, as well as coffee, cigarettes, and dog food. Then I'd drive through the narrow main street to the other side of town, hoping that Tatsuda's grocery parking lot was fairly empty. It was a smaller store and had a tighter lot with smaller spaces for parking. It didn't take long to get what I wanted. Although I hoped somebody would speak to me, often the only words I heard were from the checker as I was leaving.

I was lonely. I also found the unknown scary and angry. The thunder and lightning of the Colorado foothills had little prepared me for the storms in Ketchikan. The night of the first torrent of rain that accompanied gale-force winds saw me huddled in bed with the dogs. I tried to ignore the bangs and thuds of the unknown outside, and the next morning, with the storm still raging, the power went out. I couldn't even sew.

Usually, I sewed a lot. I'd brought several boxes of fabric that I'd purchased before we left, as well as patterns for jackets and shirts and dresses and pants. I sewed many of my own clothes when I taught in Colorado, and it was a hobby I enjoyed. In Colorado, I sewed some evenings and on weekends. Here I sewed daily. Every day, every night, trying to use up the time that I found so heavy on my hands with something positive.

The electricity went out twice that day. Not only couldn't I sew, but I also couldn't watch TV. I tried to read, but even that felt foreign. When I went outside with the dogs, the gate was flapping in the wind, banging against the fence, as its latch had broken. I had to accompany the dogs out every time they had to go, for I didn't want them getting loose and running onto the highway that our property abutted. Soaked and steamy, I wondered many times during that day why I had accepted Don's invitation to accompany him to Alaska, even though he didn't realize he would be leaving me alone in the storm. Better times seemed far removed, especially when I couldn't sew. So I wrote letters. I filled that southeaster with activity that I hoped would quiet my unease.

Eventually, as our storms do, this one abated, and the sun eventually shone on my world again. However, I continued to write.

I wrote a lot. I bought post cards and sent them to all the former students who'd given me their addresses. I wrote letters to everyone in my address book, telling them of our new surroundings, asking them to let me know how they were, hoping a letter would show up every now and then in the mail. Very few ever did. Don's mom wrote. So did mine. Maybe once a week. Of course Don's letters to me were of primary importance. However, his came only once a week or so, too, and when I was hungry for company and conversations, these communications seemed a poor substitute.

In early October, though, I opened one letter that filled me with excited anticipation. I'm sure the dogs thought I was crazy when I returned from my daily visit to town and began talking to them.

"Tammy, Shadow, guess what?"

They didn't answer.

"Your daddy has sent for us." I grabbed Tammy's forelegs and danced around the living room with her. "He's coming to get us next week. Are you excited?"

Shadow seemed puzzled as he just sat and watched us. So, I went to him and danced with him, too. "We have to get ready for a plane ride. We're going to all be together!"

Don had to fly in to Ketchikan for a "small high school" meeting where all the high school teachers in the district were gathering to discuss their curriculum and enrollments. His trip into town would be financed by the school district.

The trip out was another issue. We wouldn't have to charter a plane, as his trip coincided with a family's decision to leave camp. With three teenagers, who were also Don's students, and two dogs and their personal possessions, they needed a Grumman Goose, which was the largest floatplane available. We could pay seat fare for the trip out there and have plenty of room for our belongings and the dogs.

***

Don and I watched as a crew loaded the boxes we'd packed onto the Grumman Goose that awaited us at the Ketchikan dock. They packed a couple dozen boxes, filled with groceries, clothing, and sundries to provide us for several months, before we and our two small poodles climbed aboard. Our freight occupied but a small space on that plane. Two long benches lined both sides of the plane's body, and we, combined with our possessions, left room for at least a dozen more people.

We settled in, each of us holding a dog on our lap, and waited for takeoff. The huge engines revved up, and soon we were skimming across the water, throwing rainbow-laden water roostertails behind us, the noise growing louder and louder until we were airborne and the pilot pulled back on the throttle.

I looked out the window. Ketchikan spread below me, truly a city several miles long and one or two blocks wide, the houses stretching along the shore of the island we were leaving. We flew north and then west, across Clarence Strait, a large expanse of water that I was to find on stormy days a challenge to cross. But this day was calm and sunny, and we flew across it with nary a bump.

We reached Prince of Wales Island and began our ascent. As the plane climbed higher, tree-covered mountains filled my view. Streams cut through the passes, and narrow roads snaked along the hillsides leading to patches of a lighter green color indicating where loggers had been. Hilltop followed hilltop as the plane glided high above this wilderness. We flew up to a snow-capped rocky peak that I later learned was Mount Calder, hugged its rough ledges, and then began our descent to land in Labouchere Bay.

When the dock came into view, I saw that it was filled with people. Teeming, actually.

"Wow!" I said. "What a reception!"

"They're not here for us," Don said. "Remember what I told you? The family down there with all the suitcases is leaving, and people here really hate to see them go. This gathering's for them."

Don and I were met, and our belongings off-loaded after we left the plane. The family's possessions were then stowed aboard as they exchanged hugs and handshakes before boarding themselves. As the plane roared off, we climbed into a pickup where our boxes filled the truck bed. The camp boss drove us up the ramp and down the winding road back to camp, depositing us in front of a little building. We hauled our boxes to the front door and waved goodbye as the truck left.

Labouchere Bay. The school is the larger building toward the left.
Courtesy of Rick and Georgia Brown

Labouchere Bay

"Welcome home," Don said.

It was, as Don had said, "a nice little place." I thought it was much nicer than the place we had bought in Ketchikan. That could have been because we were together and I didn't have to worry about water damage in the kitchen, under the calendar, or the water pump or the lonely bumps in the night. The great room held a couch and an easy chair, a kitchen table and several wooden chairs, and washer and dryer.

The bathroom was rather unfinished. While some of the walls were lined with paneling of one sort or another, dark and light, there was a spot near the door that had nothing but plywood. It seemed as if whoever had put the place together had just run out of materials.

The house was not very large, but it was square, which was pleasing after the month I'd spent alone in a narrow trailer. So was the togetherness.

The dogs loved the little spot of lawn between the front door and the road, but since it wasn't a fenced area, I usually accompanied them so they wouldn't go exploring.

That evening, we were invited to Myrtle's trailer for dinner. Myrtle was the principal teacher, teaching grades four through eight.

She was also a devout Adventist, seriously celebrating the Sabbath on Saturday. She did not eat meat.

JoAnn, the teacher of grades one through three, also came to dinner. She brought the "you know what," the name we called the chicken, roast, turkey, or whatever meat was part of the ensuing teacher potluck dinners.

That gathering was a lovely introduction to the teaching situation there. While the two women were congenial and we eventually became friends, I was amazed at the differences in our philosophies of education. When I mentioned it to Don later, at home, he remarked that it was a good thing he taught in a different building.

JoAnn and Myrtle shared a school trailer on the same level of the camp as our housing. All they had to do in the mornings was to walk a few steps toward the bay and climb up some stairs. They were then in their shared classroom—JoAnn and her students sat at one end, and Myrtle and her students at the other. Entering the doorway, one could not escape noticing a sign on the opposite wall: SILENCE IS GOLDEN. I remember thinking, "Hmph. These are kids!"

Don had to walk across the street from the elementary school to get to the much smaller trailer that was his classroom. He and his high schoolers enjoyed the freedom away from the ladies, as some revelry was encouraged. He had a wry sense of humor and, every morning, placed some funny thought on his blackboard. One of my pleasures was sharing it with him over breakfast—his favorites came from a book of collected quotes by Laurence Peters. For example:

> *Speak when you are angry--and you will make the best speech you'll ever regret.*
> *Against logic there is no armor like ignorance.*
> *If a cluttered desk is the sign of a cluttered mind, what is the significance of a clean desk?*

His students really enjoyed starting the day with a chuckle, but these could also form a good springboard for discussion and critical thinking.

Although Don and the rest of the school population did not go to the King Tut exhibit in Seattle, they did take a field trip to Juneau. A week after I arrived, I was again left alone with the dogs.

However, this time, I was befriended by a young neighbor, Gail, who at twenty-one had seen more of Alaska and life than I would probably ever experience. It was with her that I wandered down to the shore, happy that the last purchase before leaving Ketchikan had been XtraTufs, the brown rubber boot that it seemed everyone wore. They had sturdy bottoms, needed to tread the rocky shale layers that had eroded unevenly and stuck up under our feet. Every now and then, a vein of white quartz wove through the shale, creating an interesting lined pattern.

When the tide was out, Gail encouraged me to find tidal pools, poking under rocks and watching what swam, crawled, or slithered out from under them. Crabs, fish, worms, all were to be found in those pools. And starfish, not the five-armed yellow kind but purple and orange varieties with way more arms. Clams and their shells also littered the beach. I was particularly enamored with some small pink empty shells and collected them.

We walked the dirt roads around camp, and she pointed out the different types of ferns, the edible and inedible mushrooms, the trees, the plants. While I didn't pay much attention to all she was telling me, I found a few of the plants that held my interest. I collected and pressed some of the ferns that grew along the roadway. She showed me a plant called Labrador tea, told me I could pick its leaves, dry them in the oven, and make some tea. This I did, too. I was happy to have somebody to walk and to talk with, and the nights alone were much cheerier, even without a TV.

I had purchased a portable sewing machine, and this was the perfect time to unpack it. Some corduroy fabric and a pattern nestled in one of our boxes. When I unearthed them, I cut out and sewed a pair of slacks for myself during the week Don was gone.

Sue Jones, a small Korean lady who lived at the top of the hill on the way to the office, became a friend, too. She and her husband, Ron, a truck driver, lived in a teeny little trailer that they'd purchased. They'd sent it to the camp on a barge along with a huge pickup truck that Ron used to drive around the country on the company's day off. The truck was longer than their little home. Evidently there wasn't a trailer to rent when Ron was hired, and this was the solution that allowed him to bring his wife along. They also had a white toy poodle, named Winkie, that followed Sue wherever she went—except when she came to see me. I don't think she wanted to expose her sweet dog to my two.

Sue also wanted me to sew for her. During the days when our husbands were gone, she'd come over, and I'd fashion patterns out of paper bags and measure them to her body, adjusting them and then placing them over the fabric to cut out. We made dates for "fittings," and I'd pin the vest and pants pieces on her before making the seams. When the outfit was completed, it fit her well enough that she wore it often. I was a successful seamstress.

I wasn't such a successful grocery-orderer, though. It was a challenge to predict what food we might want a couple of days before the supply boat arrived on Friday nights. We had to send in our next order before the one we waited for came in. One never knew if the grocer had the items we ordered in stock or if the tomatoes would be edible. In the winter, we couldn't even be sure the supply boat would make it through to us.

When I first arrived at camp, I found myself making banana bread from all the bananas going bad in Don's cupboard. Two heads of lettuce were in the fridge, too, and I'd just ordered another. Drat! I hoped I would learn in time. But just in case, I wondered what I could make in the house so we'd have fresh produce available if the boat didn't arrive. I decided to sprout mung beans. The first batch was so prolific I didn't know what to do with them all. There was only so much stir-fry and egg foo yung that Don would stomach at one time. Sue was kind enough to take the overload off my hands.

It was at this time that I began practicing having too much on the shelves instead of too little. We had a good lesson when the King's Music came to camp that fall. This was a trio—a man who played the lute, a man who played the recorder, and a lady soprano. They were part of the Arts in Alaska program, where the state sent various artists to outlying villages to be used in the school and to give concerts/performances for the community.

As for housing guests for the school, all the men had to stay with us, no matter that Myrtle's trailer had three bedrooms and JoAnn's two; no men crossed their thresholds for an overnight stay. Of this performing trio, two were men, and we had a sofa bed for them to share. They were good sports about it, and earlier, when I had realized that we'd have guests fairly often, I'd made a curtain. Using fabric I'd bought for this purpose, I just sewed a hem at the top. Don strung a wire from one wall to the other and threaded it through the curtain before attaching it securely to the walls of our big room. This way, our guests could have a bit of privacy, separated from the kitchen area.

While this trio was in camp, the first snow fell. Visibility was nil, and no planes flew. For three days, the group was stranded there, and one of my greatest gifts was the performances the two guys gave for Don and me in our home during the evenings. I especially enjoyed the lute solos.

However, one of my greatest lessons in ordering supplies came when we ran out of toilet paper. And bread. Before the guys left, Don was knocking door to door, asking if we could borrow any TP. I was making the next order, hoping that the snow didn't keep the boat away and we could get it replaced soon. From then on, the little cupboard under the bathroom sink was filled with toilet paper, as was a corner in our bedroom closet. I also learned about the gracious generosity of our neighbors. We had no trouble finding people who would loan us what we needed.

It was not difficult, then, for me to ask Don to go door to door to see if anyone drank Constant Comment tea. It came in a nice box, and I wanted to use the empty boxes for Christmas gifts to send to our friends and family south.

He managed to bring back a few empty containers, and I spray-painted them black. When the paint had dried, I used the ferns and small shells I'd collected to decorate the side of the box, using plenty of glue. Then I filled them with Labrador tea. I lettered small tags to accompany them—With love, from Alaska.

One afternoon Don came home from school waving a piece of paper. "Here, Biz," he said. "You really oughta apply for this."

He knew that I wanted to get back in the classroom and that I felt I could be more effective in the kids' lives than some of the teachers I'd seen. It was impossible at this particular time to get a teaching job since there were no vacancies.

However, there was an opening for a special education aide.

"Who would I be working under?" I wanted to know.

"Myrtle and the special ed. itinerant," he told me. "She's the principal teacher, and I believe the lady from town, Helen Pope, will provide the program." He thought for a minute and then reassured me. "You won't have to teach in either school building for there's really no room. You'll have to conduct lessons here at home."

It didn't take me long to fill out the application, and Don ran it right over to Myrtle, who was working late in the school.

When he came back, he said, "Myrtle says there should be no trouble hiring you. You are the most qualified of all the applicants. I don't even know if she had any others to consider. The camp knows you're the best around."

He smiled, gave me a kiss, and left.

I don't know exactly where he spent the hour or two after school before he came home. He was always roaming around camp, stopping by the office to see how things were, if he needed to be aware of anything, trying to meet people and expand his knowledge of the area. He wanted to know the secrets of the sea, to harvest its offerings of fish, shrimp, crab, and more fish. Eventually, we would get a boat, and he would spend time on it. But in the meantime, he was making friends and checking out future opportunities.

I hoped my future opportunities would include teaching with Don, as he was so obviously satisfied and happy with his position at Labouchere Bay.

Shortly after I applied, I was given the special education aide position and assigned three students. Jim, the ninth grader, needed lots of special help and was assigned to me for three hours a day. The other two, Frances and Brandon, were Myrtle's students, and they walked over to my house to spend an hour with me, individually, every day. Five hours of every weekday were taken up with these special children.

Working with them sure cut down on my strolls on the beach and walks in the woods.

I remember Frances having trouble with her addition tables, and Myrtle wanted me to practice them with her. So I spent a part of every meeting doing just that, flashing her cards of combinations and waiting until she told me the correct answer. I encouraged her to use her fingers to help her figure out the right sum.

She did that in class one day, and I felt the first sting of Myrtle's wrath. "She's supposed to LEARN them, not count them," I was told.

"But, Myrtle," I tried to reason, "why else would have God given us ten fingers if not to help us with math?"

"Hmph." She stomped off.

I still believe that giving kids concrete examples for every math algorithm is the best way for them to learn, to see relationships between and among numbers, to appreciate their beauty and predictability. Maybe I told Frances to hide her fingers under her desk when she was under Myrtle's watchful eye. I know I didn't tell her not to use them.

When Thanksgiving arrived, Jim and his family moved away, and a new student replaced him. This was Sue Jones, who had petitioned my help in learning better English. For an hour a day, we practiced sounds, learned words, fashioned sentences, and spoke the language correctly. She was a willing student, but I never noticed any changes when she spoke around her husband. However, she became a more proficient speaker in my home that hour every day.

For her benefit, I had tacked a chart to my front door. It showed the alphabet and a picture, mostly animals, for every letter: an apple, a bear, a cat, a dog, and so on. It surprised me one day when Sue stared thoughtfully at that chart and then told me, "I thought that was a bad word."

"What? I don't understand what you mean."

"Well, that picture ..." She got up from the table and walked over and pointed to the F. It had a picture of a fox.

I chuckled, and we had a discussion about the difference between the short o and short u vowels, sounds her language didn't have. We also discussed what a fox was, for she had never seen one. Soon she was chuckling too.

That fall was a wondrous time in my life. Learning about and sharing this particular Alaskan lifestyle with my husband brought us closer together. When George Estrella, a jeweler and silversmith, was sent out once a week to conduct classes for several weeks, we joined the other interested adults who gathered in the school in the evenings. We made jewelry—I remember some pierced earrings that I gave to my cousin that Christmas, and I still have my first copper practice plate: a pendant with cattails cut through it. I also wear the silver oval, overlaid with a similar shape split in a curvy path, another pendant that I fashioned in his class.

George also brought me food ideas. One week he gave me my first taste of Dungeness crab, its buttery goodness still a favorite of mine. I remember he made a stir-fried dish—carrots, broccoli, onion, peppers, and other brightly colored vegetables nested in a bed of noodles. It tasted so good that I tried to replicate it. The first time, Don complimented me. "Close," he said. The second and third time it was close too. It probably still is … close.

We had ordered a radio from Sears, along with our dishes and pots and pans. While our kitchen was well stocked, we never did receive that radio, and our evenings were filled with silence, or opportunities, rather, for reading good books—Don on the chair and I on the couch—or conversations about how our days had gone and what we wanted to plan for the future or private concerts from the musicians who came to visit, especially from all the males who stayed with us. Those artists, too, offered interesting looks on the world that seemed so far away from us then.

When a visiting tenor came up from Portland, Oregon, as one of Alaska's Artists in Residence, part of our evening conversation entailed discovering people we mutually knew. Don watched as he and I tried to figure out how we could possibly have somebody in common. I had lived in Minnesota and Colorado. He had lived in places other than Portland, too. We sifted through our lives, sharing what we were doing when, from childhood on, and finally we found somebody we both knew. Sort of. The person we discovered was the mother of a fifth grader I'd had the previous year in Colorado Springs. She had divorced, and while her son lived with his father in Colorado, she'd moved to Oregon. She was a publicist with the same company as the tenor's. It is a small world.

We had mentioned trying to get a radio from Sears to our friends, Sue and Ron, and one night, they came over to help us. We heard them arrive in Ron's big pickup and went outside to greet them. They'd brought their eight-track player and several music cassettes they thought we'd really enjoy. They weren't going to leave the items with us; they were going to stay there and help us have fun. They'd even brought the whiskey.

That evening, I was introduced to country and western music in a way I'd never expected. Never one of my favorite musical genres, it didn't sound so bad after a couple of whiskey-and-7-Ups. We got out the cards, sat around the table, and played pinochle while the twangy melancholy of the music drifted over us all. When they chugged off, much later, with their machine, music, and much emptier bottle, Don and I shook our heads and headed off to bed. Snuggled in our blankets, we agreed that moving to Lab Bay had been a good thing. We'd received blessings we had never even imagined.

***

As the snow came and went and the calendar pages turned, we shared Thanksgiving dinner with Myrtle and JoAnn. This time it was our turn to bring the "you know what" (turkey). We practiced for the Christmas program, and I helped the elementary students make illustrations to accompany "'Twas the Night before Christmas." After the program was over, school was ready to vacation, and so Don and I left camp for Ketchikan.

In what was to become routine travel, we boarded a floatplane and flew back across the island to Ketchikan. On that trip, we found ourselves with a few problems in our trailer. From a little reservoir created by somebody's homemade dam, a hose stretched across the neighbor's back yard and entered our back room to the water pump. The water came from a creek, and while we'd had no problems with it the few weeks we'd lived there, the ice cubes had brown centers, and sometimes our glasses looked as if we were drinking ginger ale. The water didn't stain our laundry, and it flushed the toilet just fine. We were used to the special coloring, but now, the water had frozen up. There was no heat tape wound around the hose, as Don would later find provided a solution to this problem, so we "roughed it."

Don went next door with a few pails to bring back water for flushing and washing, and the next day we bought some bottled water at the store, along with several lengths of heat tape.

Don hadn't stocked much wood either, so the wood stove wasn't pushing heat into the other parts of the trailer. We hauled our mattress in front of the stove, plugged in our electric blanket, and spent our nights with the dogs cozied up to our bodies, enjoying the warmth they created. The next day, we purchased a small electric heater.

So we had left more comfortable surroundings out at camp than we'd found in our home, but one thing was better. I'd sure missed TV.

***

Soon we were on the ferry to Prince Rupert, British Columbia, driving toward Colorado and Laurell—to spend Christmas and retrieve the rest of Don's toys. While we had driven north on our way to Ketchikan the previous July, we had towed the toy Don thought he would enjoy the most: his tri-hulled boat. We had honeymooned on that boat five years earlier, driving to Yellowstone Park and boat camping on Yellowstone Lake. Don also used it in Colorado for waterskiing on the Pueblo Reservoir. I don't think he realized that the tri-hull design was not intended for the Alaskan waters he wanted to explore, so shortly after he was hired to teach in Labouchere Bay, he traded his tri-hull for a smaller boat, one that had only one V instead of three. He planned to learn the waters in that boat and then move up to a larger model as his knowledge base grew.

However, he'd left the other toy, a 1932 Model A Roadster, in storage in Colorado Springs. Now that we had a home—and a carport—he wanted to continue the restoration that had been his at-home hobby for the previous two years. Knowing that he'd eventually be pulling it to Alaska, he'd had a trailer custom made, and he was eager to have it moved.

It's a long drive from Prince Rupert to Colorado Springs in good weather, but in the winter, the weather is not always pleasant. On our way south, we encountered a few icy patches, especially on the narrow winding one-hundred-mile road that followed the Skeena River between Prince Rupert and Terrace but had no other road hazards or major storms on our way to Colorado.

However, when we returned in January, our good luck ran out. We had driven through Wyoming, Idaho, and much of Oregon when snow began to fly. Soon it was swirling, big flakes twisting in front of our headlights, quickly covering the freeway. Don began to feel the trailer fishtail and became concerned.

"I wonder when the snow's gonna end," he grumbled.

He drove slower and slower, looking for a town ahead.

"What are we close to?" he asked me.

"The Dalles."

He began looking for an exit sign that would lead us into the city. We turned off as soon as he found it and looked for a place to stay the night.

We found a motel, checked in, and Don asked about weather conditions. The front desk clerk said they were filling up fast because people were turning around, having trouble making it over the pass ahead. He also told us that the blizzard was predicted to rage for a few more days.

"Biz, I can't take that trailer on slick roads, especially on mountain grades," Don told me later. "I'm going to try to find a place where we can leave it."

He was eager to move on, having been contacted while we were at Laurell's by the school district. His school building had burned down right after Christmas and was declared a total loss. The superintendent wanted him to get out to camp as soon as he could to start assessing the damage and plan for the ensuing semester.

The next day, Don unhitched the trailer with his Model A, leaving it in a storage unit in the city, and determined we should try to make it over the pass.

"It's sure to be better once we get to Portland and head north. But we still don't know what we'll reach before we get back to the ferry." He wanted to travel miles while the miles could be traveled, feeling that every hour was important. However, our safety was important, too.

When we reached the foot of the pass, the snow plows were in full force. They had cleaned the highway but had to make sweep after sweep as the snow still fell. Chains were required. Don pulled off to the side of the road, noting that the semis seemed to be traveling with ease, although at a slow speed. He attached the chains, waited until another of those huge trucks began its ascent up the pass, and settled in behind it. Don's conversation stilled as his hands gripped the steering wheel, and he concentrated entirely on the task at hand. Although there were moments I caught my breath when I felt the car skid, he seemed to be driving with less concern. We did make it over the pass and down to Portland safely. However, Don wondered when he'd see his Model A again.

We eventually arrived in Ketchikan, picked up our dogs from their babysitter's, and arranged for a floatplane trip back to Labouchere Bay.

1-21-79

Dear Mom,

We are back in Labouchere Bay—finally. The trip from Colorado Springs seemed to last forever. Your saying—All's well that ends—is very applicable to that trip. As you can discern in the photo the high school was a total loss. Everything burned and completely. We are cleaning out the recreation hall at the road construction camp and will use it for the remainder of the school year. Having so few students is a blessing. I will need to reconstruct their records—much from memory. I had their records up to date when I left, so I don't think it will be a big problem.

Our mail may be very slow coming and going after February 1. The air taxi outfit that serves this area may be out of business. If that occurs our mail will come and go on the supply boat, which comes once every two weeks.

JoAnn (she teaches grades 1-3) arrived back with her husband. He was originally to have been the high school teacher, but had a back operation and had hoped to obtain medical retirement. His doctor would not okay it. This does not jeopardize my job.

The school district immediately re-ordered all school books. They are being shipped air freight, so we should have them fairly soon.

I'm going to apply for a hand troller permit for commercial fishing. In two years these permits will be restricted so I figured I'd get in while I can. I can also supplement our income that way.

Our visit was so enjoyable. I hope we didn't leave you with too much food that it might spoil before you can use it up. Thank you for a lovely stay and the monetary help. If you want to mail me the oilers and lock—okay—although don't bother if you don't want to. If there is anything there you can use, keep it. Give everything else to anyone else you know that can use it.

Take care and all our love.

Don

We were now into the new year, and Don was in a new building. He had to wend his way up the hill, past Ron and Sue's trailer, past the logging camp office, and into the construction camp's territory to get to its recreation center, his new classroom. It was a trailer that had contained a pool table and several chairs, but now, the district was moving tables and chairs and boards into it, shaping it into a makeshift classroom.

Don and his students met every day there, and I used the facility during the evening. I had left Colorado with a couple of hobbies other than sewing, and I wanted to share them. The evenings were often long, and people tired of reading books. First, I thought I might share calligraphy. Don helped me fashion a flyer that would ask people if they wanted to learn how to do this fancy lettering.

Imagine my surprise when over twenty responded. And not all of them were adults. Many of the elementary and secondary students wanted to learn the skill as well, so Don found more chairs to haul up the hill. Parents supported their children in this endeavor, and I collected enough money to order ink, paper, and a set of pen points for each student. When they arrived, our classes began.

We met once a week, and in-between our meetings, the students were supposed to practice what I'd showed them. We learned how to line the paper depending on the width of the pen, how to hold it at a forty-five-degree angle, and practiced a simple italic print with felt markers to begin. Then we advanced to other types of writing: Old English, Roundhand, Uncial, Bookhand, and others. Each had its particular slant and letter formation, and some were easier than others. When I ran out of ideas, our class stopped.

But people kept lettering. "For Sale" signs on the company bulletin board were more carefully scripted, and one student offered to letter the graduation programs that year. Folks made birthday cards with more skill and enthusiasm, too, when they didn't have any store-bought ones on hand. Even as late as two years ago, a former calligraphy student lettered me a one-page note, showing me that he was still using that skill.

The next year, when we returned, I asked if I could offer some high school classes based on the success I'd had with calligraphy. Students didn't have home economics and art, and I thought they'd be fun to teach. Since I had my teaching credential, I was given permission, understanding that I would still be paid at an aide's salary.

I designed, planned, and taught these two classes in our trailer.

We had moved out of the little house during the previous spring, as the district purchased a brand new three-bedroom trailer for us. It was hauled in, and the hill was removed between JoAnn's trailer and the little house. Our trailer was squeezed in, and we spent a few weeks there before the summer. It was a good thing we didn't have to stay there long and could have the windows open. New trailers smell funny from lots of glue and fire retardants, maybe, or chemicals I can't imagine. The smell seemed to tone down over the summer.

The first semester, I taught sewing, and only three girls registered. We set up folding tables in our living room, and the district provided three portable sewing machines. The girls made aprons first, just as I had done in my eighth grade home economics class, and then graduated to patterned shirts. We ordered patterns and fabric from the shop in Ketchikan, and we pinned and cut, sewed and ripped, and talked about life in general and sewing in particular. It was not too hard to put the machines next to the folded-up tables at the end of the class every day, but finding the wayward pins that fell into the shag carpeting was more difficult. Every now and then, Don would find one with his bare foot and suggest (order) me to have the girls be more diligent in their cleaning up before they left.

The second semester was on cooking, and that garnered a male student, Adam, along with the three girls who were continuing their home economics course from the previous term. We made breads and cookies, we read recipes and measured ingredients, and we increased and decreased serving sizes. We ended the semester by planning and serving lunch to their parents and the other teachers. Of course, we had to be careful because Myrtle was a vegetarian, the only one of our guests.

We decided to make vegetable soup, homemade rolls, and a dessert. The soup was the most memorable. It was the young man's assignment to make the soup base from bouillon cubes and water after he'd washed and cut up the vegetables. I noticed Adam had grabbed the chicken bouillon cubes instead of the vegetable ones, and I quickly exchanged them. He realized the error of his way but chuckled and said he had one chicken cube already in there.

"I think that's okay," I told him. We were making well over a quart of liquid, and one out of six to eight cubes didn't seem to matter much to me.

As the adults filed in and sat down, the students served their meal. They were good hosts, inquiring as to what folks wanted to drink, water or juice, asking if anyone wanted seconds, clearing dirty plates, and bringing the dessert when all were through with their soup. As their guests left, the kids grinned, accepting the comments of appreciation, feeling good about their lunch.

"She never did notice that meat in her soup," Adam chuckled after Myrtle thanked him for the soup and left.

***

That was the semester I learned that Don wasn't totally happy with our situation out at camp. I found out one night after dinner.

We were sitting in the living room, sipping our drinks when he said, "Biz, I think we should go back to town. We have that old trailer that leaks and freezes up. It needs lots of work."

"Can't you work on it during the summer?" I questioned.

"Well, I could, but look at this." He handed me a brochure.

I looked at a drawing of a geodesic dome and read about its merits. More heat efficient. Stronger with the triangular construction. Buckminster Fuller had invented something that Don wanted to build.

"The kit is only five thousand dollars, and we have enough money, more than enough," he assured me. "And we can draw from our savings to purchase the other materials. The labor will be minimal as I'll do it myself."

Okay, I thought. We can live in the living room while he tears things apart and puts up his—oh, our—dome, and what will I do?

"I'm going to resign," he told me. "I want to go to town."

Briefly I was taken back to our dinner table in Colorado Springs four years earlier where a similar conversation had taken place:

"Biz," Don had begun. "I'm tired of teaching here, and this town is growing too big for me."

I had stopped what I had been doing and given him my full attention. We'd been married only three years, and I had had no idea that he was dissatisfied.

"Biz, I'd planned to move before I met you," he had gone on, "you know, after Doris and I divorced."

I hadn't known this.

"Now I don't like my job, and I don't like the town, and about the only thing that's working right now is us."

I had been happy to hear that. "So ...?" I had encouraged.

"I'm moving to Alaska," he had said. "Do you want to come with me?"

Wow. During dinner he'd talked about a fire drill that day at the high school in which he taught. He had witnessed conversations he hadn't liked between the principal and some students, yet he had felt powerless to say anything. He just had wanted to leave. But he would give me two years to get used to the idea, and I did.

And we moved. Things had worked out.

"You're awfully quiet," Don finally said, bringing me back to the present.

I was staring into space, I guess. "Okay," I said. "It's your decision. You really think we can afford to live without a job?"

"I might pick up something on the side," he said, "or you might. I don't see you staying home while I take apart our house and rebuild it."

He had a point there.

With that, Don submitted his resignation. He wrote to his mother after the superintendent came out one day to talk to him.

2-14-80

Dear Mom,

I have had some potentially interesting developments in my job situation. This past Tuesday, the superintendent was here to observe. He asked me again to reconsider my resignation. My reply was a flat no. He then threw out a possibility—would I be interested in a job in the office in Ketchikan developing and directing a program for health and physical education for the school district, to which I replied yes. This is very tentative, but it is what I had in the back of my mind when I submitted my resignation so early. The super is obviously an intelligent person for not wanting to lose me. Whether or not this works out, it will be nice to be in Ketchikan full time. In a lot of ways, it is a jerk-water town, but looks pretty *good after being in a logging camp for two years. I have ordered our new house addition. The company offered to pay half the shipping costs if I would order now—so I did. The shipping costs will amount to $1000-1200 so that offer was a significant one.*

Today is Valentine's Day. Biz made cute cards for all the high school students with appropriate sayings for each—such as "May Cupid's aim be better than yours" for one boy that shot himself in the leg playing quick draw. This is not exactly a Valentine's Day sentiment, but I like it:

A wonderful bird is the pelican.
His mouth can hold more than his belican.
He can take in his beak
Enough food for a week.
I'm darned if I know how the helican.

The winter has been relatively mild so the logging camp may open this month, which is quite early. The pulp mill in Ketchikan is crying for logs. There are several proposals before the legislature in Juneau for tax relief of Alaska residents. At the present time, everyone gets a $300 tax credit—whatever one owes in Alaska income tax, they are allowed to subtract $300. One legislator wants to send a check to every Alaska resident and get rid of all the oil royalties ($900 million). This would amount to $2250.00 for every man, woman, and child in Alaska. I'm sure it will not be passed. Some of the legislators act almost like a kid with a new toy in trying to figure out how to spend all that money. 'Twas ever thus. I certainly hope they don't move the capital. The voters have voted that down twice, but the powers to be that want the move (as everywhere else) ignore the rank and file when it is in opposition to their wishes. The capital move would use all the oil revenues plus a great deal more.

I have received several one-liners from Dick—usually a cartoon with one line from Dick. Take care and see you this summer.

Love,

Don

So we began slowly readying for our move back to Ketchikan. Meanwhile, I enjoyed camp life, although that spring brought a couple of new challenges. One was a late and huge storm. The winds and snow howled and swirled for a week straight. They brought layers upon layers of snow to shovel. In fact, paths to the school were about all Don could muster, and when finally the snow did stop, it was waist deep.

The dogs had to be careful where they stepped to do their daily duties. If they didn't follow the narrow path Don had dug, and a few times they didn't, they moved directly from the top step of the porch into a three-foot pile of snow. I felt I had to be there, ready to rescue them as they fell, their questioning eyes and soft whimpers creating immediate sympathy.

However, once Don decided to see if Tammy could create her own way out, and as they were walking down the path, he picked her up. Then he deposited her an arm's length over the top of the snow into a soft virgin area where his shovelfuls hadn't reached. She tunneled her way back to the path, stood in front of him, and shook herself. Then she looked up at him, tail wagging, as if to say, "That was fun. Do you want to do it again?" That was our outdoor fun—shoveling and walking along the paths and watching the dogs.

Besides the paths, Don and other men shoveled their trailer roofs. The weight of the snow threatened the strength of the trailer construction. Pushing the snow down the slight slant on either side of the trailers' roofs created a playground for children on either side of their homes. Some afternoons, their shrieks and laughter filled the air as they clambered to their roofs and jumped off, landing feet and butt first into the huge snow piles. It was a rare treat for them and a joy for me to hear their happiness.

However, it was an effort to get to where the paths didn't go, and we didn't jump off roofs, so we didn't do much outside. Instead, we read a lot, and the radio reception (yes, we finally had our own radio) was clearer than it had ever been. Don scrounged in the bowels of the school's storage area and found two partial Scrabble games, fashioned a complete set, and we enjoyed an occasional friendly competition in the evenings.

Planes couldn't fly, so there was no mail. We'd heard that planes had started out from Ketchikan on both the first and second days of the storm, containing both our mail and passengers, but were forced to turn back. Then the air taxi service waited out the weather with us. There wasn't even a Saturday night movie that week.

As the clouds cleared and the weather warmed, life returned to normal. Don flew to Ketchikan for a small high school meeting, and I was able to substitute for him. I made more in one day for five and a half hours than I earned in a week teaching my two one-hour classes. It was irritating. Sometimes I felt overworked and underpaid, but on the other hand, I was happy to be involved again with teaching, however the disparity in pay seemed.

We continued to interact with the folks at camp. We housed artists and enjoyed their talents. We received camp folk company, and we visited a few as well. However, we kept an eye toward the future; the day when we'd leave crept closer and closer.

I wrote to my mother-in-law next.

Sat. April 19

Dear Mom,

Just got in the mood to practice some printing though I think it'll pass quickly—my hand is already beginning to feel the strain—it's been so long!

It's hard to believe there's just over a month left to go—I know it'll pass quickly. It'll be most interesting to see what our meals will be—have quit ordering so's to use up what we have. Know any ways to jazz up kidney beans? I must have ordered a gross at one time and have used only two cans!

The mood did pass! We're waiting for Greg Drivers, a poet from Anchorage, the next artist-in-residence, to arrive. He was supposed to be here yesterday, but the high winds along with rain, snow, and sleet prevented any planes from flying. Don and I are enjoying what privacy we can get!

It was funny last night though—since our guest didn't come, we thought we'd have a quiet evening and go to bed early—only it didn't turn out quite as we'd planned. A mother came over to invite us to her place for dinner tonight (her husband is in Anchorage with one daughter attending the state spelling bee). While she was here, a couple of bunkhouse guys came down to talk to Don about high school and college correspondence courses. After they left, another guy came by to invite us to a going-away party (for one of the maintenance men) tonight. Then the mother's other daughter came over. We NEVER had company like that! What a surprise—made it to bed by 10:30—late for us.

Don said you're getting eager to have your walking cast. Any idea when it will happen?

I have to bake something—there's to be a baked goods auction Tuesday night. I told you about the little girl who broke her hip, didn't I? And she's in a full body cast? The family had no insurance at the time of the accident so this auction is a fund raiser for Heidi. She had to fly to Seattle for her medical treatment—was charged 3 fares for passage back (she took up 3 seats as she was lying down!). I guess I'd better wait tho—to get some eggs. My last grocery order was supposed to arrive last night on the supply boat. Only it broke down sometime last week and is running a day late. It should be here sometime tonight or tomorrow.

While Don was in town, his substitute got sick. The other teachers and I took turns covering his classes—what a bummer! Still, it was MUCH better than my doing all the subbing. I still had my own regular classes.

Did Don tell you when he called that he bought me a "new" car? A '74 Subaru—bright red with black upholstery. I'll sure be happy not to have to drive the International any more.

Not much else is new here—freaky weather. Lots of gusty wind and rain with brief periods of calm and sun. Don went to check the boats during the sun and came home soaking wet. He hopes to get some fishing in tomorrow.

I should be defrosting the refrigerator or grooming Tammy—but decided to write letters instead. Don's taking a nap—think I'll join him.

Hope all is going well—take care.

Love,

Biz

All too soon, we were on the dock saying our goodbyes, a Beaver having flown across the island to pick us up. We had boxed much of our belongings and shipped them on the supply boat and didn't have much to carry. Just the dogs and a few suitcases. As they were loaded onto the plane, we said our goodbyes. I was tearful, but folks promised to look us up when they got to Ketchikan. Because they would have to take a jet from the Ketchikan airport to go anywhere, we knew it wasn't a goodbye forever.

Back in Ketchikan

Once he was in his own home, Don began his projects. He had ordered the dome and had stored the pieces in his huge workshop behind our dinky trailer, and he was ready to begin. He had the Model A calling, "Restore me, restore me." Don had given some of the ladies of the school district office a ride in it right after we came into town, and they were encouraging him to enter it in the Fourth of July parade.

He also owned a forty-foot wooden boat I called the *Amityville Horror*. It had been built in Amityville, New York, and Don had bought it in Seattle the previous summer. He and two friends had piloted it up the inside passage to Ketchikan, taking a couple of weeks, and then we had brought it to camp.

It was an old boat, sturdy though, I was told, but having a few quirks. One was that if the engine quit, it wouldn't restart until it had cooled down. Don had learned that the engine quitting was something the boat did whenever it felt like it, and there was only one way to restart it.

We brought that "horror" out to Labouchere Bay the previous fall, choosing a calm and sunny day to travel. We left early in the morning, and in the middle of Clarence Strait, a few hours into our journey, the engine quit. While I nervously paced around the small galley and watched the temperature gauge, Don told me to relax and watch the scenery. We were in the middle of this big body of water and not floating toward any land masses. We were safe, he was trying to tell me. For the time being is what I thought.

We eventually got underway again, turned into Sumner Strait, and continued on toward Port Protection, only a little way from Labouchere Bay; it was a better harbor, and most of the privately owned boats from camp moored there. I think Don took that boat out once or twice during the school year, and he brought me out on it once.

That year, he thought we should go in to town during our Christmas break by boat. Days are shorter in December, and we knew it would be a two-day trip to Ketchikan. Don looked at his charts and plotted a course for Steamer Bay on Etolin Island. It was about half the way to town, and we'd be out of Sumner Strait. We planned to anchor there for the night. The next morning, we could travel down Clarence Strait to Ketchikan.

We arrived in the bay without incident, dropped anchor, and slept. The next morning, Don looked outside and muttered, "Holy crap." Then he continued, "Biz, we've gotta get out of here. Look at that kelp rushing by—I hope nothing's got caught in our prop." So he started the engine as I tried to stow things where they'd be out of the way, pulled up the anchor, and we were off. We found nothing to block our forward progress—until we left the shelter of the bay.

There was a winter storm in full swing, and the waters were raging. Don decided we'd make a run back to Port Protection—he thought Sumner Strait might be smoother than Clarence Strait at that point. Making a run is not what we did. On flat calm seas, the *Horror* maxed out at ten knots. We'd be going much slower over the bumpy waves. I had no idea how long the trip would take but wanted only to get out of the boat and onto dry and still land. As quickly as possible.

So we chugged up the strait, bucking wind and waters, pitching first up, up, up, and then down, down, down. Again and again, we'd ride the waves, Don holding onto the wheel as I righted the stools that fell over, put away the binoculars that leaped off the ledge, and wiped the mist on the windshield that the green water left behind. Green water meant that we plowed through a wave instead of atop it, and I prayed that the scuppers were working, those drains on the boat's side. It was a rough trip, and I had remembered an ore boat going down in Lake Superior, being torn in two by the wave action. It was a scary vision. *Please, Lord, let us get back safely.* That thought tried to replace the other picture.

Hours later, as we approached the left turn into the protected waters, Don asked about the tide. It was high so he wouldn't need to navigate around the rocks that, at low tide, guarded the bay's entrance. However, his comment, "Biz, I don't know if I can turn this boat without swamping," set my heart to beating and my prayers to intensify. I watched as Don turned the wheel, little by little, to the left. Riding wave after wave, still turning, we finally were able to approach the dock.

Thank you, Lord, I breathed. But it was too soon.

Don maneuvered the *Horror* close to the dock and then let it swing in as he went to the stern to jump off, as was his habit. He would grasp the stern rope, jump off, and then tie the boat up before he retrieved the rope at the bow to finish securing it.

Unfortunately, this time, the boat wasn't as close as it should have been, or Don misjudged the distance to the dock, or something. He jumped right into the water, and as I watched, the boat swung closer to squeeze his body between it and the dock. I hopped up to the throttle, pushed it into reverse, and when I looked up from my task, Don was standing on the dock with the stern rope in his hand. Thank God, we were tied up. On shaky legs, I walked toward the camp with Don.

That was the one and only time in my life I touched the throttle of any of Don's boats. Although he would have been the first to say the boats were "ours," I enjoyed the water only when it was flat calm. I hardly used the boat, for he often motored alone or invited others to go with him. He did not ask me to accompany him when he brought the boat in after he'd quit teaching.

I did not mention this trip to Laurell, ever, either.

Don did not seem eager to take the boat out much when he had the Model A and the dome to play with. He played with them whenever he could, too.

However, he had a real job. The position of health and physical education program director had not materialized, but a GED (Graduation Equivalent Degree) program needed a teacher/director, and Don had agreed to do that. He sat most days in his office, waiting for people to come for help, but hardly anyone ever did.

That was probably a good thing, as he needed to miss a couple of weeks to sit on a jury. He was one of twelve that would decide the guilt or innocence of a man accused of raping a young woman on the Schoenbar Trail—a poorly lit trail from the junior high school up the hill to a housing area.

4-7-81

Dear Mom,

I am sitting in my office at work bored to death. I have worked with several people and made a number of phone contacts, but business is slow and sporadic. The young man who is paralyzed passed his GED tests, and I'm done with him. Otherwise, everything is going well. Had the little boat out for the first time this season last Friday. Everything operated very smoothly.

The Model A is slowly being sanded preparatory to painting. I am shooting toward being in the 4th of July parade here. A fellow stopped by the other day to ask if he could borrow the trailer I hauled the Model A on to go to Wrangell and pick up a Model A he is buying. In return, I'm borrowing an engine hoist from him.

The progress on the house is quite slow, but I'm to the point now that I can better afford to move slowly. I saved $5.49 and it only cost me $50.00 to do so. Used an old plug-in for the stove from the old trailer instead of buying a new one—burned out the timer-clock on the new stove because plug was defective—and had to buy a new one anyway. Finish work on the house is slow and tedious—a lot of it will not get done for a long time.

4-13-81

Saw the first two hummingbirds of the season yesterday. They hovered right where the feeder was last year, but had not been put up this year. I immediately mixed some nectar and hung the feeder. We have had four seasons' worth of weather today—sun, snow, rain, and wind.

The young man who was accused of rape (the jury I was on) was sentenced today—8 years with 3 years suspended and no parole for the 5 years. The older brother will be sentenced later.

Dave and Roxanne Reinke plan to come up in early August—Wendlands in July sometime. Unplugged heat tape on water line last week—following morning line frozen, although thawed quickly. Will leave heat tape plugged in now.

Love,

Don

Don pursued all his projects with great enthusiasm, although sometimes he believed his skill was lacking. He had posted his favorite saying in his workshop: "I may do poor work, but I'm sure slow," and he'd point to that when he had visitors out there with him asking how things were going. He appreciated the hours of his "real" job being cut in half as he had, then, more time to do things "slow." Eventually, his job was eliminated altogether. But that worked out well, too.

Don could work in earnest on our house. The geodesic dome kit came in bundles of boards with painted ends. The red matched the red, yellow the yellow, and blue the blue, giant tinker toys for Don to erect. He tore down trailer walls, leaving the bedroom and bathroom for last. He checked out property boundaries and planted the footers, and soon he was putting the dome together.

I found a job clerking at the local fabric store, the Silver Thimble, and as I went off to work each day, I prayed that Don would have no accidents while I was gone. When I returned, I'd make our dinner in

Beginning to erect the dome
Reprinted with permission of the Ketchikan Daily News/Diane Zink photograph

the electric skillet that sat with the coffee pot on a cupboard against a wall in our living room, which was filled with our two chairs, the television set, and my sewing machine. I didn't bring home much of my salary for I fell in love with many of the new fabrics as they came into the shop.

After dinner, Don would show me the progress he'd made on the dome, and I'd ask appropriate questions and mumble appreciative responses. Then we'd toss the paper plates we'd used into the wood stove, and I'd take the frying pan into the bathroom to wash it in the tub.

For months we camped in our living room until finally the day came when we could move into the dome. Even though the huge ceiling was clothed only with three-and-a-half-inch thick shiny insulation, we enjoyed the comfort the extra space afforded.

Thank goodness, Don had enclosed the dome and finished the electrical and plumbing work before he received a phone call from the superintendent in early spring.

"Don, do you have six weeks to spare?" Mr. Hill began. He told Don about the teaching situation in Labouchere Bay as he saw it. "One of the high school teachers got himself in trouble with John King, and now John wants him out of there. Pronto. And John asked for you to finish out the year. What do you think?"

John King was the logging camp manager and ran things with an iron fist. If a logger crossed John or broke one of his rules or even had a personality conflict with John, that logger was flown right out of there. It seemed as if John wanted to extend his authority into the school.

As I understood it, one of the male teachers had entertained a female artist (from Alaska's Artists in the Schools program) in his trailer, perhaps overnight, and this was verboten—from John's point of view anyway—and so he wanted this teacher gone. And the superintendent was eager to keep peace with John King.

So Don talked it over briefly with me, and we agreed that he'd fly out the next weekend. I would go out there toward the end of his six-week contract for graduation since I knew several of the students who would be there.

We shared this news with Laurell. Once we moved in to Ketchikan, we called her every Sunday because we could. It was a way to keep her updated about our life in Alaska. She learned of sweet Shadow's passing when we had to put him down after he had a stroke. The phone call about burying him under the maple tree in the front yard was heart rending. She heard about the snowstorms and the heat tape and the new hot tub that Don erected behind the dome. And when Don accepted this temporary position, of course it was the main topic of conversation in the last phone call before he went back to camp. Still the letters continued.

May 5, 1981

Dear Mom—

Since we talked to you on Sunday, not much has happened.

Don left yesterday for Lab Bay—a beautiful day for flying. He was really looking forward to spending a few weeks out there—I hope to get out there for a couple of days the end of May—for graduation.

I'm not looking forward to being in charge of the wood stove and checkbook—but will probably manage just fine.

Tammy's missing Don—she had him trained just the way she wanted—and I'm not quite so accommodating. She gets to go out in the front yard—fenced—not visiting the neighbors as usual.

I'm missing him already too. Am thankful I have my job to give me something to do.

Weather's been delightful—no rain, very little wind, and lots of sunshine. It's amazing how warm 60° is here—and how chilly 40° is when it's raining. Didn't need the wood stove today.

That's it for now—take care.

Love,

Biz

A few weeks into Don's absence, I was surprised by a call from the superintendent.

"Hi, Biz," he began. "No, Don's all right." He must have read my mind—*He never calls me!* "I wanted you to know that Myrtle has decided to retire after this school year is over, and that will leave an elementary opening at Labouchere Bay. I mentioned it to Don when I visited yesterday and asked him if he'd continue teaching high school next year. I am offering you the job that Myrtle's leaving. Would you be interested?"

"What did Don say?" I wanted to know.

"He'd leave it up to you," was his response.

I had always wanted to teach, but my experiences with Myrtle and JoAnn made me realize that working in such close proximity with somebody whose methods and philosophies were so different would not be fun. Although JoAnn and her husband had transferred to Kasaan, a site where they could both teach, a new couple had been hired to replace JoAnn and Don to teach with Myrtle the previous year. I knew nothing about them, except that they would stay to teach with Don and me.

"Can you wait for an answer until I get out to camp?" I asked. "I'm planning to go for graduation, and I'd like to meet the other teachers we'd be working with."

"The Packards?" Mr. Hill said. "Sure, that would be fine. But I want an answer before the first of the month."

That was fine with me. I could talk with Don and the Packards and determine if this would be a situation that I hoped it would be—one where I was finally teaching in a place that suited both Don and me, one where we'd be happy.

When the floatplane that brought me out landed and I walked up the ramp, Don was waiting to greet me, as was John King. Perhaps it was intended as a homecoming of sorts, to make me feel welcome and want to return. Mr. King, who'd never talked to me much before, made an effort to be friendly.

"Welcome back," he said with a smile on his face.

"Thank you," I responded.

"We've enjoyed having Don here these past weeks," he continued, "and I hope you will consider coming here to teach next year."

Then he grabbed my bag, and Don and I stepped up into his pickup, and he drove us to the trailer where Don was staying.

"My word, what is that?!" I couldn't help but exclaim as we came into sight of the new school. A huge square building had replaced the trailer that Myrtle and JoAnn had shared, blocking the view of the bay from the road.

After Don brought my bag inside his trailer, he took me over to the new school. As I entered, I was in awe of the structure. Off to my right was a half-sized gym, its floor covered with a kind of Astroturf—not hardwood, but not the grassy kind either. The high school kids were playing basketball with a tall and broad stranger who Don told me was Bob Packard. He was covering for Don as he had been given time off to meet my plane, and the Friday afternoon bell was due to ring in just a few minutes.

Turning to the left, I went down a hall. On one side, two doors opened into classrooms. These were where the elementary students were. Don brought me to the second door, Myrtle's room, where I was greeted with a hello and a hug. The SILENCE IS GOLDEN sign still hung over the class, and the students looked my way, invisibly tied to their desks and quiet. Some smiled recognition. I said hi before noticing that the classroom wall to my right was an accordion pleated door. It was shut tight.

"She lets her students talk out loud," Myrtle told me quietly. "I won't have them interrupting my students' behavior."

"Really?" I responded. Obviously the primary classroom was on the other side of that door.

Myrtle went on. "I don't like her and how she runs her classroom. She lets those little children practically run wild."

I knew then that whenever I met with the Packards, our conversation would be interesting.

Our meeting took place that Friday evening when the Packards invited us to their trailer for dinner. Karen had made a taco salad, a delicious easy one that I make often today: a layer of iceberg lettuce lining the plate, then a hot combination of beans, hamburger, and onions mixed with Catalina dressing piled on next, topped with more onions, fresh tomatoes, and cheese. An open bag of Fritos in the center of the table invites diners to sprinkle some over the salad, and voila! Dinner is served.

Packard's three boys joined us, and over the hum of conversation and laughter, we all enjoyed the meal. Then the boys went to their rooms for their favorite Dungeons and Dragons games, and we began to talk about school. Well, Karen and I did. As the guys moved into the living room with their drinks and lit up their cigarettes, Karen and I lingered at the table, sipping our wine, talking about our mutual experiences.

She had taught kindergarten in an open concept school in Ketchikan before coming out to camp; I had taught grades four through six in a similar situation in Colorado Springs. Although we didn't agree totally on how children learn best, our discussion was lively and positive, and I thought we'd be a successful elementary team. We could have the accordion door at least partly open to begin the school year.

It helped to hear Bob's big guffaws in the distance, prompted by something Don had said. They were getting along too.

When we returned to town, we signed contracts to teach the following year at Labouchere Bay with the Packards. Then we got on with the summer.

It was busy, with much company. Don's niece Carol was the first to visit, followed by friends from Colorado Springs. Dorene and Ralph Wendland were active in the Coast Guard Auxiliary there and had a boat they patrolled the Pueblo Reservoir with. They wanted to bring it up to Alaska, so they trailered it to the West Coast, put it in the water, and came for a visit. Other Colorado friends, Don's backpacking buddy, Dave Reinke, and his wife also made plans to visit that summer. With our guests and our regular routine, the summer passed quickly.

Soon I was writing to Laurell about our plans to return to Lab Bay.

August 11, 1981

Dear Mom Laurell,

It's started—packing time. We've started to think about what to take and what to leave behind. And time to collect boxes—we leave a week from Friday—the 21st—but have to have the boxes ready on Wednesday as they'll go out on the "mail boat"—or Island Trader.

We will leave a temporary change of address with the post office, so we should get our mail—all of it—eventually.

I'm really excited about teaching again—it's been a LONG time. Major social studies subject this year will be Alaska—so have decided to pick up six credits via correspondence from the University of Alaska—History and Geography of Alaska. Should be most helpful.

The fellow who said he was buying the big boat said he'd changed his mind a couple of days ago, so Don told our neighbor, and he bought it. Nice to have it sold before we left town.

Heard from the Reinkes—they won't be up as Dave is having problems due to a whiplash injury suffered last spring—still undergoing therapy trying to avoid surgery. Too bad—and did I tell you that the Wendlands had their share of boat troubles while they were here—got a phone call—they'd finally gotten back to Washington where their truck and boat trailer were—A long drive home in store for them.

Hope all is well with you—Take care.

Love,

Biz

Our summer came to a close as I finished saying goodbye to my co-workers at the fabric store and Don winterized our dome. Even though much work was still to be completed, it would be safe when we were gone. We'd scheduled Tammy's last check with the vet, too, as she'd had a couple of teeth removed when they were abscessed. We boxed up the dishes and pots and pans that we'd taken with us out to camp earlier and stocked up on groceries. These boxes we delivered to the supply boat, the *Island Trader*. We packed our bags, and Don made one last check with the school district. Our housing was ready for us.

Labouchere Bay to Ketchikan and Back Again

Although we left a day later than we'd planned, when we arrived at Labouchere Bay, we were ready to work.

August 25, 1981

Dear Mom Laurell,

Well we made it out to camp on Saturday. The boat with all our stuff was supposed to be running a day late—at least we were told it was—and we didn't want to arrive before all our stuff got here. So we came a day later than we'd planned. Only to find that the boat had gotten in on Friday, as originally scheduled, and other people unloaded our piles and piles. As Don remarked, he was sorry that we weren't here but not too sorry. They sure saved us a lot of work. As it was, we spent all of Sunday unpacking and putting away.

Monday and today we packed away and sorted out stuff at school. It's starting tomorrow. Both of us are pretty excited—in fact I haven't seen Don so "hyper" for a long while—especially to teach. This other couple, Bob and Karen Packard, are fine people. Bob and Don, when together, are quite the "bullshitters." I spent an evening with the two of them before Karen got into camp, and couldn't squeeze a word in edgewise. Almost like Don and Dick together. It's good to see Don feeling so positive about the beginning of the school year. And I'm excited too—I think that Karen is a great teacher—and we think alike on so many things. It's been hard fun getting the room together.

Tammy's not too happy—kind of hard on the "old lady" being uprooted to a new place. She had a few teeth and cysts removed before we came out—getting her healthy before we moved. She'll do okay as soon as she gets acclimated.

The people out here have really received us with open arms—got a bucket of clams to steam from one gal—venison from another—halibut from still another. We sent back tomatoes—we'd stocked up on fresh fruit from the Idaho fruit truck when we were in town. Looks like I'm out of paper.

Hope all's well with you—we're great. Take care.

Love

Biz

September 6, 1981

Dear Mom Laurell,

Don's out in the pouring rain scraping the barnacles off his "new" boat. Did I tell you that he got a good deal out here on a canvas-topped v-hull boat? Three bunkhouse guys wanted to sell it so Don got it. The teachers are the only people out here making money.

Yesterday he and a group of other men spent the whole day installing playground equipment that had been removed when the new school building was erected.

They dug holes and poured concrete all day long, not even stopping for lunch.

The first full week of school is history—and I really think I'll be earning my money. The ten kids in my charge are, as a group, the least self-disciplined, self-motivated children I've ever met. There are probably three exceptions. I'm really glad that we have only two days of school this week—Labor Day off, teach Tuesday and Wednesday, and then three of us are required to attend district in-service meetings in Ketchikan. Don isn't required to go, but since Bob Packard plans to close school down, he decided to come along. We have a high school student to Tammy-sit.

We had the start of the social season in camp yesterday—had a Bon Voyage party for a girl who graduated last spring. She's heading to Washington to attend cosmetology school. It was a hen party—first time I've had the chance to talk to some of the women there. So it was enjoyable for me.

We both totally enjoy the company of the other two teachers. I'm working in the same classroom with Karen Packard—she's a terrific teacher and has been a pillar of strength and suggestion when I've needed some moral support. Bob and Don get along so well—

Have run out of paper. Hope all's well—take care.

Love,

Biz

That year, teaching went so very well. Karen and I were working together, sometimes combining our classes, but more often talking about our craft, giving and taking suggestions that helped each of us improve our work with the kids. And either my kids or I had a lot of improving to do. Don and Bob, too, were sharing the junior and senior high school tasks without discord; in fact, we often heard their laughter all the way down the hall in my room. It was a good professional year.

One Friday, Karen and I had forgotten to pass out notes to our students. After school, we put on our raingear and braved the nasty weather to walk to the homes of our students, knocking on the doors and delivering our messages. We were at the top of one hill when we heard a floatplane's engine.

Who'd be flying in this wind and rain? We looked at each other in question and then scanned the sky for the plane. Swooping out of nowhere, the school plane whooshed through the trees, its wings catching a few branches, as it sailed toward the water and a smooth landing.

When the pilot soon walked toward the school, both of us berated him.

"What do you think you're doing, flying like that? You could have been hurt or killed!"

His answer: "Yes, but I was alone in the plane. I wasn't endangering anyone else, and I knew I'd make it."

He was an excellent pilot, the best around, for that's what our school district hired with so many lives hinging on his skill. But still, it was a sobering thought.

***

That year, many artists visited us. A bluegrass band, a woodwind quintet, a percussionist, and a pianist were some that just popped in for a classroom lesson and then a concert before leaving again. Others stayed for a few days. Jon and Joemy made their first appearance with us at Labouchere Bay, although they were popular and came to see us again when we were in Fire Cove later in our teaching careers.

Jon was a mime, and his wife, Joemy, was a master of the hammered dulcimer. Between them, the kids learned music and drama, and they helped the kids write and perform a play based on *Romeo and Juliet*, which had applications to our residents' situation. Families were located either in the logging camp or the road construction camp. John King, the logging manager, assumed control of the entire area with his iron fist. This created hard feelings, and the two camps were rather like the Montague's and Capulet's. Performing as Juliet was a young man from the road construction camp, wearing a blond wig and speaking in a high falsetto, while Romeo was portrayed by a beautiful young girl from the logging camp. The kids had written a comedic farce, and the whole audience roared and applauded at the performance. I think even John King appreciated the effort.

Jon and Joemy wanted to see some of the area, and Don wanted to test out his new V-hull boat. So one evening, he decided to take us all to Point Baker. We had to walk about half a mile to Port Protection, get into the boat, and journey up the bay until there was a narrow channel leading north to Point Baker. There we would find a restaurant (sort of) and bar. Bunkhouse guys often took their skiffs to load up with beer. I was told that there was very little freeboard (area of the boat above water) on their return trips.

The four of us made it there, entered the restaurant, and ordered hamburgers and beer. The hamburgers came from the freezer, meat enclosed by buns wrapped in cellophane, and were microwaved. They tasted amazingly good to me—since I didn't have to cook them. Then we prepared to return, as Jon and Joemy had been invited for a duck dinner at the home of one of the loggers.

Don couldn't get his main engine to fire. Something was wrong with the starter, and so he used the kicker (the smaller horsepower engine for emergencies on most Alaskan boats) to get back. The twenty-minute trip turned into one of an hour and a half. We stopped by the dinner hosts' home to apologize for causing the artists' late return and were invited to join the party.

What a feast—much better than the Point Baker hamburger. I had my first wild duck. First pressure-cooked, then baked in a brown gravy, the duck was served with mashed potatoes and freshly baked rolls. With the company of such a kind family and artists, it was a wonderful meal. Delicious food and heartwarming fellowship—what a gift.

Another gift, a performance, planned by our music teacher, Kris, was a musical play, *Gulliver.* It was an all-school play, and the kids tried out for parts. Of course, the older kids got the speaking parts, but there were many choruses that everyone could sing. Kris had delegated authority well, as the junior high kids and I painted backdrops, Don and his woodshop class made the stage and props, Bob figured out the lighting, and Karen helped all soloists learn their parts. It was fun planning, creating, and producing it. It seemed a good gift for the community, too.

During that year, Don and I received gifts from Laurell in her care packages. I think she had a challenge with ideas to gift my husband since he was on the lookout for fishing gear and boat stuff, items hard for an elderly lady in Colorado Springs to buy. She probably had an easier time selecting gifts for me. When we had visited her before, she had showed me a lovely blouse that was decorated in embroidery that fastened small mirrors to the yoke. When I mentioned that I might want to add some mirrors to a shirt or two of mine, I received my share.

Laurell also added surprises. We received mirrors, pretzels, skin cream, mirrors, chocolate chips, Applets and Cotlets (a Washington-made confection), bungee cords, and more mirrors. I finally had to tell her that interest in camp for using those mirrors with embroidery on clothing wasn't very high. However, I was beginning to paint on denim. So some of the boxes contained denim and quilting fabric.

While Don puttered around in the woodshop or on his boat, I continued to sew. This time, I was crafting quilted wallets from denim, painting Alaska figures on them—forget-me-nots and rainbirds mostly. (The rainbird is Ketchikan's unofficial logo—a raven carrying an umbrella and wearing XtraTufs.) These I wanted to give for gifts—and as things turned out, they would be useful to sell, too. Only I didn't know it at the time.

However, as the academic year ended, Don let me know. He wanted to quit again for a while to work on the dome. We brought our belongings back to Ketchikan as I followed him. This time, I found my friend Barb wanting a partner in a consignment business on Creek Street, the old red-light district of Ketchikan and a thriving tourist center. So I made things the tourists might want to buy and tended the shop as Don continued to work on his projects. My wallets came in handy, and I branched out into making toddler-sized jeans with the Alaska motifs on them.

When Laurell found out, she began to help us, too. She knit small bells that people might want to wear on their lapels. She knit small mittens that she made into ornaments. It was interesting that people would buy Colorado-made items as a remembrance of their trip to

Alaska. Barb painted china miniatures, and I painted denim, from which I made hats and baby clothes. I also tole-painted recipe boxes, and we brought in others' art-and-craft items for consignments. We took turns managing the shop.

While Don worked on his projects and I worked on mine, the summer and the next academic year passed as we lived in Ketchikan.

June 28, 1982

Dear Mom,

We're finally settling in nicely—have found places to put most of the junk we brought back with us.

I've been sewing—trying to finish some denim hats I'd promised to have ready for sale by May. Not <u>*too*</u> *late—am also making some billfolds. Get to try quilting my own fabric for the first time. It'll keep me busy.*

Don had the parts for the engine waiting here when we got in—maybe he told you that on the phone. He hasn't gone back to the boat yet—who knows when he'll do it.

Bob Packard and one of his sons were in town last week looking for a boat. I guess they found one that cost more than they wanted to spend (don't they all?!!) so don't know if they got it or not. Their whole family tentatively plans to come into town for the 4th of July. We've offered to house them.

Lisa Schwartz—remember her? A former student—called last week from Anchorage—she plans to visit Ketchikan over the 4th, too. We may have LOTS of company. Lisa has gotten engaged—wedding set for November. It'll be fun to see her again. She was special.

Our weather continues beautiful—extremely dry and hot. The fire danger is extreme, too. We've been enjoying the dryness though—lots of airing out and Lysoling furniture to get rid of the mold and mildew smells.

Hope all is well—take care.

Love,

Biz

Letters I wrote throughout the time we were in Ketchikan were newsy and upbeat. We did have company for the July holiday—the Packard family stayed with us. Although we only had one bathroom and their family numbered five people, we were able to function just fine. We even didn't run out of hot water.

Keeping in touch with people from camp was important and gratifying. Not only did the Packards stay with us yet another time or two, but also the Monreans, another couple we'd met in Lab Bay, became good friends. We'd share occasional evening meals, and Sharon took me to garage sales—her favorite Saturday activity.

A family from camp came to town with no job, no money, no housing, no car ... and stayed at a trailer court down the highway from us. They had two little kids, and the wife was a beautician. I traded rides to run their errands (get groceries, register kids for school, check at the employment office, pick up mail) for a new perm. First time with curls, and I liked it. In fact, I kept up with perms and curls for several more years.

Lisa Schwartz didn't visit us on the Fourth of July as planned but called to ask Don to give her away at her Thanksgiving-time wedding. She didn't want to ask her biological father, with whom she'd had limited contact, and her stepfather had said no when she asked. Don was pleased and touched to be involved with something so special.

We purchased tickets to Anchorage and reserved a hotel room. Don even bought a new navy-blue suit, and we headed north on a Friday. We'd never been to Anchorage before but didn't have time to see much. Lisa and her fiancé met us at the airport, brought us to the hotel, and invited us to the rehearsal dinner that evening. The time blurred by as we helped them get ready Saturday morning, or perhaps tried to stay out of their way, attended the afternoon wedding, and answered folks during the reception.

"How do you know Lisa?" Many wanted to know.

"I was her high school teacher," Don replied.

"He must have been pretty special," they told me when they met me.

"Of course," I replied. "But Lisa was pretty special in that logging camp, too."

She was worth the trip, the time, the expense. It was with a warm feeling that we boarded the jet the next day and came home.

We really were working on the dome. Laurell had asked what she could do for us, and Don allowed her to purchase the tiles for the kitchen counters. We had selected them from a catalog, and she purchased them and had them sent. However, Don decided we needed a sauna before winter set in, so he put in a small two-person sauna before he brightened up our kitchen.

Laurell had also given us a maple bed frame and easy-chair rocker when we had left Colorado Springs. I decided to strip the chair and recover the cushions. Finding a soft light-blue, plush upholstery fabric, I replaced the red print. I also just stained the wood once it was unfinished, and that, too, lightened up our room.

Don found no shortage of projects that year. In addition to building the sauna and setting the tiles, he insulated the utility room, worked on his Model A, finally fixed the boat engine, stained and installed the cupboards, and sanded and refinished the teak table we'd brought with us from Colorado. Whenever the weather was sunny, Don ran outside with a can of paint and his brush to touch up places here and there before deciding that the touch-up made the surrounding area look too bad. So his touch-ups became bigger painting projects.

We both worked on paneling for the dome ceiling. In his shop, Don cut the triangles we needed and brought them into the dome. I stained them on the unfinished plywood floors, never minding if I also stained parts of the floor. When they dried, we stacked them against a wall to install later. Although we both were tired of the aluminum-bowl look that the silvery-papered insulation caused, those panels didn't get installed for several years.

During this time, our aging gray poodle, Tammy, now completely deaf and almost blind, began convulsing. After watching her struggle for a day with her new challenge, we decided to make a trip to the vet's. It was lonely for a while without her—I'd had her for nineteen years. We didn't replace her … instead, we looked for jobs.

Yes, Don had decided that we should go back to work with the school district again.

We had submitted our applications after talking with the Packards one day. They had transferred from Lab Bay to a floating logging camp located just north of Ketchikan. That way, they could more easily come to town in their boat. It was a forty-five-minute ride. Traveling to Labouchere Bay entailed either almost an hour-long floatplane ride or, now that the road was punched through to Craig, a six-hour car ride followed by a three-hour ferry ride. I think the Packards were already trying to find work in the Ketchikan School District, which they eventually did.

We were invited to replace Bob and Karen at Lab Bay, this time with a woman who transferred from Thorne Bay, the bull cook's wife, Rosemary. (Her husband kept the camp in working order—one of the two top jobs under the boss. The other was the side rod—the one who kept the logging operations going.) Don would teach junior and senior high school, Rosemary elementary, and I would try my hand with the primary kids. Having never taught those grades before, I was most thankful for the year I worked so closely with Karen and observed what she did with them. Her kids learned, and mine did too.

However, Don wasn't happy here, either. He struggled with several of his students as well as Rosemary's leadership. She had been named principal teacher, and her methods and Don's were quite different. He began to weigh the options of teaching again versus quitting. One of his difficult students would be graduating, making next year easier. But it was doubtful Rosemary would leave. I tried to ease our way by making our home life as normal and happy as I could.

Eventually, we both put in requests for transfers and waited to hear what the next school year would bring.

April 29, 1984

Dear Mom,

Early morning here and looks like the beginning of another sunny day. It'll be 5 in a row if it continues—even the puddles have dried up! It was so nice yesterday that I was in the mood to wash windows! Did the kitchen and the living room before the mood left.

Don arrived yesterday—back from a high school teachers' meeting on Friday in Ketchikan. In fact, Friday was a day at school with 2 subs and me. I took my kids nature walking both in the morning and afternoon, so if anything went haywire, I wouldn't be there. We had a good time—looked at all the stuff we'd collected under a microscope when we returned.

We spent part of last Easter with some Catholic friends in camp—ate with them after mass. There's a priest—Father Mike Nash—stationed in Thorne Bay, who flew a float plane to all the outlying areas here in Southeast for services. His parents were visiting him last week and flew along to meet his parishioners. When they came here, it was the 4th Easter service that day, and rather than going to church, they sat and visited with us. You'll never guess where they were from—or maybe you will, since I've spent such a long time on this subject----That's right—Friday Harbor! Another example of what a small world it is ... anyway they said that Dick was a member of the Catholic church there and they would bring him our greetings when they returned. From here they were flying to Hobart Bay—we know some teachers there, so sent a little note along to them, too.

We have two young pretty Shakespearean actresses as artists in residence for two weeks. One's from Hoonah, the other from Juneau. (It's the first time in a long while that we've actually had Alaskan artists!) They've been working with the kids toward a performance this Thursday night. They've made quite an impact on the young men in school—there are only 3 girls in grades 4-12, with 12 boys. Those older boys especially have become very helpful!

Don decided to finish this letter too, as his mom had asked him to tell him something more about his brother, Dick.

Hi! I'm back from our high school meeting. Among other things, we decided to recommend that all high school students be required to have 3 years of math and 3 of science along with 4 years of English. Education is making another cycle back to more fundamentals which I'm sure is for the good. We will be leaving Lab Bay again at the end of the school year. I don't know at this time whether we will transfer to another location or be layed [sic] *off or quit. I suspect that many changes will occur before the next school year starts with the state of the logging industry now and the changes in the school district. We shall see.*

Love,

Biz & Don

We asked the school district to consider transferring us to Hollis. We really wanted Hollis, as it was on the ferry terminus, making Ketchikan available to us on a three-hour boat ride. It wasn't a logging camp, and it needed two teachers: one elementary and one secondary. As it was on the ferry terminus, it was also on the Prince of Wales road system, making drives possible to Craig, Klawock, Hydaburg, Thorne Bay, and other population centers on the island. It would make for fun weekends with the flexibility of travel. After filling out the transfer paperwork, we settled back into our school year and waited.

I kept busy with my projects—teaching two tole-painting classes that spring after school to interested students and adults. I had been asked to letter the diplomas for the school district and also the graduation program for Lab Bay. And I assigned my primary students to make pictures on fabric, using special crayons, which I made into a baby quilt—an end-of-the-year gift from our class to our pregnant aide.

A week or so before school was over, John King led me down as I drove the logging road out of camp. Women were not allowed to drive, according to John's rule, except for Rosemary. Every morning, she'd drive in the school van from her trailer up the hill and park in front of the building, driving home for lunch, and again after school. However, I was allowed this once to drive the school van to Hollis where my students, chaperones, and I would catch the ferry for Ketchikan and a field trip. John made sure we were kept safe from approaching logging trucks and left us once we passed the area they were working.

After everyone met at the school and boarded the van, we drove on down to Hollis, waited for the ferry, and then drove aboard. We were on the boat for three hours before we docked in Ketchikan.

When we arrived in town, the first thing I had to teach my students was "curbs and gutters." They had no idea that we were not allowed to go off the curbs, except after we had looked both ways and been assured that no traffic was coming. They also fit right into the open-concept school that I had asked to visit for a few days. Valley Park Elementary had a K-1-2 classroom, and our 1-2-3 students melted right into the population studying the sea that week. The school also housed the physically handicapped students, and it was a wonder watching the little girls and boys from the bush learn about wheelchairs and white canes from other little girls and boys. The third reason to visit this school was its swimming pool. We used it every day we were there, and my camp kids relished the relative warmth of the water and the lack of salt to wash off later, although they noticed the smell of the chlorine. We got back to camp, everyone having had a good time.

Don took his kids on a picnic on the beach one of the last days of school—a Monday. It had rained all weekend, hard and sideways, and on Sunday afternoon, one of his girls came down to ask if she *had* to go on the picnic. But Monday cleared, only clouds appeared, and they had a good time, apparent by Don's couple of hours' afternoon nap sleeping off "Smear the Queer" (a childhood tag game) and other such foolish beach games.

July 9, 1984

Dear Mom,

We're still marking time, waiting for word to go out to Lab Bay and move to Hollis before heading south. Hopefully that word will arrive sometime this week. Don and I are both enthused about the transfer.

Our 4th was spent with the Massenburgs, watching the parade and picnicking; we watched a remote-control plane and boat show at Ward Lake and even got a little walking done. It was cloudy and sprinkly all day—weather hasn't cleared up at all yet, and I'm really looking forward to being in a climate where I don't need to wear my turtle necks under my shirts. In fact, I've got soup stock on the stove simmering for supper. It's presently windy and rainy.

Don had a nice birthday yesterday. I got him a do-it-yourself bathrobe kit (fabric and pattern—I couldn't surprise him with it as he always asks what I'm sewing) and we had bought an electronic keyboard a couple of days before. He plays "Greensleeves" so I can recognize what it is already. We're both having fun with it—and who knows—someday Don might get to play a big organ yet!

He lost a crown on a tooth—has a dental app't tomorrow. I hope to have one this week too—

Not much else—hope your energy is returning.

Take care—see you soon.

Love,

Biz

Fire Cove School

We waited and waited for word of our new assignment, but we also purchased tickets to fly. Colorado and Minnesota would both see us arrive and leave in rather a whirlwind fashion. First, we went to see Laurell. When we were in Colorado Springs, being spoiled and enjoying her mothering, we received a phone call from the school district office. The superintendent told us that we'd been assigned to Fire Cove School and reminded us that school began August 2, and we needed to be there by the first to prepare for class.

While we were disappointed we wouldn't be on the road system, we had mentioned to the superintendent that we wouldn't mind being assigned to Fire Cove. It was the float camp where the Packards taught after they had left Lab Bay, and they enjoyed it. It was also not quite an hour's boat ride north of Ketchikan. We could park our new truck in the marina north of town and drive the boat to the camp. Then, whenever we wished to come to Ketchikan, we could reverse the process. So we'd be able to travel more, although we were dependent on weather for good seas. We looked forward to the move.

We changed our reservations so that we could attend my twenty-fifth high school reunion in Minnesota on July 28, fly back to Ketchikan the next day, and still have a day to try to organize our stuff before flying out to camp. It was more of a tornado-like visit, but we managed to get back in time to find we had a day to spare at our new school.

We arrived on July 31, two days before school was to open. Deciding to book a floatplane instead of bringing our boat was Don's idea. He would get an idea of the "lay of the water" between Knudsen Cove and Fire Cove, and also find out where the cables and water lines of camp might be before venturing forth by boat.

Landing in a de Havilland Beaver with time-experienced packing behind us, we brought only the necessaries and carried not nearly as many boxes as we had on our first floatplane trip. I followed Don out the door and down the steps onto the airplane float where we helped the pilot unload our provisions. Soon we were joined by the camp's owner, a short man with a cigar in his mouth, sporting frayed, high-water logger jeans. They were held up with suspenders over a plaid flannel shirt, and he was wearing red XtraTufs. He held out his hand, and his eyes sparkled as he shook our hands.

"Hello. I'm J.R., and welcome. Let me show you around." He led us down the walkway to the playground and our trailer before taking us over to the school. "Have fun. If you need something, just ask. Remember where the office is?" With a smile and a wink and a flick of an ash, he was gone.

Gildersleeve's float camp in Fire Cove

***

Gildersleeve's float camp, located in Fire Cove, nestled near the coast of a protected inlet. Tied to the trees behind the camp and anchored to the sea bottom fathoms below, it was home to about two dozen families. Most of us lived in trailer houses bolted to large rafts, which were lashed together with heavy metal cables.

A six-board walkway stretched from one end of camp to the other, terminating on the sea side at the owner's home. We lived closer to the shore side of camp, near the incinerator and generator, each of them having a float of its own. Our trailer shared the float containing the playground; a set of four swings, a rounded red jungle gym, a balance beam, and monkey bars sat outside our front door, spaced far enough apart that the kids could ride their bikes between them.

On the other side of the walkway, the school hunkered over the entire space of its large float. It was really two buildings: a half-sized gym attached to a structure that had been remodeled into two classrooms. (That structure had been an adjoining boathouse, salvaged when an Alaskan lighthouse was dismantled years before.) Don taught junior and senior high school in the near room while I worked with elementary kids in the other.

Judging from the size of the desks inside, we knew which rooms were ours, and I went into the back to see what I could find. On the bookshelves were the texts, neatly arranged, and I leafed through them, finding familiar lessons. Then I began to organize. Moving the desks into groups of two, pushing the teacher's desk to the rear of the room, and carrying books from one shelf to another, I began to sweat and ache. Kneeling to find the crayons and markers, I was preparing to make some posters when I heard Don's voice from behind the door.

"Biz, come here."

Thankful to leave the tasks of the teacher, I opened the door and walked toward a tall woman standing next to Don. She wore a denim skirt and clean white blouse, her slightly graying hair combed smoothly into a short pageboy. Her brown eyes sparkled as she extended her hand. Wiping my hand on the butt of my jeans, I shook her hand.

In a well-modulated, pleasing voice, she introduced herself. "I'm Beverly." She glided over to a table on which a tray sat. "I heard it was your anniversary, so I brought you something to celebrate." She gestured toward a bottle of Asti Spumante, two plastic wine glasses, and a paper plate filled with chunks of smoked salmon, each pierced by a toothpick. "I want you to enjoy your time here," she said as she left. Before she closed the door, she looked over her shoulder and smiled at us. "You can bring the tray back to the house anytime."

I glanced at Don, my eyebrows raised.

"That's J.R.'s wife," he told me.

Our celebration waited until we left the school and went home, slightly marred by the bouncing of the trailer as the kids jumped and swung and laughed and played on the playground just outside our living room.

"What a welcome," I said. Don just sipped his wine. We were happy.

August 11, 1984

Dear Mom,

This is the first letter I'm trying from the new Macintosh computer that we got on our way home. It's going to be a fun tool to learn to use.

We really had a good time visiting with you. It's too bad that our time was so short.

This is the first time I've had the time to sit down and write, and I feel a little guilty as there is still a lot to be done to get things ready at school.

We are enjoying the Fire Cove community. Everybody has been most welcoming to us. We had a pot luck dinner last Monday night so everyone could get to meet us and we could meet everyone. And the food was delicious. Especially Beverly Gildersleeve's cheesecake—freshly baked and covered with freshly picked huckleberries and blueberries.

There are presently 20 students enrolled at school. I have 11 and Don has 9. It's still a bit of a madhouse as we haven't got all our materials and we haven't had the time to look around to see where the Packards may have stashed things. We plan to spend this weekend moving books and papers to see just exactly what is here.

This place is something else. The whole camp is a series of rafts tied together securely. There are little spaces of water between the trailers and the walkways ... The kids who haven't passed their swimming test (something that the camp has set up—maybe the distance from the float to the shore) must wear their life jackets outside. It's second nature for them to do just that.

We can tie up the boat on the side of the playground—right next to our trailer. So there isn't a long distance to haul things when we bring them by boat. (It's a longer way from where the plane lands, and they have a dolly available to use.)

We didn't have any trouble finding the place when we came back by boat from Ketchikan last weekend. There's a marker just outside the bay in the main channel. It only took us 45 minutes to get here. The water was smooth enough for Don to run with the engine wide open. He said that we could probably make even better time with an empty boat.

While I'm thinking about it, there is no telephone here, but there is a marine radio. If an emergency arises, call the school district office and ask them to get in touch with us at Fire Cove. They can do that.

We are nestled in at the end of a large bay—when the tide is low, we have several islands in view about 20 feet from our bedroom window. When the tide is high, they completely disappear. We are surrounded by high, tree-covered hills.

The radio reception is not good and the TV reception is nonexistent. We have taken a few pictures and will send you some when we get them developed.

Don woke up Thursday night with a toothache—he's at the point where his teeth are really starting to go in bunches—and flew into town Friday morning, saw his dentist, had some x-rays taken, got some pain pills, and was back the same evening. He has an appointment for next Friday to get a crown put on a tooth he had lost the crown for in July, so will get this aching tooth taken care of at the same time.

I hope all's going well with you—take care.

Love,

Biz

We had purchased a Macintosh computer, a small boxy thing, during our stopover in Seattle, and I had begged for it to rest in my classroom. Not only did I have two Apple computers for my kids to use, but I had a printer as well. Don agreed, and soon the elementary kids were keyboarding on all three. The school newspaper that Don's kids had started (the *Fire Cove Log*) was printed on that computer. Even Don ventured forth to try his hand with its bells and whistles.

8/22/84

DEAR MOM,

I AM WRITING YOU THIS NOTE ON OUR NEW MACINTOSH COMPUTER. MY TRY AT THIS LAST NIGHT WAS A WASHOUT. I COULDN'T GET THE DARN THING TO PRINT. ONE MUST BE SMARTER THAN THE EQUIPMENT THEY USE, BUT IN THIS CASE I AM NOT—AT LEAST NOT YET.

I'M STARTING THIS PARAGRAPH WITH A DIFFERENT STYLE AND SIZE OF PRINT. BIZ AND I are just fine. My visit to the dentist is complete and the teeth are in good shape until next time.

Here Don stopped to write a note in his regular cursive writing as the rest of the first page of his letter was blank.

Some of these print styles are hard to read. I shall try to remember that for the future.

Then he resumed experimenting with the fonts of the new computer. The second page begins:

I went ahead and printed the first part of the letter and it worked OK so I shall proceed.

We are enjoying our new location, but are working hard getting used to a new school and new kids. Biz has 10 kids. The five youngest are boys and the five older all girls. Several of the boys are giving her fits, but they seem to be slowly adjusting to what she expects. I have no complaints. My biggest difficulty is giving them enough work to keep them busy.

I was hoping to have my ninth grade girl enter some cross-country running meets in September and October, but the meets are on Saturday and she is a Seventh Day Adventist—so no meets for her. About half of the people in this camp are Adventists. The only thing they seem to observe religiously is their Sabbath. I don't get the impression they are fanatics about many things.

The weather the past several weeks has been magnificent. It's one of the few times (perhaps the only time) that Biz has complained of being too hot since we came to Alaska.

It's nice being about 50 minutes by boat from town. We are planning to go in about every other week to check on the house and grocery shop. I'm parking the truck where we park the boat so getting back and forth on water and land is convenient.

There is a notice posted on the camp office door to the effect that the crew probably faces a short shutdown which indicates a move is probably *imminent. At least one family is planning to leave next week for a 10 day vacation. How soon they will be ready to move the camp is not known yet, but I understand we all stay aboard and continue our regular activities as we roar off at about 2 m.p.h.*

I am enclosing some snapshots and an article about Sally Jesse Raphael.

Love,

Don

That little computer stayed in my classroom the entire length of our teaching at Fire Cove School, six years. It became a habit for me to write a letter to Laurell every weekend we were in camp. But, I found added joy in the ease with which I could answer any letters we had received during the week. With only a few keystrokes, the typing changed from "Dear Mom" to "Dear Kathy" or "Dear Joe and Ann," and I had another letter to print off. Of course, I might have to add a little personal note at the end, but what a great way to let people who cared know how we were doing.

Don's Illness

We were doing just fine, too, until one November Don was struck in the classroom with a sudden, sharp, throbbing, and unbearable pain in his gut. Excusing his class, he stumbled his way to the office to see if he could get a plane into Ketchikan to see the doctor.

Beverly, however, had other plans. Her ex-father-in-law was a surgeon at the Seventh Day Adventist Hospital in Portland, Oregon, and she made arrangements for Don to fly there. He left that day to be met at the airport by this man, transported to the hospital for an immediate examination, discovered colon cancer, and scheduled for surgery the next day. I was on the next jet.

We did tell Laurell about the removal of part of Don's colon. "They got it all," Don told her.

That was a lie. The cancer had already spread to his liver.

So, after this, Laurell did not receive the entire news. There was always a part missing from her letter that everyone else received.

February 10, 1990

Dear Mom,

Back to the old grind again. We just hit the halfway mark, 90 days, and look forward already to the end of the year.

When we got back to camp, the water lines had just thawed after being frozen for about a week. Talk about good timing. The men were working on our line when we walked into the door and within a few hours we had running water again. The school still doesn't have any—although there's water running in camp, it hasn't been hooked up to the school yet. So the kids run home every time they have to use the bathroom. They're pretty quick about it, too, as they have to make up the time they miss after school.

Along with the thaw came lots and lots of snow. Over two feet accumulated on our float, and since it holds the playground, it was LOTS of extra weight. The float is riding about 6 inches lower, and although our trailer is about two feet above the float, the playground is only a few inches above the sea. (Usually it's about 8 inches above.) We've had the kids shovel the playground for a couple of their p.e. classes, just to get some of the weight off before it accumulates some more. Yesterday it rained, and the areas that had been shoveled melted, and the other areas compacted. The snow on the roof has been sliding and dropping off. You don't want to be under it when it falls! Last night we were awakened to a big thud when a large amount came down—the trailer shook for a second—just like it does when we're being buffeted by winds. Forecast is more snow and cold. Time to keep the water running.

Today Don is working on the dryer—it doesn't dry anything. The heat is on but the clothes stay wet. We have a goodly pile of laundry and need to get it washed, and we don't have any clothesline here. I've been wearing jeans to school—with my boots—and they take forever to dry when they're slung over a chair.

Each of us received another student over the winter break. Don's is from the camp just down the bay—parents wanted to move him here because he wasn't doing anything in the school there. In fact he would skip school and hide under a skiff all day just to avoid detection! The superintendent asked Don if he'd take him, and Don said he'd give it a try. (My inclination would have been to say no, but then I'm not Don. He now has 7 kids; I have 13.) One of the fourth graders moved away at break and a new first grader turned up. He's the 6th first grader, and he's a peach. He can read, write, cipher, and listen. One of the little girls latched onto him though, and the biggest problem I have is separating the two of them as she doesn't let him get his work done. Talk about hen-pecked at an early age! One of the first grader's journal entries last week was that she saw them kissing on the playground. Causes some chuckles in the classroom with the older kids and me—guess it's good humor for us all.

We came back last Saturday, in time for a camp pot luck on Saturday night. Everybody seemed pleased to see us, and the food was delicious! Sunday was a work day, and the week seems to have flown by. We both have terrible colds, so sometimes the nights aren't great—interrupted by stuffy noses, coughs, and aches and pains, but they seem to be getting better. Kids are catching it, so if we don't relapse, we'll do okay.

Karen and Ron, Kathy, Joe and Ann, and Caroline all had this added to the paragraph:

It's making Don's recovery from surgery especially difficult, but he's on some medication and hopefully will be okay by the 23rd, when he's scheduled to begin the next chemotherapy. It'll be through a pump—and so I'll go in with him to find out how everything works.

Then Laurell's letter continued.

We had the special ed., the music, and the speech teachers out yesterday. Evvy, the special ed. teacher, came out Thursday and overnighted. She brought the makings for shrimp fettuccine, and Don and I were in seventh heaven! (It's way too full of fat and calories for me to make it for just the two of us! But we sure ate our fill anyway!) On Friday, after school, one of them said that they bet we were happy to see the weekend come so we could get some R and R. I said that I could hardly wait for them to leave so it could start! Not nice, but almost true!

That's it for the first week of school. Take care—we love you—
Biz

I was careful to write Laurell's letter first before adding the parts about Don's cancer and his treatment. I carefully folded her letter and sealed it in an envelope addressed to her before moving on with my other letters.

I continued to do the same with subsequent letters, leaving these parts out of what I sent Laurell.

February 17, 1990

We'll both go to Ketchikan next weekend. That's when the new chemo is supposed to begin. Nothing to tell about it yet, since we don't know anything about it.

March 4, 1990

Don stayed over since he had to get the medication in his pump refilled. He rolled over in his sleep and found a staple from his incision—and got part of it removed on Friday, without any anesthetic, but there's still some more there. He was a little down when he came back on Saturday—seems like there's always something. But he's pretty good today.

March 17, 1990

Don went to town last weekend to have the pump removed and the catheter flushed for cleaning. I think I told you about it last weekend when I was stuck in camp by the weather. When he returned, he said that I could come in with him next week and we'd both learn how to refill the medication and flush the catheter so he wouldn't have to go to town so often. That's great—especially since the next go-round will be three weeks on and three weeks off instead of the two/two he's having now. He'll enjoy the time off, but the time attached to the pump is not fun for him.

Earlier that spring, Don and I had been talking, discussing possibilities for the future. He decided to retire and said he would support my efforts if I wanted to continue teaching. So began a hunt for a new school. Laurell received the part of the letter that said:

I have accepted a teaching assignment for the next year at Polk Inlet, which is a floating camp also owned by Keaton Gildersleeve, but run by his cousin Richard. It has a smaller number of kids in grades 1 through 8. Keaton and Richard both asked that I be transferred there, and since the place I really want, Hollis, doesn't appear to be opening up, I said yes to Polk Inlet. It is only a couple of miles further down the channel from us, and we've visited the school and seen the housing and it was fine. Now both the superintendent and the camp boss want to turn an unfinished bunkhouse into a school for there and get a new trailer. It's full of exciting possibilities, but because of how slowly things move around here, I have visions of opening school the middle of August teaching reading, writing, arithmetic, and then shelf-building, bathroom construction, carpet-laying, etc. We'll see.

The Polk Inlet camp is situated right next to a Forest Service road, which will be nice for walking. The road also connects to Craig and Hollis and the rest of the island when snow doesn't close it. So that will be nice, too. There are rumors that the camp will be towed to Chomley soon, but we've been there before with this camp and there are roads to walk there too. Not connecting roads, though. And so far it's just a rumor.

Gildersleeve's smaller float camp at Polk Inlet as seen from the sort yard

We had heard about the opening at Keaton's other camp earlier that spring. Before school one day, Keaton Gildersleeve, the owner, came into the building where we were both working and called us into Don's high school classroom.

He settled himself atop one of the students' desks as I strolled from my classroom into Don's and sat in a chair nearby. Then he looked at us both and smiled.

"You're retiring, right?" he said to my husband. When Don nodded, he went on. "Well, we'd like to throw a potluck in the gym for you, show you a little bit of appreciation for the years you've been here."

Then he turned to me. "So what are you doing next year, young lady?" I wasn't as young as Keaton, but sometimes he talked that way.

"I don't know. I've been thinking about applying for Hollis, but I don't know if there are any openings right now." (Hollis was a school on the Prince of Wales Alaska ferry terminus.) He knew that I would continue to teach after Don retired and whatever the future brought our way.

"Well, now, I might have something for you."

The teacher working at his other float camp, a smaller place requiring only one teacher, was not going to return. Would I consider that? I couldn't stay where I was—that camp required two teachers because of the large enrollment, and only one housing unit was available. The school district had always hired married couples for this school.

I looked at Don. I knew that his health was failing, that the cancer he'd been diagnosed with two years before, which was first removed from the colon but then spread to the liver, was taking its toll.

Keaton and his wife, Colleen, had waited with me in Portland the previous December as Don had a surgery that we hoped would cure the cancer. A method to cut the infected part out of the liver had been developed there since it had been found that the liver would regenerate by itself when freed from the disease. The operation that had been planned for eight hours had taken only two, as the surgeons had discovered that Don's tumors were not in places that could be cut away. Instead, a shunt had been installed that directly administered the chemo to his liver, and he was now wearing a pump twenty-four hours a day in the hopes that the inevitable would be postponed a while longer.

Keaton and Colleen had enveloped me with their arms and their love when the doctor had emerged from the operating room to let me know. I think we all had cried.

"Let's go for a walk down by the creek," Colleen had suggested. "And then let's have lunch."

As we'd strolled in the cool sunlight, their conversation, reassuring and comforting, had helped soothe my spirit, and I'd actually been able to savor some soup when they'd showed me one of their favorite bistros. Later we'd returned to the hospital to find Don emerging from the anesthetic. They'd left, and as soon as Don had regained his strength, we'd come back to Alaska and continued teaching.

My thoughts returning to the present, I replied. "I'd like to talk it over with Don a bit more first, but thank you for offering. We'll get back to you soon."

We were anchored in Cabin Creek, only a few miles' ride from Polk Inlet, so that next weekend, Don brought me down for a visit. It was a sunny Saturday, and the water was calm, my favorite boating conditions.

Don had bought a new twenty-four-foot Bayliner when we had been in Fire Cove a few years earlier. After starting the engine, Don helped me into the cabin, and I nestled myself onto a bench by the table while he untied our mooring lines. Then he stepped in, took the wheel, pushed on the throttle, and we were off. We chugged past the bunkhouse, past the cookhouse, turning the corner where the two Gildersleeve houses were located. As we began to roar down the channel, I watched the scenery pass by.

What a beautiful place in the sunshine! Both sides of the inlet were lined with trees, marvelous green cedars and hemlocks, spruce, and alders. Here and there, the fragile white buds of blueberry blossoms and pink splotches of salmonberry flowers were barely visible. Although we checked for signs of life along the rocks near the shoreline, no deer or bears appeared. However, an eagle or two soared across the landscape, and water birds, scaups and petrels, scooted out of our way. The clean spray splashed white and foamy above the wake we made, and all too soon, the other camp came into view.

As Don slowed the boat, I looked around. The float camp looked like a smaller version of the one we'd just left, only with different buildings in different locations. However, at each end of the string of floats, a long stiffleg (series of logs tied tightly together to form one long piece) extended outward in the water, forming a sort of triangle with the camp, and we entered through the unconnected vertex of these logs. Attached to both sides were various outbuildings and, on one float, a machine called an A-frame. (I was to learn later that camp life would be almost impossible without that piece of equipment, capable of moving things on the water—logs, buildings from one float to another, even anchors, whatever needed to be rearranged.)

"Oh, look," I marveled out loud. "The camp has suburbs!"

Don cast me a look that softened his eyes and brought a faint grin to his face, the kind that meant, "What a weird dork you are to think that!" But I loved seeing that look and was always happy when I caused it.

I hadn't seen it much lately—those intimate glances that said our souls joined. But then, we hadn't exchanged many intimate moments of any kind in the past two years. Our marriage changed dramatically with the invasion of Don's cancer. I was busy seeing to Don's comfort and trying to keep life as normal as possible, and he was busy in his own way as well—dealing with the disease and trying not to let it disrupt our lives, when in reality it did just that. It erased those moments that made our marriage magic.

Sure, we said "I love you" every night before going to bed—Don to his recliner so he wouldn't bother me with his restlessness, and I to our lonely king-sized bed. We became more like comrades in arms, struggling to make a good war against cancer—Don never suggesting the possibility of losing, I leaving that possibility to fester in my mind, and both of us making a conscious effort to guide our waking hours by ignoring our powerful enemy as much as we could.

We eased alongside one of the walkway floats, and Don tied us up. I smiled my love at him when he came to the boat where I was waiting. Perhaps I grasped his hand a little more tightly when he offered it. I don't think he noticed. As Don helped me out, his head turned toward the camp.

"Wonder where everyone is?" he said, as the place looked deserted. The only sound we heard was the roar of the generator. No children, no booming laughter, no shouts across the water.

We meandered along the walkway, past the generator, past the old brown and crumbling schoolhouse, and found the ramp to land. A bunkhouse guy was just heading down, a fishing rod and a couple of fish in his hand.

"Where is everyone?" Don asked.

"It's Saturday," the guy said. "People go to town," as he jerked his head in the general direction of Craig.

Later we were to find out that there had been a cross country meet scheduled on the island as well, and the school population, including the teacher, had taken off to participate. So we talked to only one person before we finished our walk-through and returned to the boat.

During the next few weeks, we continued to discuss our future as new information arrived.

After Don returned from one of his normal Friday chemo appointments—he had the drug refilled in his pump every week at the hospital in Ketchikan—he brought sad news. When the regimen had first been prescribed, the doctor had said it wasn't a last-ditch treatment but the last, best, most effective treatment of Don's cancer. After a few months, he was still complaining of low-back pain, so his doctor prescribed a CT scan, a bone scan, and several more tests. They showed no cause for the pain, but he was told that he had degenerative arthritis and apparently the tumors were growing. The results were being sent to Portland for a comparison with what they had found that previous December.

Don did grumble a bit, as it was difficult for him to be connected to that pump twenty-four hours a day. What torqued him the most was how it limited him from jet skiing. Although neither of us came out and flat said, "It's not working," I know I had a sense of foreboding after we talked. However, it was our practice to try to forget Don's cancer whenever we could, so we didn't mention this appointment again.

Instead, we continued teaching, counting the days until the end of the school year.

I received word from the school district that no positions in Hollis would be available for me, so the offer of a position at Polk Inlet School began to look really good. A knock on our trailer door one evening brought Keaton to visit.

He came in, followed by a tall burly guy with a beard on his face and a twinkle in his eye. Keaton introduced us to his cousin Richard, who was managing the other camp. They sat on the couch, and Don offered them a drink. He had been enjoying his 7 and 7 sitting his recliner and knew Keaton would join him. Richard accepted a glass as well. As we relaxed around the living room—I had brought in a kitchen chair and was sipping a glass of wine—the conversation ran to fishing, one of Richard's passions; boating, another of his since he'd just bought a new Grady White; and children, as Richard had two, a daughter ready to begin kindergarten and a much younger son.

"Have you thought about what I asked, Biz?" Keaton eventually asked.

"We'd love to have you join our ranks," Richard added. "We're much smaller, and we only qualify for one teacher. Our students are young—they'll be in grades one through eight, and Telitha will begin kindergarten. I'd like to know her teacher is as well thought of as the folks here think of you, and I'm hoping you'll like us well enough to stay on."

How could I say no?

Here I was, going to teach grades one through eight at Polk Inlet School the following year and looking forward to the change. The camp was situated next to a forest service road, which would be nice for walking. The road also connected with Hollis and Craig and the rest of the island. That would allow us to drive to many places we hadn't yet seen. There was also a rumor that camp was going to be towed in the near future to a new site in Chomondeley Sound, but that was just a rumor.

Another weekend, this time on a Sunday, we boated down to the camp again. Richard met us and brought us to the school. It was old, its brown frame deteriorating from years of abusive weather, and the float had grass growing up between the chinks of the logs. He took us inside and told us about going to school there as a kid.

"Many a time, I got my hair pulled or my hands slapped," he recalled. "Teachers were strict, and while I might have been a handful, I learned a lot in this building." He gestured toward the two blackboards along one wall and then encompassed the entire space. I noticed the opposite wall lined with books before my eyes turned upward.

"What is that hole in the roof for?" I asked. It was covered by a piece of wood that looked as if it could be lifted up if one could reach it.

"That was our fire exit," he explained as his eyes crinkled and a smile appeared. "A rope hung from the ceiling, and we would shinny up it. Then we'd open the hole cover, and find the ladder leading down the sloping roof toward the lowest part of the building. We could jump down without being hurt."

I didn't ask him if this were true or not but, instead, asked if he'd share his memories on the first day of the new school year. He gladly agreed and did so on the first day of school.

"Only one thing," Richard continued as we moved toward where our Bayliner was tied. "There's no housing available right now. With folks coming and going like they do during the season, I'm sure something will be available in August when school starts. We'll look forward to seeing you then."

He helped me into the boat, and as Don started the engines, he untied the boat, and we were off, back to Fire Cove School to finish our last year there.

Keaton offered to retrieve a float with a small building on it from Polk and set it up temporarily next to the gym, right across the walkway from our trailer. That way we could put our belongings in it, and it would be pulled back to Polk Inlet and tied up in the suburbs. Whenever housing opened up for us, we would have all our stuff available. It was going to make moving much easier.

The end of the school year came in a rush. We were packing and moving boxes. We were dealing with students knowing there were only a few days of confinement left before the freedom of summer. We were clearing the refrigerator, and not mentioning Don's cancer.

The morning of the big farewell potluck, the second Sunday in June, arrived in calm blue-water sunshine, the birdsong loud and the preparations beginning early. Four barbecue grills were set up on the playground, right next to our trailer, and the activity outside spurred me to check our remaining provisions.

"Don, I can only find red Jell-O and some old, freezer-burned raspberries and strawberries," I moaned. "I have to make a Jell-O fruit salad and hope it will taste good!"

"Don't worry. This party is for us, remember?" he said. "Nobody will care if we don't bring anything, much less that it's a red, fruity sweet thing."

Thus reminded, I set about making sure I had something to contribute, as Don hurried outdoors to see how he could help.

We couldn't use the gym, as it was still decorated from the previous night's eighth grade graduation and dance. Kids had been too tired to dismantle it, so Don and the men brought tables and chairs from the school onto the playground, mingling them with the grills and the swings and the monkey bars. Around noon, people began to congregate, loading their potluck donations onto the table across the walkway in the shade of the school's shadow.

What a delightful meal. While I tried to down a taste of everything, I don't know that I managed among the potato salads, the green salads, the grilled fish and hamburgers and ribs and hot dogs, the chips and dips, the pies and cakes and cookies. But people piled their plates high. Even the red Jell-O concoction I was so worried about disappeared.

Eventually, Keaton got up to speak. His words, most audible over the silence of the crowd and the quiet of the birds, were thoughtful and kind, grateful and hopeful, words of wisdom and grace. The community presented me with a gift certificate for two lovely dinners at one of the finest restaurants in Ketchikan, but their gift to Don brought happy grins and laughter from us all. As Don opened the box Keaton presented him, a blue-and-orange garment fell out of the wrappings. Don held it up to his body and smiled. It was a dry suit, and now he could Jet Ski without the worry of soaking his chemo pump.

As soon as we worded our thanks, Don hurried into the trailer to change. He reappeared, a vision in skin-hugging blue and orange, and headed off toward the edge of the float, where his Jet Ski was parked. A turn of the key, a rev of the engine, and he was off—Jet Ski spray moving around the end of the camp and out toward the opening of the bay. Soon another engine joined him, and we wandered across the walkway to the back of the school and watched as he and Keaton cavorted through the water, their roostertails weaving figure eights through the water as they dodged and drove, happy in the sunlight of the afternoon.

I returned to the playground where many of the women were beginning to clean up the crumbs of our potluck. Sitting at a table, I was soon joined by Teddy, one of my walking partners, and we talked.

"How are you doing?" she asked.

"Okay. I guess. It's good to see Don so happy."

"How about you?" she pressed.

"I'm okay," I repeated. "Moving is coming along. I'll miss you though." In addition to being a friend and fellow walker, she was also the custodian, an aide, and the mother of two of my students. I could count on her whenever I needed help, even when I didn't know it.

***

Just the day before, Teddy had stopped by to ask if I'd like to go walking. Since we'd been in the Cabin Creek location, I hadn't gone at all because the roads were unavailable except through a tedious hike through the forest and then the logging slash (the huge piles of branches and twigs that are piled on the outskirts of the logging site—like a giant nest formed by a creature that doesn't know how to weave things together smoothly).

I had time and wanted exercise and her company, so off we'd gone. I was surprised how easy it was to begin, but then we had to balance on fallen logs to get over creeks and rivers. She encouraged me across—I envied her balance, but I didn't fall in. Then we had to move straight uphill before we arrived at the slash. Managing our way through branches, around holes, and over sticks, we finally reached the road.

We walked awhile and then met a machine that was sorting logs, sitting right on the road and blocking our way. I suggested we turn back, but Teddy waved both arms until the guy in the cab noticed us and paused.

"Can you stop and let us through?" she asked.

He smiled, gestured toward the bit of road his machine didn't cover, and we continued on our way. We went to the sorting yard, where the logs were arranged before they were dumped in the water.

It was low tide, so no logs were going in, and we thought we could use that intertidal region to walk back to camp, thinking it was like a beach.

We jumped onto the rocks at the edge of land and began picking our way back but found that this beach was made of little rocks, big rocks, and mountains. Not much sand. There was no easy way back, but we managed. And it took us only two hours.

It was a good trip. I didn't realize that I needed to get away before the big party. I believe Teddy did.

***

At the table, Teddy continued. "I think you'll really like the other camp," she said. "You know Joe's brother worked there for years, and he got along well with all the people there." (Joe was her husband.) She spoke slowly, trying to form her thoughts into carefully chosen words. "I don't think that it's… well… I think that people feel more equal there."

Perhaps she was referring to Keaton and his father before him, as they really were the leaders of the camp, almost like benevolent dictators, a favorite term of Don's when he was asked how he managed his classroom. They had their upper echelon, the bull cook, the side rod, and the guys who had worked for the company for years. Those trusted and true workers were treated with a bit more consideration than the newcomers. I was happy to be almost a part of the upper echelon—not working for the company but with friends in the high places.

***

The school year ended, and on Friday, amidst many goodbyes, I boarded a plane for Ketchikan. I had enrolled in a class that began the following Monday and wanted to get our home in Ketchikan cleaned out and stocked up for our summer there. Don was planning to bring the boat in as soon as he found out why it wouldn't run.

I left him at camp trying to figure out what was wrong with it. He thought maybe it was the fuel pump, and he might have to order parts before it would work properly and he would feel safe to take it across Clarence Strait.

So I was surprised when I received a phone call from Don the next day. He was at the air taxi office in town and would I please pick him up. He had decided to leave the boat in camp until some parts he had ordered arrived and join me in town.

When I returned home on Monday after my class, Don was waiting in the living room. He was holding a letter in his hand.

"What's that?" I asked.

"I heard from Portland," he said. "Here, you read it."

His oncologist reported that the drug wasn't working; the tests showed that Don's tumors were growing. Two other drugs were available, but they had had little success and large side effects. The oncologist recommended that Don drop all drugs and "consider quality of life issues."

The next day, Tuesday, Keaton came by in the afternoon to offer Don and our town neighbor Keith (who was a crackerjack mechanic) a ride out to camp so they could fix the boat and get it into town. I was told later that he also reported an alternative cancer treatment available in Greece that his accountant had mentioned. He gave Don the relevant information, and when he returned from camp in his boat, which Keith had helped fix, Don called this person who had found healing. Greece became an alternative.

Wednesday, Don went to his local doctor to return the pump and discussed seeking treatment out of the country. His doctor suggested a second opinion at Swedish Tumor Institute in Seattle.

Thursday brought a friend from camp, the former side rod who now had his own company; we had run into him in the grocery store. He had heard about Don's status and offered, "I have a cousin who went to Greece for treatment two years ago, and he's still going strong. You really oughta consider it. I think it works." He gave Don the cousin's phone number, and when we returned home, he called.

The cousin and his wife had saved everything on their computer and were going to send us a printout. But that phone call revealed the following information: the doctor was a microbiologist who discovered something natural that would battle cancer cells. He had it mixed up in Switzerland and operated a clinic in Athens, Greece. He treated all cancers the same, a series of injections, which made the patient feel he was "getting a sunburn from the inside out," for twenty minutes each. However, the treatment was not recognized in the United States.

Nonetheless, the week had swept us up on a wave of optimism, and when Friday evening came, we totally enjoyed Don's retirement party, his second, this time given in Ketchikan.

Not only were Keaton and Colleen there, but so also were many of our Ketchikan friends and school-district personnel. I had written to Laurell:

> *Don's retirement party was fun—building many warm memories—when so many friends' faces showed up. I spent the evening laughing and crying. Don's secondary supervisor was the master of ceremonies. Keaton Gildersleeve gave the first speech, and it was all "thank you's" for things Don had done during our six years at his camp, and he presented Don with a Gildersleeve Logging Company jacket. (Rarer than hens' teeth, I'm told.) Then Don Alderman, the music teacher, gave a speech and presented Don with a gift from the district, a Native art print.*

Throughout the evening, I watched Don gracefully accept his due. I was filled with thanks that he was appreciated, he knew he was

Here's to you , Don!

appreciated, and he was gratified and fulfilled. It was a good retirement recognition party.

I had added to a letter to my cousin Kevin—which Laurell never saw:

> *The way it looks, we'll make a quick trip to Colorado first. I hope this time Don finds the opportunity to tell his mother about his cancer, but we'll see. Then we'll*

> *go to Seattle to Swedish to see what they say. While we're there, we'll get some passports, just in case. I imagine if they confirm what Don's been told by his oncologist in Portland, we'll make plans to go to Europe.*

As we waited for the papers about the doctor in Greece, Don decided to get his teeth pulled. I think he felt he had a reprieve, and he wanted to get on with his life. He'd been bothered by all the dental work he'd needed, as it seemed as if hardly a month went by when one of his fillings fell out, one of his teeth ached, or one of his crowns cracked. He had decided, before his cancer diagnosis two years earlier, that he wanted false teeth. So as I went to my class, he had most of his teeth pulled, first those on the left side and then those on the right. Then he spent the rest of the summer chewing only with the teeth still left in the center of his mouth. He also spent the time fishing, puttering about the house, driving his Model A roadster, and planning steps for his cancer treatment.

When my class was finished, we left Ketchikan and spent a bit of time visiting Laurell in Colorado Springs. Don had never told her about his colon cancer: "She's got enough to worry about what with her own health issues and Dick's brain tumor." I think Don also felt that his mother's concern would reach bounds that he would be uncomfortable with, especially since he'd had another brother who died of spinal meningitis before Don was born. His mother cared deeply about the two sons who were still with her, and when the older was fighting a serious problem, Don just chose to ignore his cancer in the presence of this woman. Although many times I asked him to tell her, he never did.

On our way back to Ketchikan after this visit, we stopped in Seattle so Don could see the cancer specialist at Swedish Tumor Institute. Don was given an MRI; lying still was difficult to endure with his severe back pain, but the results showed a slightly herniated disc but no spread of the cancer. He was told to rest and give the disc an opportunity to heal itself. The doctor also told Don he'd review the results of a previous CT scan and write a letter giving him "the best guess" of the time he had left. He prescribed a drug that might slow the cancer's growth that Don agreed to take before heading off to receive the Greek doctor's treatment. However, we learned that we didn't have to go to Greece to receive it. We could find it in Mexico.

Hope in Mexico

We began making plans for a Mexican Christmas. The doctor from Greece had trained people in Mexico to use his treatment, and a brochure explained that we could stay in a hotel in San Diego and be bussed daily into a clinic in Tijuana. It sounded so much easier than traveling to Greece and gave the same hope for a cure. Thus, we were actually looking forward to the trip

But first, there was the commitment of teaching in Polk Inlet. As the school year began, housing was still not available there, so Don and I stayed in a small trailer at their other camp in Cabin Creek. Every morning, Don boated me the three miles, helped me onto the boardwalk in front of the school, and I'd teach.

The powers of camp were in the midst of bettering our situation. A new school was being transformed from a bunkhouse; it would become a beautiful facility. We were told that a two-week delay existed, and we had to refurbish the old school, the one that Richard had taken me through, with furnishings and equipment. They had been stored in a little building on a float in the "suburbs," so one day the boom boat moved it close and tied it up, and Don and I began packing desks and books into the old school. We decided to leave the computers stored away until we could settle into the new building.

Sheri and me with our students in front of the old school

When school opened, Richard came to talk to the students—his uncle J.R. had built the structure in 1956, and both he and his cousin Keaton had attended school in this very building. One of their teachers, curiously enough, had been Myrtle, whom Don and I had taught with when we first moved to Alaska, in Labouchere Bay. I imagine she had required "golden silence" from them, too. The nine students in grades one through eight were attentive, sitting at their desks and looking at the blackboards Richard said he had stayed after school to clean.

I had an aide, Julie, a blessing because of her experience. So between us, we got school started. It was not an easy start. The kids were good, the books were adequate, and learning was taking place. However, I was living three miles away from school.

In a small trailer still in Keaton's camp, Don and I set up temporary housekeeping. He usually picked me up by boat when I was ready to leave. It was not the best arrangement, and we both eagerly awaited the arrival of our new housing. In one of my letters, I noted:

Don just called me to come and look at some floats that were being pulled by here on their way to Polk Inlet. Our new teacher housing is on it, a double wide trailer house with an attached shop, and a little greenhouse. I think the present owners will be living in it for awhile, but they're buying a house in Ketchikan, and when they move out, we'll move in. I'll be happy not to be commuting.

The weather's been just beautiful, and the water's been calm, so I've enjoyed the boat rides. Since I don't drive the boat, it's not like driving a car, and although Don's been real good about showing up when I tell him I'll be through, sometimes I'm not, and he has to wait around. He doesn't complain though. Still, the weather's not going to be beautiful forever, so I'm looking forward to moving from Cabin Creek down to Polk Inlet. It's about three miles away and the ride takes only 10 minutes. There's not much traffic, either.

After Labor Day, if we're not moved down there by then, I'll need to hitch rides to and from school, as Don will stay in Ketchikan to be with Dave and Roxanne, who don't leave until Tuesday, and then to put the truck on the ferry to Hollis to drive it to Polk Inlet on Thursday. I think I can get JR to give me a ride down there in the mornings, and the eighth grader, Caleb, has a skiff and likes to visit Cabin Creek, so I think he'd give me a ride back. In rainy weather I'll get wet.

I wasn't looking forward to being at other people's mercy as to when I could and couldn't get to work.

Dave and Roxanne were good Colorado friends of ours, and we hadn't seen them in a long time. They were coming to visit over the Labor Day holiday, and they wanted to go fishing. Don and I bought flightseeing tickets for Misty Fjords National Monument, and as Don would be in Ketchikan, I wanted to spend the long weekend there too.

Don was still busy fighting his cancer—chemotherapy had caused swelling and redness around the site of his portacath leading to the hepatic artery, and he either flew or boated to Ketchikan every week for a Friday appointment with his medical team. They were trying a new drug, and we were hopeful it was retarding the cancer's growth. Of course, Laurell didn't know that, but Dave and Roxanne did. In fact, I think that everybody we knew except Laurell was aware of Don's struggle with this disease.

Laurell knew that Dave was Don's best friend from Colorado—they'd been best backpacking buddies, going into the mountains, fishing for brook trout, sitting around a campfire, telling lies every chance they had. Dave and Roxanne had moved to Maine around the time we moved to Alaska, and Don and Dave hadn't seen each other since. Dave also told me later that he was coming to say goodbye to Don. We had told them about the progress Don was making—or wasn't making—with the cancer.

It was good to spend time with old friends, even though the goodbye seemed to be just that—not "So long," but "Thanks for coming." I cried after they left.

September through December passed in a foggy rush, at least for me. I was moving into a new teaching situation, from one school to another. I was moving, too, from one home to another to yet another. And I was trying to be the best support and wife I could be to my dying husband. There was a lot on my mind.

I don't remember any of the academics I taught, but I imagine my experience served me well. The students were good, well mannered, and hard working, and their wonderful behavior covered any mistakes I made.

One very new wrinkle in our lives was that we were now on the road system. That meant that students could participate in the cross-country events, and they were used to doing so. At least three of the girls in the elementary school were serious runners and wanted to practice every day after school. Don, who had worked with one of his high school girls the previous year, said he would take them out on the roads and time their runs. Once he brought the pickup from Ketchikan to Hollis and drove it out to Polk Inlet, he could also drive runners to the meets. Julie, my aide, also provided transportation. Her girls were two of the runners. At least one or two Saturdays in September and October, we were on the road, driving to the cities where the meets were held. And always the girls ran their best.

I had agreed to participate on the teachers' negotiating team with the school district. That was a big mistake. It did get me into Ketchikan once or twice at the same time Don was there for his chemo, but I wasn't emotionally prepared to argue for my job. I never enjoyed the combative process that school districts and teachers' unions seem to use, and when ours went to arbitration, I was told I was too negative to be of much help. So I resigned after only two months of service.

While I was in town the first time, I asked Julie to sub for me. She did, but the day after I returned to camp, she said she was leaving and was taking her two girls with her. She assured me it wasn't me or subbing, but I wondered. I'd been told that she had some marital problems, but I didn't know anything for sure. So I hired another aide, Susan, who didn't want to sub. So I asked the mother of the third runner. She said she would, and she did. But when I returned from a trip to town, she too said she was leaving, at the end of November, but it wasn't because of me or subbing for me. We were playing a bit of musical helpers there for a while.

We finally were able to transfer from the old building to the new. There was no heat in the old school, and as the days grew cooler, the crew worked harder and longer on the remodeled bunkhouse. Finally, it was towed to the edge of camp, and on one fine weekend, Don and I and all the students who wanted to help moved.

We toted desks from one building to the other. We toted books. We dove into the little building and brought out the computers. And finally, we put up the shelves and began to sort and put away the lovely library books that were in so many boxes. When we began the school day in the new building, we almost had to wear sunglasses—the walls and carpet were so bright after the dinge we had been used to.

Don was almost an unpaid second teacher. He helped me work on the paperwork that the principal teacher of every school was required to fill out. He reminded me if I asked too often how to fill out a particular form or how to get the district (or the camp) to provide something, "Biz, it's something you've got to get used to."

I didn't like hearing that. Not only was I not as outgoing and outspoken as he was, I also wasn't sure what I would become without him. I wanted to utilize every asset he possessed. He also painted and puttered around the new school once we were able to move in, as well as listened to the kids read a couple of days a week. When the track meets were on a school day, he'd take the runners and their parents to the site, allowing me to stay in camp and teach. We were still a two-teacher team in many ways.

When we received word that we could move to Polk Inlet from the little trailer in Keaton's camp, we rejoiced. We were assigned a bottom unit of a duplex on the front row, next to the generator, only a short walk from the school. It was a square living space, a pleasant change after the narrowness of the trailer.

The little building holding the belongings that we'd packed up the previous spring was towed to the edge of the walkway, and Don and I spent one weekend moving in. Although we still had boxes piled almost to the ceiling in one of the bedrooms, it was good to be able to use the things we could. We left the freezer and the Jet Ski parked in the building as it was towed back to the suburbs until we could move into our new and larger residence.

The apartment was interesting in that the floor sloped. One day when I taught, Don baked one of his favorites—a chocolate cake. He showed it to me when I came home from school, chuckling because it was three inches high on one side, and only a half inch on the other. He measured! The floor slanted toward the rear, and that was where the bedrooms were located. So it made for an easy trek to get ready for bed at night but required more energy to get up and going in the morning. The difference was noticeable.

Late in the fall, we were finally able to move our boxes for the last time. The double-wide trailer became our housing. When we walked inside, we were amazed at its space. We would have a huge living room, a kitchen and a dining room, and two bedrooms and two baths. There was a sort of workshop built onto the back. However, it had no furniture.

Don flew into Ketchikan, and on Keaton's bill, purchased a blue couch and coordinating recliner, along with a couple of queen-sized beds and one table with four chairs. I loved the living room that was created: a smoky-blue carpet surrounded by off-white walls and now containing comfortable furniture in my favorite color. Don did well. We didn't live there long before we had to deal again with his cancer.

***

Too soon, fall closed in on winter, and we were on our way to Mexico. Flying from Ketchikan to San Diego was tiring, and when we finally reached our hotel, we gave thanks for one day's grace before we'd be riding the bus across the border to the clinic.

During that day, the sun shone, and Don slept. I ventured outside toward a marina near our building and walked around the harbor's edge, admiring the view and questioning the future. Had we made the right decision? Would the next two weeks be a turning point in Don's struggle with the disease? Would I function well in this situation? When I returned to our room, Don was much refreshed and suggested we visit the dining room before turning in for the night.

The next morning, a bus picked us up from the hotel. Loaded with Don's medical records and our identification and money belts, we were on our way. Every seat was taken, and most faces looked hopeful, apprehensive, afraid, and/or concerned. I imagine ours did too.

We were all going to the Contreras Cancer Clinic, and riding on that bus made it easy. The entry guards at the boarder talked briefly to our driver before motioning us through, and then I watched as the rest of Tijuana passed by. Quickly, from the freeway, we saw large cardboard boxes snuggled up to rock formations, clustered in various communities along the way. Somebody told me they were villages of Mexican people.

The freeway turned into a busy avenue, and soon other Mexican homes appeared. These were stuccoed mansions, colored in yellows and creams, their properties fenced with huge wrought-iron gates guarding the entries. It was in this neighborhood that the bus pulled up to a large institution-looking building, albeit clean, bright, and new, and stopped. We were ushered out of the bus and into the clinic.

We found seats in the crowded waiting room and waited. We were in a very busy center, sorted and sent to wherever it had been determined that we go.

"Señor Robbins," announced a female voice from behind a counter.

Don rose, I with him, and we followed the sound. We were led down the hall to a doctor's office where a dark-haired man waited for us. That began a series of tests, and I returned to the waiting room until Don was finished.

"Biz," he began when he emerged from the hallway, "we're going to have to move from the hotel to the clinic here."

"What? But the brochure said we could be transported …" I protested, not wanting to be in this place for the two weeks Don's treatments were scheduled.

"Yes, but I'm going to need surgery," he continued. "They can't use the portacath that was installed earlier. The chemo burned the skin around it, and they want to install a new one."

"What about that Greek doctor's regimen? I thought that was just a series of injections?"

"Well, that's the other thing. The doctor said that the type of cancer I have will respond better to another treatment. I'll get a new shunt, and then you and I will learn what they want us to do when we leave."

"But do we have to stay here the whole time?" I was still reluctant to remain.

"We can stay in the same room." He assured me that the hospital had accommodations for patients and their spouses, as that's how most arrived.

So we returned to the hotel, the next day moving in to the clinic for a two-week stay. We paid ten thousand dollars cash and were told that covered Don's surgery and our room and board for that length of time.

Our room was on a floor circled by patients' rooms. In the middle was not only a nurse's station but also several comfortable couches, tables, and chairs, perhaps an effort to make a living room out of the clinical setting. It was where I would go when Don was sleeping (which was often) or being seen by his doctor. It was also where I met a couple of other wives.

Raimie was from Canada. Her husband suffered a rare form of cancer in his kidney, and he either would have had to wait a very long time for treatment or would not be seen at all if they'd stayed home. They figured he would be dead when, if ever, he was allowed to see a doctor in Canada.

Jennifer, from California, came with her husband, too. He had exhausted all the available options to treat his brain tumors. They had read about the Mexican clinics that provided alternative cancer treatment and decided to come to "the best of the bunch." This was their last-ditch chance, too.

Somehow, we ended up in the living area at the same time most days, and we'd talk about the progress, or lack of it, that our husbands were making. One might have had a good night's sleep; another might have had good numbers one day and then bad numbers the next. We were a support group, keeping each other's spirits up in the midst of hope and care and optimism that was laced with an unspoken sense of futility.

"Are you going to follow the diet when you get home?" I asked. Patients were encouraged to eat a vegetarian diet. Fresh vegetables were stressed, either steamed, baked, or juiced. I was encouraged especially to juice carrots and to use the pulp to make muffins. Carrot juice and carrot muffins were always on the menu, along with steamed vegetables and fruit plates. I knew that at camp such fresh produce might be difficult to obtain.

"They'll be hard for me too," Raimie agreed, as where she lived in British Columbia was also rather remote.

"Jay really likes meat," Jennifer added when she said that she'd have no problem in the Bay area. "I don't know what to do about that."

"What about the medical protocol?" I wanted to know if their responsibilities might be the same as mine. Don had been placed on a procedure that required taking some pills containing enzymes by mouth and being injected with laetrile. My heart sank as I heard this for the first time. I remembered Steve McQueen, the movie star, and the publicity surrounding his seeking a cure for his cancer in Mexico. He also was prescribed laetrile; he didn't live long.

Now here Don was being given the same medicine. Daily. I would have to learn to inject him, in the center of the new shunt where his skin had grown over. It was scary. Not only would I need to be careful, feeling to see where the needle needed to go, but also I would be praying that Don's outcome would be more positive than that of Steve McQueen's.

"I don't really have to do much," Jennifer said. "Jay will just have to take his pills and continue on the diet for three months. Then we'll return for more treatments here."

Raimie, too, had different medical procedures to follow. She didn't seem as nervous about going home as I was. But it was a gift to be able to talk to these women.

It was also a gift to be able to exercise. Every day, I would leave the hospital and walk the couple of blocks to the nearby bull ring. As I walked my ten laps around its perimeter, I would marvel at the shapes of the clouds in the blue sky. Or I would wonder at the top of the ring—why it was laden with broken bottles and barbed wire. Or I would think about what Don had been doing that day. Or that night. Or what our future would be. Or even if we had a future.

Often that surgeon's question returned: "Do you want to tell him he has a couple of years to live, or shall I?" She had asked me when she came to talk to me in the waiting room after Don's initial colon removal when she saw that the cancer had already spread. It had been two years.

When I counted to ten, or sometimes twelve, a half-hour had passed, and I thought I should return.

Often I found Don waiting for me outside the building. He had pushed and pulled the wheeled cart containing the IV drip he was prescribed to the doorway and through it. Smoking a cigarette in the sunshine, he always had a smile.

"Enjoy your walk?" he'd ask.

I always said that I did.

Eventually, we left and flew home to Ketchikan. I carried a brand new suitcase filled with syringes and medications; Don had a brand new shunt inserted into his liver. I had been instructed to inject Don daily with the medication and to provide freshly juiced vegetables, especially carrots, and steamed vegetables for his meals. We tried this at home, and when school resumed, I left Don in Ketchikan, as I needed to get back to teach.

In my absence, Don decided to have the remainder of his teeth pulled. Because he had already lost the teeth in his right and left sides, he thought he would enjoy food more if he were fitted with false teeth. Although the dentist advised caution and I said, "Don, don't do it," my husband could be a stubborn man. He had his remaining teeth pulled and came out to camp with a set of false teeth in his mouth, a faint grin on his face, and only a very little time left to live.

He no longer had the strength to meander about the camp, staying in our trailer, usually in the little back room with his 7-Up and cigarettes. He became weaker and weaker, and when visitors from the school district noticed, contingency plans were drawn up for the time when he would have to be hospitalized. That time came when he was unable to move from that little back room to the main trailer section without falling up the small step that separated them.

Don Alderman, the music teacher who noticed his tumbles, said, "I think it's time, Biz."

That following Friday, we flew out of camp; Don never returned.

I was left writing to Laurell, trying to prepare her for what was coming, although I didn't realize how quickly Don would die. And I didn't tell her that Don had cancer.

March 4, 1991

Dear Mom,

I'm sorry I haven't been writing lately but I've been so busy … finally solved most of my time problems, so your letter is the first item on my agenda.

I've asked for a couple weeks off from teaching—I have bunches of sick days—in order to stay in town and look after Don. His back is still a problem, and although he's been trying physical therapy, it's not working real well. With him in town and me out at camp, he's not eating well either. He hasn't gotten used to his dentures, either. So I'm in to be with him and to nag and cook, and help him get his back and diet in shape so he'll be able to go back to camp. He's lost weight, too, so I'm going to spend time making healthy, succulent meals.

Out at camp, my class load has been on the increase, with one family returning from south and another family moving from another logging camp. I started in January with 4 kids, increased to 5, then 7 by Valentine's Day, 9 the following week, and last week the first high school student arrived! Talk about keeping on the run. The high schooler is taking English (easy for me to fit in), algebra (fun to teach), biology (no teacher's manual yet), Alaska Native studies (LOTS to read and prepare), French (no NOTHING available except some videotapes—I took German in college, so gave the responsibility of this class to my aide, who's having the student teach her French), and band (no problem—she's an excellent flautist and practices after school in the kindergarten room).

I found I wasn't doing a good job in the classroom with my concerns about Don, and wasn't happy with my relationship with Don because of my concerns in the classroom. So my stress level rose, and I decided I needed a break from one of my two commitments. And Don wasn't the one. So I feel a big load has been lifted from my shoulders.

This wasn't exactly a lie, but it was certainly a big fib. I had shifted all my concern to Don, who was struggling. When we arrived in town, and as I wrote this letter, Don had been given morphine to ease his pain, and it was working. However, it was also causing him not to be able to eat. He couldn't keep anything I fixed down, no matter how tantalizing, succulent, or bland it was. I wondered what would happen next as I continued my letter to Laurell:

> *We left camp last Friday; it was not a good day for flying with lots of wind, but Don had only 3 pain pills left, so he took 2 before we got on the plane. We made it in just fine—our neighbors had started a fire in the woodstove so the chill was off the house. We stopped by the drs. office and then the pharmacy for more pills.*
>
> *It's been really cold—camp froze up the night before we left. By Friday there was running water into one bunkhouse, where we can at least pack fresh water into our homes and take a shower and use the flush toilet—so it could have been worse. Our neighbors plugged in our heat tape, so we have running water in town. With the cold we've had beautiful sunlit days and icy clear stars at night.*
>
> *I left our computer at school, Don's suggestion as the kids really enjoy using it, so writing all the letters I owe is going to mean they're not as long as they'd be if I'd type them.*
>
> *In fact my brother and my cousin haven't heard from me, so I'll close and get started on their letters.*
>
> *Hope all's well—take care.*
>
> *Love,*
>
> *Biz*

I mailed it promptly, but by March 4, Don was already in the hospital. His reaction to the morphine, plus his deteriorating body, necessitated around-the-clock care. He quickly succumbed to the plagues he was fighting and died on March 7. His death certificate reads "respiratory arrest—5 min.; colon cancer—3 yrs." I don't know if Laurell received my letter before her son was gone.

Don's brother, Dick, lived in Texas at the time, still battling his brain tumors. Don had told his brother about his disease, so I called and told him about Don's death and asked if he could please drive to Colorado Springs and tell Laurell. I quelled my anger with Don for never even hinting to his mother that there was something wrong, leaving me to deal with this lovely lady who never had a chance to say goodbye.

We arranged a plan: I would take Don's ashes to Colorado Springs, and until I arrived, Dick would stay with Laurell. Once I was there, the three of us would sprinkle Don's ashes.

While Don was in the hospital, I had asked him what he wanted done with them. He was past speaking at the time, so I suggested I take them to Colorado and sprinkle them in one of his favorite trout streams. He nodded and smiled or maybe winced—it was hard to tell—but he knew that is what we planned to do.

The trout streams were too hard for Laurell to reach, requiring a rather strenuous hike off the beaten path up into the mountains, so Dick found another place. As we drove west toward the streams, we went through the town of Buena Vista, right past its city park. One of the picnic areas led down to a river, the Arkansas, and while Laurell and I waited on the bank, Dick waded in, turned the box that held Don's ashes upside down, and uttered some words that were lost to the wind. As Laurell and I hugged each other, Dick waded back, and we returned to the car. We'd said our goodbyes.

Life without Don

I flew back to Alaska and to the camp I'd left a month before.

Me heading down the boardwalk, alone, to my trailer

My neighbor from Ketchikan, Robyn, wanted to come along to support me as I returned to this place, this lifestyle, that had been such a good fit for my husband. I hoped it would be a good fit for me as well.

When Robyn and I deplaned, Marilyn and Maggie, parents of my students, greeted us from the airplane float. I slowly walked to the end of the camp, to the last float which held my trailer, and after climbing the few stairs, entered the living room and deposited my bag. Robyn, Marilyn, and Maggie had followed, carrying the boxes of groceries I'd brought. They set them down, gave me hugs, and the sisters, Marilyn and Maggie, left.

Robyn began to unpack the groceries, planning to keep me company for the first night back. She baked cookies and prepared our dinner meal while I decided to check on the students. Wondering what I'd find and also if I'd done the right thing in returning, I left my trailer and crossed over the little bridge to the school.

Inside, Mrs. Lonners was saying goodbye. She had been a blessing, coming to substitute for a whole month, living in a floating logging camp and teaching students in grades one through eight. She had arrived the morning of the day I had needed to leave with Don. We had discussed the students, the ways of getting groceries, the nuances of keeping the trailer and the school functional, and anything else that was on our minds. I was grateful to her and the school district for allowing me to leave with the intent to return when I could.

While I'd been gone, the powers of camp had moved the float with my house to an outside row. The view was wonderful. Overlooking the water and hills toward the mouth of the inlet and combined with the comfortable furniture they'd provided, sitting inside and staring outside became a favorite pastime. Even the rain was nice when I could watch seals frolic and fish jump. Whenever a plane taxied over to the airplane float, I noted who got off and who got on. It was a good place to be, a safe place.

During that first week, itinerants paid me visits—first Don Alderman and then Evvy Fernald, the special ed. teacher. They both overnighted, and we talked late into the evenings. Both Don and Evvy were good friends, and while their presence eased my way back into the camp teaching situation, these nights also were but the first in a series that would help me determine how I dealt with death and aloneness.

During their subsequent visits, we'd talk as friends do, they making evaluations of my emotional and mental health. Of course, their official visits were supporting the educational program we provided for the students.

I still wrote to Laurell:

April 13, 1991

Dear Mom,

It was so good to hear from you. I'm glad your sleeping pills and Xanox are helping. I received a thoughtful note from Harriet Winn, which I answered today. It would be nice to take her to lunch when I'm in Colorado this summer.

I have signed my name to three pieces of mail from various banks and mailed them to wherever they went. My memory fails—but I do remember there were three. One required a notary and was difficult to understand just how to fill it out, but since it hasn't been returned, my guess is that I filled it out okay.

She was suffering as much as I, and her friend Harriet was trying to make the grieving smoother for both of us.

I really didn't know what I was doing—just signed the papers people told me to sign and tried to keep myself together—myself the teacher and myself the person. Many tried to help. Robyn had helped me ease into the community again and also baked some lemon cookies and a root beer cake. I promised myself to keep in touch with all those who'd sent their love and sympathy. One, however, surprised me. I told Laurell about it.

A sympathy card and short note arrived the other day from Heather. She's in Phoenix. I answered her note, and who knows if she will decide to try to establish a relationship with me or not. But I left the door open if she wants to give it a go.

The card and note were from Don's daughter, Heather, whom we hadn't heard from since before we left Colorado. She had lived with us for a while when she was sixteen before she ran off with her boyfriend to Florida. She had heard about Don's death from her mother and contacted me. I don't remember if she was inquiring as to a legacy Don might have left her or asking how her dad's life had been in Alaska or just sending condolences. I do remember trying to offer my friendship, a link with her dad, if she wanted it. We never did become friends.

I continued writing to Laurell.

> *Weather's been rainy and windy. Lots and lots and lots of rain. I guess it's been snowing on the higher elevations where they're logging, but I'm sure appreciative that the pipes haven't frozen and the water is running. Especially with all the overnight company I've been having. Only problem has been the furnace. The book Don gave me for Christmas, How to Fix Damn Near Everything, doesn't have a furnace chapter. It has something on mowers and blowers, but I think I'll get the district maintenance man out to see about it. It's been a problem ever since we moved into the housing before Christmas.*

While I appreciated receiving the book as a Christmas gift from Don, I am not at all mechanically minded, and I don't care to spend my time learning anything about how to be. This furnace and, later, a water heater would prove to be the most difficult problems I had to solve in Don's absence. What to do when the district's maintenance man said it was the camp owner's problem and the camp owner said the problem was the school district's? That was my dilemma. It remained unsolved for quite some time.

Spring arrived and, with it, some energy. My housing float held several flower boxes and one claw-footed bathtub, all full of dirt. The tub also held strawberry plants, white blossoms promising lots of fruit, but the boxes were empty. I thought I might fill them with seeds and see if somebody would tend them over the summer when I would be gone.

When I shared this with Don Alderman on one of his overnight trips, he sent back several gardening implements after he returned to Ketchikan along with this poem:

> *Mary, Mary, quite contrary, how does your garden grow? With silver bells and cockle shells and a whole bunch of weeds.*

He knew how to bring out a smile.

I asked the students if they'd like to help with the flower boxes, and they were eager to help. A letter to Laurell in May said:

> *It's a beautiful Friday afternoon in Polk Inlet and I've been out on the float getting my hands dirty working the soil in some planters the former tenant left behind. Some of the kids want to tend vegetable gardens this summer, so I'm helping them. They can use the soil and boxes—I even have seeds and fertilizer, so when school starts up again in August, maybe they'll share the fruits (or should I say vegetables) of their labor.*

The kids and I began counting down the days until the end of the school year. They had activities: a dance for the older kids at the other Gildersleeve camp, a "sea week" field trip at low tide to play in the ocean and learn at the same time, and a program to present to their parents. I ordered materials for the following year, helped Keith and Robyn find all the boat parts when they visited so they could help me sell the Bayliner, and typed up the programs for the school end-of-the-year production.

Toward the end of the school year, the superintendent asked if I would like to transfer to a larger school. Remembering that I had requested a transfer earlier when Don had retired from teaching, I wondered if I still wanted the camaraderie of other teachers, sharing a school with others, and so I asked my friends for their opinions. Both Don A. and Evvy suggested I stay where I was, noting that I was getting comfortable with my situation there. Marilyn also supported my return to camp the following year; she and other parents were pleased with the education their children were receiving. So I declined the offer and planned to return the following fall.

Returning to Ketchikan, to our dome home for the summer, I tried to ignore Don's absence. I fertilized all the plants we had, I washed everything washable, I rearranged my clothing so it took up Don's space, too, and I scrubbed all the walls and floors with a Borox solution. My cousin, Karen, who was allergic to mold and mildew, was coming for a visit. The house would be spanking clean for her.

While I waited for her coming, my friend Evvy was made a widow. Her husband had been killed in a traffic accident outside one of the totem parks. I tried to help her, and in truth, she showed me in her grief how to grieve more deeply myself. We spent a great deal of time together before my cousin came.

Then I made plans to visit Laurell.

> *I'll probably be in Colorado the third week of July—if all goes according to plan. My cousin Karen (Kathy's sister) will be spending the first two weeks of July in Ketchikan with me. I'm real excited about that—she's never been here before. Then, I'll leave on the same jet with her and we'll spend a couple of days in Seattle before she goes back to Minnesota and I come to Colorado.*
>
> *I found all the tax information I think I'll need. Don had last year's stuff all in one packet and I found it when I was going through the desk. Trust him to be organized. So I gathered all the similar information that he had put together—hope it's the right stuff!*
>
> *It's also possible that I won't come alone. Evvy Fernald, our special ed itinerant teacher, has relatives in Colo. Spgs. And Castle Rock, and was mentioning today that maybe we should travel together. She lost her husband last Friday, so she's still in a state of whatever it is when we first learn of the loss of a loved one ... Anyway, it would be nice to come to Colorado with her,*

if indeed that's what she decides she wants to do. She still hasn't made it out to her house to stay overnight, and I volunteered to stay with her whenever she wants to go. I remember my first night without Don in the house. I have a friend from camp here staying with me, and although I didn't realize I needed someone at the time, I did.

It seems that my letters seem to be filled with nothing good. Let me tell you some good things that have happened lately.

On the last day of school each student arrived with a carnation and a hug for me—I have a lovely bouquet on its last legs even as I write.

Laurell and I talked over the phone about once a week. I think we were mourning together. However, we didn't grieve in the same way.

You asked about the pain pills Don had. He had some morphine, but I flushed it all down the toilet. He used up all the other pain pills he had, so the strongest I have right now is Tylenol. I'm sorry. But I didn't want that strong stuff around the house.

I'm home most of the time—if you want to talk. I've been spending a lot of time splitting and hauling wood. It's great exercise and good therapy. My biceps hurt! I didn't think I had any, but am slowly getting some.

It's fun to watch Jeopardy—3:30 my time. I find some enjoyment in that and the $25,000 Pyramid.

Otherwise, I move through each day, not teaching makes life more strained, but like you said, each day the sun rises. I wish the pain would go away. Does it ever?

With that question, I raised my fear that I would never recover from Don's death. Perhaps it raised a similar feeling in her. I don't know. But I did visit her in July, and I thought we had a good time.

Strength and Healing

School began in mid-August 1991, and I returned to camp a few days early to prepare. I wanted to see how many students I had and which grades they were in so I could get the classroom ready. I knew I would throw myself into my work with as much energy as I could muster. What I didn't know was the strength and healing I would find just doing my job.

I found eight students enrolled—in grades one, two, and three and eight, nine, ten, and eleven. Wow, I thought. What a stretch. Sheri, who had taught kindergarten the previous term, had no students but was willing to be a classroom aide for me. Julie, who'd done that the previous spring, had moved away during the summer, so the position was open.

Thus began a relationship that grew stronger, both personally and professionally, with time. Sheri, tall, blond, and outgoing, had experience in Oregon working with younger children before moving to Alaska. She was fair, strict, and knowledgeable in the ways kids learn. I was lucky she was there.

Sheri was my right hand and my left. When she moved up with Telitha, the only kindergartener (now the first grader), to "regular school," we worked together most of the school day. She regularly expressed her concern over each of the kids she dealt with, and we ended up planning how best to serve students' needs together. Her time at the school totaled way more than she was paid. Between the two of us, though, we provided a very good place for children to learn. And this we provided for five more years.

That first fall, we set a pattern that became our way of school. I planned all the lessons for all the students, but Sheri taught the younger ones, and I, the older. With this group, that meant she worked mostly with Telitha in first grade, Craig in second grade, and Bret, her own son who was in third grade.

There were five in the older group: Cindy and Evan (Sheri's other son) were in eighth, Caleb in ninth, Melissa in tenth, and Brian was in eleventh. This was the first time I'd taught high school, and two of the junior high classes were new to me as well.

When the textbooks arrived a week after school began, it was a real challenge to stay ahead of the students. I was teaching oceanography, US history, literature, grammar and composition, algebra, geometry, physical science, and world cultures while also overseeing computer science, small-engine repair, journalism, health, and band. I vaguely remember the tremendous planning and reading I did every night just to stay ahead of the kids. For fun, we all read and discussed *Huckleberry Finn.*

That fall I was busier than I had ever been. When I had been gone the previous winter/spring, Mrs. Lonners had noted that I had thirty-three preps per day when she took over for me. Now, my preparation for class was a positive way to use my time, and I used up an awful lot of it this way. I was at school by six thirty in the mornings, having the younger students arrive at eight. That way, I spent some time with them alone, as the high school students and Sheri began their day at ten. We staggered our half-hour lunches. Sheri and the younger kids went home first, followed by the rest of us, and likewise for the afternoon dismissal times.

I spent time working after school, usually locking the door between five thirty and six to go home, arms filled with US history, physical science, and other textbooks to read. After dinner, I'd take a text into the back room, sit in one of the folding chairs, light up a cigarette, and read a book as I sipped my wine. When I felt sleepy, I turned off the lights and took a book to bed with me. I usually didn't get much of that one read. Instead, I slept well most nights.

It was a better way, I knew, to end my day than I'd begun practicing that previous summer.

***

After Don's death, I spent the summer living in our geodesic dome home in Ketchikan. Before dinner, during dinner, and after dinner in that empty house, I'd sip my wine, smoke my cigarettes, play solitaire, watch TV, and sink into a place of such pain and loneliness that I found myself sipping more wine, smoking more cigarettes, and wondering why I didn't feel better.

I mentioned my concern about my own behavior to a friend I trusted. She suggested that, when my pit of depression threatened to swallow me, I write. "Whenever things go wrong and I want to stop my world to get off, that's what I do," she said. "It helps."

I told her about trying that, sitting at the kitchen table and pouring my emotions onto a tablet, only to have the tears fall, obliterating all the words and making the paper a pulpy mess. "Besides, it hurts too much," I said.

"Why don't you try writing on your computer?" she asked. She knew that I had a small Macintosh that I enjoyed writing letters on. "That might make it more impersonal and hurt less."

I did try. I sat at my Mac and typed. Just whatever came out. In those drunken evenings, I spewed heartache, anger, venom, and hate toward God, toward Don, toward his doctors, toward everyone I could think of that could be blamed for his death. Even myself. I was consumed by guilt at times for not juicing more carrots, for not being able to prevent him from having his teeth pulled, for a million things I might have done differently from the day we'd married. I filled pages and pages as the summer drew to an end.

I brought my computer to camp and had set it up in the second bedroom. I still typed away some evenings, grieving for what I'd lost and fearing for the future. But those evenings grew fewer and fewer as

I filled my time preparing to work with those children who became my reason for living.

Whenever I thought of it, I wrote to Laurell, although the frequency of my letters dwindled. There just wasn't the time, and perhaps I was pulling away for some reason.

In the following letter, I wrote what I thought she would like to hear:

August 14, 1991

Dear Mom,

With two weeks of school already over, I can tell I'm going to be busy. I needed this, I think.

Here, I told her about my class and the subjects I was teaching before getting on with other topics.

Today I mopped all the floors with a new mop, and it was almost fun. I still have the dusting to do, but I decided to come over here and get some letters written while the school was empty. Everybody likes to use my Macintosh, and the [printer's] ribbon is getting pretty threadbare—thought I might get quick notes written before it wears out completely. I was told that the school is getting its own Macintosh sometime next month, and we can all hardly wait.

The pickup started right up last weekend when I headed off to Hollis to see the teachers there—Judi and Sharon. We went in Sharon's car to Craig to shop and have lunch. It was a fun break for me, although I did feel a little guilty about not being in camp. I will get over it though because it's something I've promised myself to do more often. And I'll get used to the truck that way, too …

The weather's been warm, making being in school difficult because of the stuffiness. We open the windows, but because there are no screens, we also invite yellowjackets and pesky flies. It's been raining some in the evenings so that's cooling and nice. Yesterday a small thunderstorm came through camp—a rarity. Saw one flash of lightning and heard one clap of thunder.

Fish are returning to spawn and the bears are fattening up at the streams for their winter hibernation. Walking requires care and caution, and I haven't been walking much. Not because of the fear of bears, but because of lack of time.

My neighbor's parents are visiting, and "mom" has been bringing me a piece of blueberry pie and a small loaf of bread every now and then. She spends a lot of her time picking berries. They traveled by boat to an island several miles away and were entertained by a pod of humpback whales. She thought they got a little close to the boat (they were about a football field away) and I can understand her wariness. There was a picture in the paper a few weeks ago of a skiff that was dented by a killer whale's fluke …

Dick advised me to write regarding your will. If you remember, when we discussed it last month, I suggested you leave everything to Dick. I don't need any money, but someday I'd like to receive all the letters I've sent to you that you told me you've saved. They'd bring back warm memories for my legacy, and would be priceless source material should I, one day, try to write a book. If you would leave me something, those letters I would like to be given. You have my love and support no matter what you choose to do.

I hope the medication is easing your pain, and that life is easier for you these days.

Next week sees our district inservice in Ketchikan. I'll try to touch bases with you by phone.

You're in my thoughts—take care of yourself!

Love,

Biz

This was the last letter in Laurell's box. She was dealing with her own struggles, her health deteriorating, necessitating a move. Dick lived near her, but he, too, was not in the best of health. At this time, I was dealing with my situation as best as I could. Although I continued to write, the letters were further apart, as I didn't make her as high a priority as I had done before. I was ready to plunge into this new school year. And I wanted to do it well.

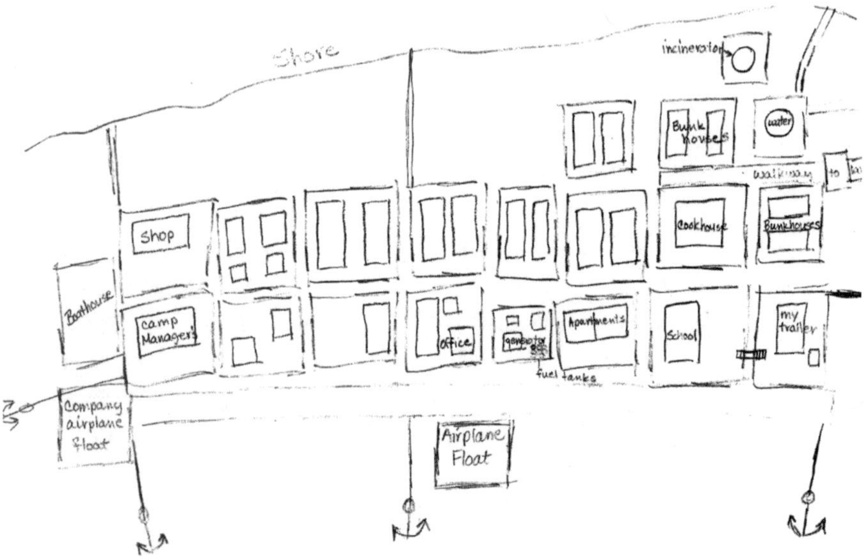

Sketch of the camp's layout

My School Family

The children became my focus. They and their families were in my world so far away from Laurell. And as time passed, they became my family, too.

The children belonged to people who, in one way or another, worked in this camp. Telitha, the first grader, was Richard and Marilyn's daughter. Richard, I didn't see often. Being the camp manager, he was out in the woods with the loggers, or he was off in his boat fishing, or he was in Ketchikan at the office, working with the others on logging-camp business, trying to make the business profitable. However, he was very much the leader of the camp when school activities occurred.

Richard's big frame dominated the schoolroom whether he was dressed in a Santa suit to give out gifts to the children after our Christmas program or sitting at a table, holding a gavel, running an auction of baked goods to raise money. Every so often, the school advisory committee spearheaded bake auctions, usually to raise money for our field trips. We needed to use an air taxi service and Alaska Airlines jets to get to Sitka and Juneau, which made our trips quite expensive. Richard managed to get the bidders to pay top dollar for Marilyn's pies, my brownies, and other donations. Sometimes he even sold things twice! And of course, he always sat front row, center, whenever the kids performed. I knew he was proud of that school and what was accomplished within those walls.

His wife, Marilyn, I knew better. Small, tiny almost, next to Richard, she stood tall. She was proud of her native heritage and, at times, referred to herself and her siblings as "the tribe of Indians" in camp. With dark hair and dark eyes, her smile lit up her face. She had a quick mind, using it to create funny comments in her conversations. She could be counted on to show up at school to listen to kids read, to volunteer to bake some treats if we needed them, to contribute groceries whenever we made "stone soup" or tacos or other such Friday treats. She also became a good friend, getting to know me as we walked together after school and talked whenever we had the chance.

Telitha and her younger brother, Josh, not yet in school, were cute kids. Dark-eyed and dark-haired, they resembled both their parents in some ways. Telitha walked like her mother, a bit pigeon-toed, yet her frame promised to be large like her father's. Josh, tall like his dad, was slim and always active, like his mom.

They had the longest way to walk to school since their home was at the opposite end of camp, in the "front" row, and occupying many floats. They lived in a beautifully built cedar two-story house, its living room windows opening on to the scenic vista of the bay, sky, and land. Richard had built it himself. An adjoining float housed his shop, a much smaller building containing whatever he had in the way of machines and tools. The third contained a boathouse and wasn't so much a float as a floating shelter for his Grady White, a particularly desirable boat in these parts.

Interestingly, there was also a "live well" in his boathouse. He'd fashioned a large wire cage, rather like a crab or shrimp pot, and had attached it with a rope to the side of this float. Whenever he found some crabs, he'd bring them home, put them in the cage with fish scraps and lower it midway to the bottom of the bay. Whenever he and his family wanted that particular feast, he'd pull the cage up and select the biggest to enjoy for dinner.

On the other side of his house, still in the front row, was another of Richard's floats. The far corner held a trailer house, but near to the main house sat an A-frame. Built also by Richard, it was a delightful place—a living area with kitchen and bath downstairs and circular stairs leading to the lofty bedroom. It had been their first home, but they outgrew it with the arrival of their two children. The trailer sharing space behind the A-frame was empty, belonging to Richard's parents. A fifth float on the corner of this end of the camp held the company airplane, a green-and-white floatplane (a Cessna 180), as Richard often flew out of camp for business.

Eventually Josh, too, came to school. Although his sister, Telitha, walked down that boardwalk daily, there were a few times that Josh didn't. When he was in kindergarten, he had a bright shiny red pedal car. On sunny days, he pretended he was driving down a street to school, and he parked it carefully next to the steps. That way, it wouldn't get dented by playground equipment or tripped over by inattentive adults.

Next door, along the front row of the floats, Melissa, the tenth grader, resided. Melissa was physically very small, but she had a giant personality. With short, dark hair, flashing eyes, and a masterful vocabulary, she became the leader of the high school students; indeed, in many ways she became my role model.

She lived with her Aunt Susan, who ran the cookhouse, and her Uncle Milo Mann, a shovel operator. Susan was Richard's sister. Susan and Richard had grown up in camps, as their dad was, at one time, part owner of Gildersleeve Log. They knew of Southeast Alaska logging camp life and were happy to share their information. Sometimes it came in strange tidbits. Once Susan told me that hummingbirds would perch on my finger if I were patient, and one sunny summer day, I decided to try.

I walked to the doorway of my trailer, noting that the hummingbird feeder I'd hung nearby was filled and that birds were fluttering around it. Quietly I stood, extended my arm and pointed my forefinger toward their activities, waiting for the hummingbirds to come. I waited in the warm sunlight, but nothing happened. Voices from the walkway grew closer, and I heard, "Whatever is Biz trying to do?"

I recognized Susan's chuckle then as she said, "I think I know. Wait a minute."

My float sank slightly under the weight of her step as she left the walkway and came near. "Biz, that's not exactly the way to get a hummingbird. Let me show you."

She lifted her arms and formed a ring with her fingers, just under the feeder.

"Oh." I was embarrassed, but I thanked her kindly, and she left with her friends, hopefully explaining that there was really nothing wrong with Biz.

Then I moved to where she'd been, raised my arms, and arranged my fingers under the feeder, just as she'd done. The birds had left with her movement and didn't return. My arms grew tired, but still I trusted her example. Finally the air filled with the whir of wings again, and the whole flock of hummers returned to feed. They did stand on my fingers to dip their long beaks into the feeder's holes, and I was filled with awe. Their little bodies weighed nothing, and I watched as they fed, those wanting to get close zinging around my head, beating their wings with that drumlike sound that means "get out of my way; it's my turn." Two or three or even four of them would perch on my fingers as they drank their nectar. Finally, I could hold my arms up no longer, and I had to move. The birds left. Susan was right, for I had held hummingbirds in my hands.

Susan also helped out at the school. She was a special education aide, working with special needs students for a while, before she became head cook. And even when she was working those long and strange hours for the cookhouse, she offered to come into the building on holidays to paint faces. Kids sported beautiful green shamrocks for St. Patrick's Day and amazing tigers, lions, and other animal faces on Halloween.

While Susan was Richard's sister, her husband, Milo, was Marilyn's brother and one of the "tribe of Indians," a quiet, gentle man. He always had a smile and a kind word of greeting when we met, and I heard that he made a mean macaroni and cheese. He, like Marilyn, had a quick wit and a great sense of humor. I just didn't see it often. But I appreciated it when I did.

So sisters and brothers lived next door to each other, and the family connections continued.

Following the walkway, the next float's trailer housed second grader, Craig, and his two siblings, Cindy in eighth grade and Caleb in ninth. Their mother was Maggie, another of "the tribe"—Marilyn's sister. She, like Marilyn, was small and dark, and Craig resembled her most, with dark hair and dark eyes, flashing with energy and mischief. Caleb, the oldest, I knew as a polite young man, probably favoring his father. After Christmas, Caleb opted to live with his father and never returned to camp. While he was living with Maggie, Cindy mothered him, as well as Craig. Shy, soft-spoken, and a lovely presence, Cindy explained to me one day that Craig, even when he was being carried in his basket home from the hospital, was constantly twitching. That information came when, one day, I asked why he couldn't sit still. She also led and kindly directed Caleb, making sure he knew what his homework was, encouraging him to work hard during the school day. She tended her siblings with care.

Maggie and her first husband had divorced a few years earlier; he left the camp and lived in one of the small towns on Prince of Wales Island, and Maggie had recently remarried. She greeted planes, clerked in the commissary, sorted and handed out the mail. She was a general office-greeter person, while her husband, Darrel, was in charge of facilities. He kept the camp structure operational, sometimes in logging camp terminology called the bull cook (or the maintenance man). Next to their trailer was a smaller structure that was the camp office and commissary; on its outside wall hung a row of mailboxes. These places were convenient to the floatplane dock and Maggie's job.

Brian was in eleventh grade, a new student who'd arrived over the summer to live with his aunt and uncle. Brian was also part of "the tribe," as his aunt and Marilyn were cousins. He was big, tall and broad, and he could have squashed any of the elementary kids with his little finger. But he was kind and good natured; when he left before the academic year was up, we all missed his presence.

Finally, Sheri's children, Bret, in third grade, and his brother, Evan, in eighth, were not related to the others. They were both tall and thin, tow-headed and blue eyed; while Bret became the jokester, Evan became my hero. Or maybe his mother was. Whenever I needed something, either Evan or Sheri would see that I received it: a tank of propane, some fuel, or advice. They made my lifestyle there manageable and pleasant.

They lived in a little house, tucked away in the second row of floats, behind Richard and Marilyn's. Their float, nestled between Richard's shop and the two largest trailer houses, supported two small buildings. The first, a little house, built by Richard's parents and refurbished by Sheri and her husband, Eldon, and two boys, was the Bonines' home. This little two-story box contained a living room with a wood stove, a mudroom with a stacked washer/dryer, a kitchen, a bath, and the master bedroom on the first floor. Upstairs under the pitched roof, two bedrooms belonged to Bret and Evan. I spent time in this house, eating pizza, taking a shower when the water system froze up, going over to talk; it was a friendly place.

The other building was a small trailer housing no school kids but an important person to me as well: Rick Brown. I'd met him years ago when Don and I first arrived in Labouchere Bay. He lived alone, and I didn't see him often. But Rick sometimes stopped by the school on his way home from the woods.

"How's it going?" he'd ask. I'd tell him and ask him about his daughters, Erika and Kaejo, whom I'd known and taught at Labouchere Bay. After he told me what they were doing, he'd leave.

One day, he asked who was taking care of my sewer pipe. "I can't get anyone to do it," I replied. This was during a cold spell when the bay had frozen and the pipe needed to be freed from the ice and moved to a new spot. Then the sewage wouldn't back up into the bathtub as it had that morning. I had asked around—Darrel, Richard, anyone I thought might have the time and inclination. I had almost given up and resigned myself to a bathtub full of sewage until the weather warmed. After my brief tale of woe, Rick immediately harrumphed, turned on his heel, and went out into the darkness. About half an hour later, he returned.

"It's moved," he said and left before I could give him a hug, but I did manage to say thank you before the door closed.

I formed relationships with many of the adults in the logging camp, some close, some not so, through their children. Marilyn and Richard, Sheri and Eldon, Susan and Milo, Maggie and Darrel—these parents worked and lived on the camp as long as I did, and their children mentored me through the years I was there.

Others came—the Frabels, the McMurrians, the Inmans, and the Bussaniches, bringing their children who stayed for a year or two or three and were integral to the workings of the camp. However, a few parents who didn't log and who didn't live on the float camp sent their kids to school there, too.

Bri and Cori Graves lived across the bay in a floating unit of their own—Sea Otter Lodge. Their parents housed men who worked for the native corporation that was helicopter logging. The neat thing was that their dad also flew a helicopter. Every morning, we'd look up at the sound of rotor blades buffeting through the air and watch as the copter landed on the airplane float, the motor slowed and stopped, and their dad got out and helped the girls down the stairs. I think we all envied their form of transportation—they didn't have to walk to school at all.

Even when the helicopter job disappeared, the Graves family stayed, bringing their girls to school by boat. When the bay would freeze, they'd have to use the bow to break the ice. They'd rev their engine so the front would rise and then cut it when the boat's bow was above ice. The bow slammed onto the surface and forced the ice apart, making a small channel of water for them to plow through before repeating the procedure. This way, they slowly made a path for their boat so Bri and Cori could come to school.

Another couple who came by boat was Ron and Michael Olson. They lived about five miles away on Babe Island with their grandparents. Their dad was a fisherman and often gone, but their granddad was a master craftsman. He built boats. The skiff that Ron drove every day was a beautifully made wooden boat, and Ron drove it with skill. His brother, Michael, usually could be found in the bow, maybe watching for hazards, but more likely just enjoying the ride. The boys sometimes could not make it home after school when the weather stormed, and they had sleepovers with other students whose parents were agreeable.

Besides those who lived at or nearby camp, those who came from Ketchikan were important as well. Southeast Island School District was headquartered there.

Polk Inlet School, while important to us, was a tiny speck in the realm of the thousands of square miles in Southeast Alaska that the school district covered. Dave Dossett, former superintendent, figured the district was the size of New Hampshire and Vermont together. Whether a fishing community, a native village, or a logging camp, wherever eight children were gathered, there a school could be formed. The district served as many as five hundred students from schools like Thorne Bay with an enrollment of a hundred or more students and eight to ten teachers, to Polk Inlet and others with ten to fifteen students and a single teacher. Providing this huge area with support staff and supplies depended on the school plane.

A Cessna 206, piloted by Max Lukin, delivered our itinerant teachers, our maintenance providers, our guests, our administrators, and our books and crayons. The first inkling we'd have of the plane's arrival was when Max would buzz the camp. He would swoop down a bit, rev up his engine, and then move up, turn around, and begin his landing procedure. The white floatplane with black and orange stripes would taxi to the floatplane dock, where Max tied up the plane before helping whoever came down the plane's steps to disembark. Then he'd offload whatever freight we were to receive, and everyone on the plane would head down the walkway to the school. Max usually skipped the school and went straight for the cookhouse to see what goodies he'd find. He'd ask if I had anything to send back to the district office before he left. As we heard him take off from the float, whomever he'd brought was ready to work.

My most frequent guests were the other teachers. Don Alderman taught music, and he ran the music program in an efficient and strict manner. Coming to camp once every two weeks or so, he'd sing with the younger kids, and he brought out recorders for everyone to learn to play, teaching individual lessons. He was a hard taskmaster, expecting students to practice every day and, in his Texan accent, speaking sternly to them when he knew they didn't. It only took one or two times of "Now, I can tell y'all haven't been practicing, and I expect you to do better next time," accompanied by a glare, and he had these kids playing music.

With the older ones, he gave individual music lessons. Some learned to play the piano; some had guitars. Don was a wonderfully gifted teacher for the wide range of students we had, finding something special for each child to succeed with.

Overnighting itinerants were expected to provide food because they were paid an extra per diem for every overnight stay. Fresh produce was often hard to come by in the camps and villages, and the teachers had no restaurants to eat in, so a meal cooked by a visiting teacher who had brought fresh ingredients was wonderful payment for providing a bed, a bath, and a towel.

My second bedroom, containing one double bed, was my guest room. If I had more than one overnighter, the second used the living room couch. Itinerants brought their sleeping bags, as often they had to sleep in the schools they visited.

One night when Don Alderman was in that second bedroom, I was awakened from a very deep sleep by the sound of markers on a whiteboard. Drowsily I wondered, "What's Don writing at this time of night?" Then I realized I didn't have a whiteboard in that bedroom and listened more closely. Animals were cavorting under the trailer, possibly under my bed.

When I asked about it the next morning, Don said he'd heard nothing. Then I asked around the camp and was told that it was probably otters mating under there. They weren't quiet, nor did they sound gentle. A whiteboard, indeed.

Evvy Fernald, our special education teacher, also came about every two weeks. Since she was newly widowed, we had much to talk about personally, as well as professionally. She was an excellent teacher, and we worked well together. We collaborated to make sure that her targeted students were mainstreamed into the classroom in a way that all could benefit. (At this time "gifted" students were included with "slower developing" students—all called "special needs" and qualified for special education assistance.) For example, when trying to change the behavior of a student who did not know how to act in our classroom setting, we constructed a behavior modification program that benefited all the children, not just that "special" one. It was so successful that I maintained the program long after the behavior was modified, Evvy helping me to expand it to meet new needs. When she left, I knew how to help all students benefit from what she wanted her special-needs students to know, and her aide knew how to use the time the students were pulled from the classroom for special instruction.

While Don and Evvy were my most frequent visitors and my closest friends, others arrived often as well. A kindergarten teacher, Debbie Merle, came whenever there were students in kindergarten. I remember one year there were two of them: Josh Gildersleeve and Katy Clark, and that was as big as that class ever was. Some years, there were no students; other times, only one. Whatever the number, Debbie hired an aide, prepared the lessons, supplied the materials, and made sure on her visits that her program was being carried out. As principal teacher, all I had to do was make sure there was a space for it to happen. One room in the new school was allotted for kindergarten use.

Another regular was Steve Dempsey, the school counselor. He pulled out students individually to discuss the trials and tribulations they encountered—either by their request or by their parents' and/or teacher's. He often walked to parents' homes to counsel with them after he'd talk to the students. He also provided lessons discussing methods of healthy behavior.

Beth Stephens, the health teacher, came less often but was always armed with lessons for the students. I remember one time she also gave a geography lesson having just returned from India after attending a workshop with her dentist husband. She brought with her a beautiful sari and had one of the shyest girls in the school model it. Lacey was a beauty in the turquoise and green silk creation, crooking her elbow just so, so that part of the fabric could drape across her arm, turning slowly around for the class to admire.

The superintendent, Bob Weinstein at one point, Dave Dossett at another, came less often as did the curriculum supervisors, Ernie Hansen and Martha Jacobsen. However, they were responsive to my requests. For example, when the teaching of logarithms appeared in the high school text, I called upon Dave with his strong math background. He flew in one day to teach the lesson. Despite having logarithms introduced to me in high school, I have never understood them. Most math concepts are fun for me to teach, but this one still has me stumped, even after Dave's lesson.

When one of the high school kids worked with a piece of CAD software (as I recall it had something to do with designing and perhaps architecture) and became puzzled with the directions it contained, Ernie, with his computer background, came to help translate the instructions. (The course was supposed to be self-taught, and this particular kid was quick, bright, and more computer literate than I—I just had to ask for the materials for the most part and let him loose to learn.) The support they provided and the effort they made to schedule their trips to arrive so the curricular continuum would be maintained were greatly appreciated.

The new school was a marvel. The renovated two-story bunkhouse that became Polk Inlet School was a building that really served its purpose. One entered the building through a little wanigan, a coat room, with hooks lining the walls and a large trash can in the corner. This might contain ropes, balls, and other such playground equipment in the summer or water in the winter. Often when school was in session, the boys who boated to class threw their Helly Hansens (commercial raingear) over the top to dry out. Then, too, the hooks were filled with coats and life jackets, and often, rubber boots lined the wall underneath.

Entering through the front door, we were in the main classroom. It was quite large. One wall was lined with a bulletin board under which a countertop covered cabinets. It had lots of storage and a sink as well. Directly across from the door, a series of windows looked over to the next building. Two blackboards covered the opposing walls, and desks filled the space in-between. The teacher's desk sat off to the side. This was the room where most of the instruction was given. It was also the room that became our gymnasium when the desks were pushed to the side and our auditorium when the desks were taken out of the room.

Down the hallway toward the cookhouse, two bathrooms, labeled BOYS and GIRLS were off to the right.

On the left was a doorway to a little room with multiple uses. Smaller than the main classroom, it was the room in which the high school students received their satellite classes. It also was used as the workroom with the paper cutter and file cabinets. And it became a phone booth, too. That was quite the big deal. When the district first installed a phone, we didn't know if it would work. It operated off some satellite and seemed magical to us who hadn't had phone access for years.

The word spread, and soon folks asked if they could use the phone.

"For personal calls?"

"Yes."

"Let me ask."

The school district agreed if calls were made after school hours and the callers reimbursed the district at the rate of one dollar per minute. A sign-up sheet was placed next to the phone, and when the monthly bill arrived, Sheri checked off the calls, making sure each user had signed up. Then she made out a bill to each user, collected the money, and sent it in to the district office.

Having a phone meant folks came to my door more often.

"Can I use the school phone?"

"Sure. Let me get my shoes and the key."

I would take them over to the school, unlock the door to let them in, make sure they signed the call log, and leave them alone, trusting they would turn off the light when they left.

They never knew that I had an extension in my house. In the second bedroom a phone sat on the night table next to the bed. My computer was there as well, but not hooked up to the phone line. It wasn't a dependable connection—Internet access was a far ways into the future.

The satellite connection worked better some times than others. I think the tidal fluctuations played a role. The person on the other end always sounded as if he/she were inside a large tin can, and echoes reverberated throughout the conversation. Nobody ever complained about the quality of the connection, though. We were all too happy to have a phone line to the outside world.

People used the library/computer room on the other side of the main classroom, too, but not as often. To get to the library, we passed through a short hallway with a door on either side. One door opened into a teacher storage space, used for papers, pencils, textbooks, and such.

Through the other, we could enter another classroom, a small one, usually reserved for the kindergarten.

Then the hallway opened up to the library on the right. Several stacks of books presented a lovely sight to the eager reader. We were happy to loan books to the community, although few asked. Directly at the end of the hallway, a piano stood against the wall, and to the left, three computers were situated. After the computers, we could head up the stairs to what became, for many of us, our favorite room.

Several components made it desirable. The three windows provided vistas totally invisible from below. We could see out onto the water, notice the animals that were swimming, the boats that were traveling, the planes that might be arriving, as well as catch a glimpse of the logs that were being set into the water just beyond the corner. We could also see over my trailer, up the walkway to land, and what might be happening up there.

Brightly colored beanbag chairs dotted the floor. A few other chairs were interspersed, but it was these beanbags that we all sat on when we came upstairs. We could separate classes; perhaps the high school students came up to the beanbags to discuss Shakespeare while the elementary students stayed below and worked on their math. Or perhaps the elementary students came up to discuss their health lesson while the high school students worked on their history.

And always, the upstairs was available to students who had their work done and wanted to read silently. Even though they probably spent more time looking out the windows than reading, as long as they were quiet, nobody cared.

This room was only half the length of the schoolhouse. A doorway led into an unfinished section that held lots of shelving and was storage space. Whatever wasn't needed at that particular time found its way to a place on one of those shelves.

This was our one-teacher school.

Seasons of the School

Every year, I began school the same way, coming out a few days ahead of the opening day and getting ready. For the second year in a row, my preparation involved the pickup truck, intending to bring it back from town. Rick had helped me bring it in the previous spring, loaded with all of Don's things that I no longer needed or used at camp. I was bringing it back, stuffed with every teaching aid I could find—idea books, art projects, fabric pieces, whatever I thought would make learning fun for the kids and me.

This year, Sheri had come in to town to help me drive back out to Polk Inlet; I never was fond of driving that challenging road alone. She was going to drive the school van that we had just been given to use. When I started up the truck, it sputtered and belched black exhaust and then died. It wouldn't start, not even when Sheri tried. So I called Robyn, and she and her husband came down to take care of it while Sheri and I loaded all those boxes into the van and set out with just the one vehicle. Although I was marooned at Polk Inlet by not having a vehicle with which to drive to Craig, I found plenty to keep me busy.

There were always new children, those who had moved into camp during the summer break. I needed to assess their strengths and weaknesses, and I also wanted to learn what everyone had been up to during our summer break.

"Guys, please take out your crayons," I'd begin, "and make a picture of what you did this summer." The returning kids would roll their eyes, as if to say B-O-R-I-N-G, and shake their heads as I'd continue. "When you've finished, I'd like you to write a story about your picture."

I was always asking them to draw pictures and write stories. Making books, both individual and classroom collections, and bulletin-board displays of their work were projects they all grew to count on doing.

"You ask us to do this every year," Bret reminded me after the fourth or fifth year.

"Yes, but you always draw a different picture," I said. "Your story is never the same."

He seemed content with that, and so was I. It was a tried-and-true way to begin to learn about my kids.

As the classes began to round out, the year separated itself from the previous one. Perhaps we had a full first grade this year, or perhaps the juniors were working on oceanography and German by satellite. The coursework varied with the curriculum changes and the high schoolers' needs. One year, Cindy was south, and we felt the hole she left; we rejoiced when she returned. Another year, Melissa had graduated, and Evan took the lead.

Usually we began in August, while summer was still in full bloom. We kept the windows open, hearing in the background the toots of the boom boat as it sorted the logs that were dropped into the water. We had our PE classes outside on the area of the school float that the building didn't cover, perhaps an area of ten feet by forty feet. A four-square had been painted in one section, and the tether ball was brought out. Sometimes, Sheri told the kids to grab their life jackets, and they'd set off up the ramp to land, to hike.

When the weather was not good, we'd push the desks to one side and have our PE in the classroom. As "Mousercize" or Richard Simmons's "Sweatin' to the Oldies" tapes played on the VCR, strains of "Peggy Sue" and "Leader of the Pack" seeped out the cracks of the schoolhouse and drifted around camp. Sometimes we square danced; I had found some music and directions during my summer visits to the teacher shops in the malls, and the kids paired off and learned the steps. One summer in Minneapolis, my college roommate and I had visited a bar on the fourth floor of the Mall of America and had been drawn into the line dancing that someone was teaching. I came back to camp with several video tapes, and we line danced to give variety to Richard Simmons and our PE days.

Of course, we had a lot of regular book learning going on. Usually students were assigned to their seats and worked individually on their math and their reading. Sheri and I would introduce concepts and then expect the kids to complete their assignments without any disruptions. That was a lofty dream, and eventually, we developed a system to encourage them to keep to their tasks at hand.

We taped small papers on the corners of their desks, and after talking with them as a group about what we'd like to work on that week, we'd identify three areas. Perhaps it was ignoring other lessons being given or not talking to their neighbors or working on the task they'd been assigned. If either Sheri or I noticed a student outside the bounds that we wanted him or her to learn, we'd just put a little mark on the paper. At the end of the week, we'd count the marks, and if somebody had more than was acceptable, he/she wouldn't get to cook on Friday.

Cooking became a big reward.

I had purchased a recipe book just for kids years before. It not only contained several recipes that listed the ingredients and directions for making various dishes, but it also came with diagrams of the measuring utensils and drawings of the ingredients. It was perfect for primary children learning to read, and what was even better, each recipe was for one individual serving. Those young kids learned their fractions through their measuring spoons and cups, having to double the portions when one of us asked, "Would you make mine, too?" Both reading and math were incorporated into this activity that the students really loved. The cookbook became the Friday bible.

Elementary students took turns choosing what to make each Friday, and then they volunteered to bring ingredients. Annual favorites were pizza and tacos. In fact, I made a rule that no recipe could be repeated in a year and had to keep track of which were chosen, or we'd have had pizzas or tacos every Friday. Children made soups of different kinds, cupcakes, pancakes, peanut butter, and many other delicious (and some not so great) dishes. But the one I remember most is the one Daniel chose.

Daniel was one of those kids who lived in Polk Inlet for just a little while. The Gildersleeve/Mann and Bonine families seemed solidly entrenched, but the presence of other families was more fleeting. Perhaps the dads got fired or quit; perhaps the moms couldn't stand the lifestyle. Whatever the reason, we hoped to make their children feel the safety and solidarity of the school.

Daniel arrived after Christmas one year, his dad and step-mom having been there already for quite some time. He was a big kid, a sixth grader, who carried a wide smile and below-average skills. It didn't take much work for us to help Daniel fit in; his classmates had learned to accept others and be kind. They were his teachers.

After much study, when his turn came, he chose something we'd never had before, after he left, or ever since. It was a hot dog wrapped in a bun and cooked over an open fire. I was curious as to how he'd accomplish this marvel when he chose it as we had no open fire in the school or on the float. "Never you mind," he assured me. "I'll take care of it."

When Friday arrived, kids brought the ingredients for making the bread: flour, soda, salt, and sugar. Daniel brought the hot dogs, one for each of us at school. (We adults enjoyed these experiments as much as the children—and while this was a reward for the elementary, the older kids always participated too.) The surprise he brought with the hot dogs was a small hibachi and charcoal pellets, and as we made and rolled out our dough and wrapped it around the hot dog, he got the fire going. He had also gone up to land the day before and cut branches, sharpening one end, to provide us with cooking sticks. A few at a time, we went outside to cook our bread. We sat on the boards of the float, warmed by the sun, and held our sticks over the hibachi.

I'm not sure anybody's bread was cooked through and through, and Daniel was lucky that we were given a sunny day. But we all enjoyed the camaraderie around the "campfire."

Enjoying Daniel's Friday cooking choice

Students always appreciated the break from the routine classroom lessons these cooking sessions provided. If, when Friday arrived, there'd been that poor student who hadn't behaved as we'd expected during the previous week, he or she would have to watch us all eat. He or she would try harder the following week. This cooking helped us modify behavior.

We enjoyed our field trips, too. With the use of the school van, we could all pile in and drive on the logging road leading out of Polk Inlet to the wider roads that eventually became paved and led to the cities of Craig and Klawock.

One of our first trips was to the fish hatchery in Klawock. There, in the fall, salmon returning to spawn were enclosed in cages. They fought fiercely to move on to their spawning grounds (the hatchery itself), and while they were contained, we got closer looks, watching their muscled bodies slamming into the bars, splashing us with their water, and admiring their strength and courage.

Another trip was to Hollis, the ferry terminus for Prince of Wales Island. There, another school housed two teachers and a passel of kids. The school had been erected a long while, and it sat on flat land with a field. What a treat! We could run and play baseball and kickball in the sunshine. We could eat our lunches with other kids and make new friends. That's just what we did.

Wherever we drove, Marilyn always made sure her kids were equipped with Ziploc bags. "I've taught them to use them as horses use their oat bags," she said. "Josh and Telitha both get carsick and airsick and seasick, and they're good pukers." They were, too, never missing their target and needing to vomit every trip we took. They also never complained; it was just a fact of life to them.

As summer wound into fall, we found ourselves in a pleasant rhythm of school. At least to me it was pleasant. My right-hand aide, Sheri, and the others who worked with the children had ironed out the kinks of their teaching methodology, and the students had begun to bend toward meeting my expectations. Usually our days went smoothly.

Larger schools would be starting football and cheerleading; we began to prepare for the one team sport we could manage, given our size and enrollment: Battle of the Books. Yes, reading became our sport, and the teams were divided by grade level, as prescribed by the librarians of Alaska. Teams were assigned to read specific books and remember details, plots, characters, authors, and other such information as could be gleaned in order to answer questions when the tournament began in the spring. This sport was open to any school in the state, and many participated. Students at Polk Inlet School were assigned these books as part of their reading instruction, and although we often didn't end the year with the same students we began with, we participated by telephone in our school district's battle. One year, Cindy and Evan won the district battle and went on to the state. After I left, the team of Bri and Bret actually won the state title for junior high.

We tried to fit outdoor activities into the curriculum as much as we could. High school kids were given permission to spend the afternoon out in a skiff, motoring around the camp as they collected water samples. They looked for flotsam, jetsam, and microscopic animals and basked in the sunshine, waving to whomever they met as they were outside. They were studying oceanography.

The high school physical education course was designed to equip students to enjoy individual sports, and most of them occurred outside. They learned archery, fencing, and shooting skills when they were at Polk Inlet. Only once during my tenure, Sheri offered to take the kids up the hill to land to set up the big bull's-eyes and practice shooting bows and arrows. They practiced fencing in an empty building nearby, donning the masks and protective vests before using the swords to *en garde* and *touché*. Sheri suggested to our superiors that the students learn rifle skills and practice shooting their .22 rifles. She talked the district into providing their ammunition when each student could provide his/her own rifle. And finally, she took them walking when they had finished their quarter semester of each of the other activities.

One September, we loaded into the van and drove down the logging road to where the company was working. On our way we saw the fallers, cutting the trees off in the distance, working in groups of two. They were leaping from one mossy log to another, balancing yet kind of prancing on the fallen giants, moving on to their next assignment. Looking rather like two dancers, they held their chainsaws in one hand and something else, maybe ropes or cables, in the other.

When we arrived at the place where the logs were loaded onto the trucks, Milo was working the machine that moved them. A huge orange monster it was, and the kids couldn't wait for their turns. When Milo stopped work, he hopped down from his high seat and asked if anyone wanted to sit in the driver's seat. He was greeted with great enthusiasm: "Me … Me … I do!" The older kids were shouting every bit as loud as the younger ones. Each student had his/her chance. Either they hoisted themselves up to the door and climbed into the seat, or Milo lifted them up so they could reach the door's opening. There, they experienced the same unobstructed view of the process that Milo had and, perhaps, envisioned the day that they, too, could be riding high.

This mini field trip was supposed to show the high schoolers how logging was done since they were studying Alaska and its economy, as well as jobs that were important to maintaining it. However, the elementary students had the better time. "Milo's machine" was the main topic of conversation when we returned—and of their journaling when it was their time to write. We were lucky the weather was nice that day.

Fall saw the weather change. Sunny days became cloudy ones and then rainy ones. The winds and the rains came with increasing force and frequency, and we spent less and less time outside playing foursquare on the playground. I described the rain as "continual, heavy, and blasting," in my diary one day when the winds were whipping over the water at a speed of over seventy knots. It was not pleasant to be outside, as there seemed to be no way to keep dry. Even when we were covered with raingear, the wind and water seemed to find the smallest opening and enter our pants and our jackets. Those who had to travel more than a few feet came into school wet and cold.

We watched the waters outside the school churn into whitecaps, and those days Ron and Michael, who boated from five miles away, began to check around for places to stay the night. Marilyn and Richard were their most consistent hosts, and I felt better knowing the boys wouldn't have to venture forth in those wicked waters.

Those winds also posed a problem in the school. They forced the rain into places we didn't know would leak. One fall, drips formed around the window near the computer stations. We reported it, and on the next dry day, Darrel spread some of his magic goop along the roof and around the outside of the window. He thought he had fixed the problem. However, the next time the winds and rain blustered, the leak reappeared. He tried to fix it again, but he couldn't. That leak was something we watched for a couple of years, trying to make sure it didn't endanger the computers and staying out of its wetness. Those types of leaks were very hard to find and fix and weren't limited to just the school.

Often fall was the time more families would move here. Perhaps new hires from the spring were so homesick they up and left; perhaps guys got drunk and were fired. Whatever the reason, the bosses hired new people year round, but the school population often increased in late September and early October. (Those with children were willing to bring them up when the school year had just begun; they were more hesitant once their kids were further into the academic year.)

I remember Keaton pulling me aside once and telling me that he'd just hired a new cook. That was nice, I told him, wondering what his point was going to be. "The man has three children," Keaton announced.

I turned to him, eyebrows raised, mouth open. We wouldn't have enough desks, as we were already all filled up. "When are they coming?" I wanted to know.

"Today."

I contacted the school district maintenance man at Thorne Bay and told him of my problem. "We need three desks as soon as possible," I urged.

That very afternoon the school pilot showed up in his plane. He taxied up to the airplane float and unloaded those desks, borrowing a dolly to make them easier to transport. He wheeled them down to the school one at a time, and we set them up. When the cook's children arrived, they were welcomed and shown to their seats and began the process of fitting in.

I was grateful that the day was calm again, and the planes could fly—and that the school district staff was so responsive to my request.

The end of fall seemed to be measured by the coming of Spirit Week, which always coincided with Halloween. That particular week, we took some time to be silly, as a part of our day was given over to playing games. We also dressed up, each day in a different costume, perhaps as a nerd or in our pajamas or wearing a hat. Of course, on Halloween, we wore our costumes.

I tried to find costumes every year. Once I found a skunk hat when I was in town and accompanied it with white and black makeup crayons for my face. Another year, I sprayed my hair red and purple and went as a punk rocker. But only my head was adorned—both costumes had me wearing regular clothes, but one year I did turn up in a full-body costume.

That year, I had been in Ketchikan for a weekend and had visited my friend Sharon. She was a spectacular garage-sale shopper and showed me her finds from the previous weekend. Among them was a gray rabbit suit. "Biz, it would fit you," she said. "Why don't you try it on?"

It zipped up the front and was made like a snowsuit, except it had huge ears on the hood and attached booties. It did fit me.

I didn't want to take away her Halloween costume and told her so. When she assured me that she had planned to wear it the following Easter, I packed that rabbit suit in my duffel bag when I flew back to camp. That year, I was a Halloween bunny.

We also had special art projects. At this time of year, they usually centered on pumpkins. When I was in Ketchikan, I'd purchase a pumpkin for each child and bring them back to camp with me, a weighty box of freight. The kids would bring knives from home, and I would ask them to design a face, draw it on paper, and then transfer it to the pumpkin before they cut. Of course, we'd have to clean out the seeds first, and I'd take them home at night, wash them and then bake and salt them so we'd have snacks when we worked on our jack-o'-lanterns the next day.

Sometimes, we painted little pumpkins. When I could find them in the grocery store, I would pick them up, as they weren't so hard to carry. They were nice for a change, although the kids wouldn't have minded if we carved jack-o'-lanterns every year.

The last year I was there, we made masks. I had found some gauze laced with plaster of paris in some catalog and ordered enough for a class project. Then I asked the kids to pair up, a big one with a little one, and passed out the water bowls and strips of gauze. The little kids smeared their faces with Vaseline and the big kids cut the strips into manageable sizes before running them through the water. Then they stripped the excess water with their fingers before applying it to their partner's face. Soon we had a room full of little ghost-like visages, those young ones struggling to keep their faces still for the half-hour needed for the mask to dry.

Then it was the big kids' turn. I hoped they had modeled their plastering style well enough that the young kids wouldn't place the strips over nostrils or inadvertently hurt the eyes. They had been good models, and every student left school that day with a mask on his/her desk to dry overnight. The next few days, we added warts and scars and paint—what wonderful faces those masks became. Some even wore them on Halloween night when they trick-or-treated to the homes around camp, having fashioned costumes to go with them.

We continued with our studies, too, and I always struggled to keep ahead of the kids. Figuring out rational roots of polynomials or trying to understand the helix of DNA, I diligently read the textbooks both on the weekends and each evening prior to the next day's lesson. That the lessons of the curriculum should be an integral part of each day should not be forgotten. We were a real school, even though we were out in the boonies and operating on big rafts.

However, once Halloween passed by, the calendar rolled over to November, and we knew winter was on its way.

For me, the first time the water pipes froze signaled winter's coming. If the custodian or I hadn't left the water running a small trickle in the school and the temperatures dipped below freezing, the water line to the school quit working. When that happened, we changed the rule for using the bathroom. The kids who lived on the camp went home whenever they had to go. That left the one flush in the tank available to Bri or Cori, and Michael or Ron, all of whom traveled great distances to attend school. Once the flush was used up, a bucket of sea water was hauled from the edge of the float and placed in the bathroom. Thus the next person had water to flush the toilet.

The "if it's yellow" rule was in effect as well. "If it's yellow, let it mellow. If it's brown, flush it down." It was not unusual during the winter months for the water pipes to be frozen for a week or two at a time, even with sunny days. One would think the sun's rays would warm the ice, but they didn't. The sun was too low in the sky, and the hills rose too sharply from the coast to allow its rays to hit the float.

We waited and prayed for rain to come again and warm the air and thaw the pipes so we could enjoy running water again. Not only could we flush the toilets then, but we could also take showers and use our washing machines. There were days when the pipes were frozen and the classroom literally reeked from people smells—kids who hadn't taken showers or baths for a week or more were wearing clothes that hadn't been laundered for the same amount of time. Or more. Sheri and I cringed when we moved the desks to walls so we could jump up and down to our exercise tapes during PE time. That would generate more sweat and new scents for our room. We'd leave the windows open, allow the wind to chill the air, hoping it would take some of the smells away as it blew through the classroom. However, "everyone is in the same boat" became the mantra when we felt we came stinky to school.

Sometimes we held PE outside during these winter days. If a large amount of snow fell, we'd send the kids home to get their shovels, and we'd clear off the float during our PE time. Heavy snowfall forced the floats to sink in the salt water, and we wanted them to remain as buoyant as possible. When the float was cleared, students at times made snowmen for their PE classes, a reward for the hard work of shoveling.

Winter PE

One winter, Richard made a trip to Ketchikan in his Grady White and came back with a surprise. We knew he had intended to pick up some of the residents who'd been gone on vacation, and he did come back with them. He also came back with a snow blower.

When the next big snow fell, he used it to make a clear path along the walkway from his house along the entire camp to the school, and then he surprised me. He cleared off the playground. Kids wouldn't have to shovel that day. However, the weight of the snow left on the other side of the school float had changed the balance. When the kids came to school, the front door swung in with extra force and knocked the hula hoops off the wall where I'd had them hanging. As the students entered, not only would they have to hang up their life jackets, but they'd also need to rehang those hoops. They didn't mind—their gift was seeing the four-square site and being able to bounce their ball during recess that day.

Of course, when the snow piled up, logging stopped. The bunkhouse guys left, and the cookhouse shut down. Many of the families moved to warmer climes until startup occurred in the spring. The school population usually shrank to what we called the "homeguard," those people who lived there through the dark cold days of winter—the Gildersleeves, the Bonines, and occasionally another family or two. Even I left for the six weeks of the school's winter vacation, usually scheduled from mid-December to late January.

Besides the weather changing, another transition I noticed from fall into winter came with my birthday. Occurring the first part of November, I hadn't told anyone about it that first year. When I received piles of cards from friends and relatives outside of camp and Sheri noticed them, she gave me what for.

"Biz, you make birthdays so important for the kids, and then you don't let us help you celebrate. It's no fair!"

She was talking about my practice of making cupcakes for each child's birthday and serving them in school. I usually baked eighteen of them the evening before, iced them, and carried them to school before the day began. Using cake and frosting mixes made the task relatively easy, and I enjoyed celebrating each child as we sang "Happy Birthday" and shared cupcakes on every special day. One birthday I especially remember was Michael's.

I knew Michael, a special-needs student in fourth grade at the time, was waiting with great anticipation for his cupcakes on his big day since his two favorite things to do were to watch cartoons and eat. Also I'd expected three itinerants from Ketchikan to fly in for the day, so I'd planned to make twenty-four instead of the usual eighteen.

I preheated the oven, lined the muffin tins, mixed the batter, ladled it into the tins, and then set the pans in the oven. Imagine my surprise when I noticed the oven was still cold. I searched my microwave cookbook to see how I could still bake them and was told I had to place each cupcake into a custard dish. I had only one. No microwaving for them.

Should I carry them down to Sheri's? She lived on the other side of camp, it was dark, and I'd have to also carry a flashlight. I wasn't too adept at walking those floats in the daylight with my hands empty, much less carrying some trays of cupcake batter.

I decided to trek to the school, and I returned with the toaster-oven that I'd purchased with Scholastic book credits a few years earlier for our Friday cooking time. I used that to bake those cupcakes in batches. They turned out to be a bit misshapen, concave, and although I tried to hide their flaws with frosting, I couldn't. Michael didn't mind.

However, I just couldn't make cupcakes for myself, and it didn't seem right to toot my own birthday horn. Sheri took care of that. The next year, she came to school with a sheet cake, a few candles nestling in one corner (thankfully, not the fifty-one that would have been the truth), and she also surprised me with cards. She'd had each of the kids make me birthday cards without my knowing. From then on, she always remembered my birthday.

Of course, we had to celebrate hers in early December, too.

Once the school put on a fall program when shutdown came early, with our usual musical offerings, readings, and the play, "The Hound of the Maskervilles."

But it was the Christmas programs that I remember best. In the darkness of early evening, adults would file into the school and find seats on the folding chairs we'd placed on one side of the classroom. A curtain, created from three bedsheets of navy, brown, and white fabrics, was strung across the center of the classroom, and behind it was our stage.

We began with recorder solos, piano solos, guitar solos, whatever instruments the kids had been working on, and we interspersed the musical offerings with readings. Students read their own work or chose thematic poems they liked and walked in front of everyone, with no microphone, and read their selections. We had a brief awards ceremony too, my giving awards to students who'd achieved 3.5 and 4.0 GPAs, who'd performed as thespians, who'd worked on the school newspaper or in the school government, and who'd had perfect attendance that semester. But my favorite part came during the second half. That's when the play was scheduled.

We had plays about Christmas in the OK Corral, Christmas in Mother Goose Land, Christmas with Mr. Scrooge, but the first Christmas play we did, "Star Bright," when Sheri and I first worked together, I remember best. It was about a small star that earned its way to become the topper for the world's tallest Christmas tree. We only had a small cast, and Caleb had opted not to perform; Brian became the Christmas tree, Melissa the star, Cindy the head ruler of the sky, and the others were individual heavenly bodies: Polaris, a meteor, the sun, and a comet.

Our costumes were minimal. We had taken large cardboard boxes and cut headpieces for the meteor, the sun, the comet, and Polaris, painted them starry colors, and the actors wore them around their heads. For Brian, we'd fashioned a simple Christmas tree, about three feet tall, and cut a hole in the center about six inches from the top for his head. The tree didn't quite come to his waist, but his acting, size, and voice made him an imposing "King Conifer." Melissa had cut a large star, painted it yellow, and hung it around her neck with some twine.

The plot was simple. King Conifer was looking for a star to sit atop his tree for Christmas. All but the smallest star boasted their reasons for becoming a tree topper to Brian: one being beautiful, one being fast, and one providing light to the earth. The kids had memorized their lines, at least the best they could. And when they were supposed to speak but were silent, we had a first grader who helped out. Telitha at one point grinned, pointing to Craig when he forgot his words. Another time she stamped her foot to indicate to somebody else it was his turn to speak. She was our prompter that year.

The small star managed to become the honored star when she saved some sailors. What the play called for, I don't remember, but we made it unforgettable for the audience. Because Brian had a green boat, the *Green Weenie*, that he putted around camp with, we altered the play a bit. When the sailors in the play's script were lost in a fog, we made up a few new lines. Brian, Craig, and Bret were these sailors who were rowing in the *Green Weenie*, hoping that they wouldn't run into a rock, be washed out to sea, or have the fuel barge run over them when they were looking for a way to get home. Melissa came swirling onto the stage, twirling around that little cardboard prop of a green boat holding the three boys while a xylophone backstage tinkled "Twinkle, Twinkle, Little Star."

The boys shouted, "Look a star! … Follow that star. I know where it leads … Paddle as fast as you can!" and finally, "Look, there's camp! We're saved!" Sheri and I had rewritten this with the kids' help so it would apply to us, and when the boys finally saw camp, a collective sigh with chuckles of relief swept through the audience, many of them bunkhouse guys.

The next scene showed the Christmas tree praising the little star for her bravery in helping the sailors while berating the others for thinking that their beauty rather than their actions would earn them rewards. When King Conifer honored the smallest star to be his topper, Evan slid a metal folding chair out from behind some cardboard clouds, and Brian sat on it. Melissa climbed gingerly up onto the seat behind him and dangled her star over the tip of his tree. The curtain closed to loud applause as the cast sang "O Christmas Tree."

The curtain opened, the actors appeared onstage and bowed, and we sang a few more carols before I tried to close the curtain again. Sheri wouldn't let me—she got in my way and said, "Just a minute. We have something. Cindy? … Melissa? …"

Soon somebody walked on stage with a vase filled with beautiful flowers. Sheri took them and began, "Mrs. Robbins …," I looked at her, my face feeling hot, as she continued, "We know how much work you've put into this program," and I was thinking that everyone had, not just me, "and we wanted to say thank you." She handed me the vase and a card, and as I placed them on top of the piano, she asked, "Aren't you going to cry?"

Perhaps I would have at one time, but that evening I was riding on a heartful of smiles, and I shook my head. "No, not today. I'm in a good mood." And then she let me close the curtain.

We removed all the props, cleared off the floor, and prepared for our final act. That was the first year of the Christmas square dance.

Several years before, I'd found a Christmas-themed jingly bells square dance that I'd taped, and that became our signature event, the ritual closing of our program. The kids danced to the music, do-si-doing and circling right and left, promenading their corners, and dancing flawlessly right up to the grand right and left, which we had had to practice many times.

This particular year, all five boys and, among the girls, only Melissa and Cindy wanted to dance. (Telitha, then in first grade, found the steps too challenging.) With a square requiring four girls and four boys and none of the boys wanting to be in a girl's spot, Sheri and I filled in to complete the square. Two of the boys had to take turns. Evan and Brian traded off during practices, and for our performance, each danced only once: Evan danced the first time when those who knew the steps because they'd practiced for PE danced, and Brian braved the second time when the boys invited women from the audience to join them.

Craig, Bret, Caleb, and Brian each offered their hand to ladies from the audience—none of them to their own mothers. The ladies, good sports that they were and with encouragement from Sheri, "You can't say no," moved into the square with their partners.

As Susan was moving onstage to dance with Caleb, she, who was heading the cookhouse, looked back to the bunkhouse guys and threatened, "Laugh, and you get nothing for breakfast!"

From the first "Honor your corner," those ladies were lost. The boys tried to gently push them to where they should be, but the ladies had no idea what to do, and soon the boys lost their place in the music as well. As all square dances do, this one moved the women around the square, each time performing the same sequence of steps but with a new partner, and finally, the last time, somebody in the audience said, "I think they're getting it."

However, one of the women had left the dance floor, and her partner was all alone. Sheri again boomed out, "Dance with the invisible woman like we practiced," and I seldom again was so proud of Craig. He promenaded that invisible lady around the square, swung her, and then bowed to her. The only problem was that the corner gent wouldn't take her when his turn came, so Craig kept her for the whole dance. Of course, the grand right and left never happened, and when the music stopped, the boys wiped their brows and took deep breaths. The women went back to their seats to the laughter and applause of the mostly men left in the audience.

Some of the guys got up to leave, but Sheri said, "Sit down; it's not over yet," to Everett as he'd risen from his seat. For now was the ladies' turn to invite men up, and while Cindy and Melissa invited bunkhouse guys, Sheri asked her husband, and I asked Everett. Somehow, whether it was because we females were collectively older and wiser than the boys who preceded us or because we were more used to bossing people around, we didn't have nearly the trouble that the boys had had. In spite of some mistakes, we made it through the whole set until the grand right and left. Then we got a little mixed up but managed to go around the circle, grabbing hands whether they were right or left, and ended up with our partners. Everett and I, being slow, were behind Melissa and her partner at the end, so we forged through them at the last minute, Everett uttering his apologies.

That was the end of our evening's entertainment, and so I announced that people could get autographs from the cast before they left. I don't think anybody heard me above the buzz of the audience. One male voice uttered, "That was pretty darn good. Everybody out there chased me around the floor." He was somebody who had fun with the square dance.

Again I tried, "Anyone who wants autographs can get them from the cast." Nobody moved.

Susan said, "We don't want to leave."

They did though. Eventually.

As I shut off the lights and locked the door behind me, I thought we had been blessed, all of us, by that gathering, and I vowed to try my darnedest to make future programs follow suit.

The days that followed were rather listless, the excitement of the program having passed and the regular lessons before our winter vacation being a drag. To jazz up the day a bit, I planned art activities in the afternoon. "Let's get all our work done in the morning," I'd encourage, "and then we can do something fun in the afternoon."

Not that sometimes our routine scholastic lessons weren't fun, but art was more fun.

Every year, I'd order special projects to be made at this time, projects that took extra time, projects that were extra special and could be given as gifts to treasured adults. We made napkin holders from wooden pieces that we had to glue in place, we made special Christmas ornaments, and one year, Michelle helped us make individualized T-shirts.

Michelle was younger than many of the mothers, newly married to the camp's mechanic, and didn't have any children of her own yet. She became the school custodian and eventually the kindergarten aide, and this particular year, she showed us how to use puffy paints to decorate white T-shirts. She brought in her own bottles of paints, and I brought back shirts from Ketchikan after asking the kids what size they wanted to have, depending on whom the kids decided to give them to. Telitha ordered a huge one—maybe for her dad, while Evan ordered one for little Josh, and Bret for his mom. I made one for myself, using those puffy paints to letter each child's name around in a circle, thinking I was fashioning a Christmas wreath for myself to remember this class whenever I wore the shirt. I never wore the shirt, but I never forgot those kids either.

When I returned from town with the shirts, I also brought several boxes of graham crackers and gumdrops and other Christmas candies. We were going to make gingerbread houses. Well, graham-cracker houses, actually. I made powdered sugar frosting, and we glued the walls together, cut some crackers on the diagonal, setting them on opposite walls so we could add sloping roofs. Then we used the frosting glue to set gumdrops and candy canes and other sweets on our creations. We arranged them on the bookshelf, creating a lovely little village that we enjoyed until people began to leave.

One by one, the school population diminished as parents took their children south for the shutdown. Some visited relatives while others flew to Hawaii or maybe Disneyland for their holidays. When we were few in number, we were known to have "game times," and we played things like cribbage, Go Fish, and War, quiet games that would pass the afternoons and be more fun than schoolwork. Of course, many of us were envious of those whose absence from school had already begun and were eager when finally that last Friday on the district calendar arrived.

For winter breaks, we had a month off or more, and I usually spent Christmas with my family in Minnesota, to return a few days before school started again.

When that first day in late January arrived, I began our assignments: "Okay, guys. What did you do for your vacation?" I had papers and crayons available for their accompanying pictures and the bulletin board already titled: What I Did for Winter Break.

Bret rolled his eyes but was silent. He started writing.

***

Spring arrived on the wings of the varied thrushes. Although these robin-like birds spent the entire winter in the woods, it was in the spring when their mating trills echoed across the water. Calling from across the bay, answering from up the ramp, those birds lifted my spirits with their morning music. As I made my way across the floats with my cup of coffee to the school, those thrushes seemed to embody the season of rebirth.

Soon, logging operations would begin again. Bunkhouse guys would return, and the hustle and bustle of men working would stir the camp. The silence of winter was broken by the grinds and clunks of machinery in the nearby sort yard, out of view but not out of sound. A boom boat chugged cheerily in the water, following the splashing of the sorted logs as they were dumped, pushing them to the spot they belonged, and nosing them into place. Then the driver hopped out and chained the new batch to the rest, jumped back into his boat and backed away, perhaps giving a toot, and was ready for the next dump. Whistles and toots, engines' hum, and clanks of chain signaled the logging operation's busy activity as its new season opened.

At school, spring meant that some days were interrupted by the standardized testing the district and state required. Although it wasn't the basis for distributing money or chastising staff that it seems to have become, it was intense. Both the kids and I wanted them to do well, and so they were encouraged to eat well and get a good night's sleep before they had to take these tests, and I excused school early on the days that they were given. From what I understood, the school day had to be a minimum of four hours long. On those days, we kept to

Inside the classroom—what will we do next?

the minimum, and students' spirits didn't sag with the struggle of so much testing.

I tried to make their learning fun when I could, so I made a big deal out of the hundredth day. All year long, I'd kept a running tally on a roll of paper taped high on the walls, going around the classroom of the days we'd been in school, starting with number one. It turned into a number line, of course, and as I wrote the new number in place each morning, I'd ask for answers. "Is this an odd or an even number?" "What is it a factor of?" "Is it prime or composite?" Mostly geared for intermediate students, these questions helped everyone see relationships and learn that numbers were predictable and fun.

I also made the calendar dates for each month with some special pattern. In the front of the room, I had hung a blank calendar and put numbers from one to twenty-eight or thirty or thirty-one, depending on how many days each month had. When we opened each school day, among my practices was to put the date up in its proper place on the calendar and have the "special person" read the calendar correctly. As he/she read it, I wrote it on the board, and it was visible for the whole day as students needed the information for their assignments. A few days before the month changed, I cut some shapes out of construction paper and wrote the numbers on them, planning to match the shapes with the month and numerical pattern I wanted to use. For instance, one February, I used hearts for all the multiples of four, making the other numbers out of white squares. In December, I might have used trees for the even numbers and stars for the odd ones. Whatever the pattern, I never told the kids ahead of time. I'd wait until they discovered what they were as the numbers were posted. It didn't take long, as they became used to my tricks.

When the hundredth day appeared, usually in mid to late February, we celebrated. We were over halfway through the 180 days that we were required to attend, and were on the downhill slide of that academic year. The day before, after dismissal, Sheri and I blew up balloons, one hundred of them, and hung them under the chalk ledges.

The elementary lessons, especially math that day, were planned to emphasize that number. I had collected coins, and one year we played with one hundred pennies, trading them for nickels and dimes and quarters. Another year, I filled baggies with M&Ms and had the kids count them, graph them by color, and then we used their graphs to figure percentages. I also asked the kids to count the balloons—had we managed to provide one hundred of them? They were important, as after we finished the shortened day of lessons, we used them to play games.

One was balloon volleyball. Kids moved their desks so that the front half of the room faced the back half of the room, and they moved toward the chalkboards so that a middle space was created. Then one side hit a balloon, trying to get it across that space to the other side. If it wasn't hit hard enough, whoever was close to where it was coming down could give it a thump to help it get over. Then the other side tried to hit it back, like a regular volleyball game without a net. Oh, and without moving much either. They couldn't move their butts off their chairs, or the referee, Sheri, would boom out a reminder, "Stay seated!" or, "No space off the chair," or after repeated jumps up, "Keep your butt down!" After perhaps fifteen minutes, whoever was ahead was declared the winner.

Another favorite was the balloon stomp. We tied strings to the balloons, moved the desks to the sides, and the kids then tied the balloons to one of their ankles. When Sheri said, "Go," the stomping began. Of course, the goal was to be the last person whose balloon was unbroken. You can imagine the whoops and shouts and thumps and bangs that filled the classroom. There were also quite a few "ouch" and "oops" as balloons were missed and feet and ankles were accidentally stomped. As the numbers of kids with their balloons still intact dwindled, Sheri and I and the others who were out formed a circle and made it smaller, thus tightening the arena of play for the remainder of the contest. And when the winner was left with his/her balloon unbroken, we moved the desks back from the room's edges and sat back down, out of breath, perhaps a little bruised, but happy.

It always was a bit of a letdown when I wrote 101 on the number line the next day.

Within the next month, we began our planning for the following year, especially for the high school students. Their courses would come from the requirements they still needed and the classes that were available. One big improvement during my tenure there was the access to classes by distance.

Evan and Cindy were able to take German from Oklahoma and oceanography from Oregon. The satellite dish the school district had set up on my float was used to receive the programs, and before others came to school, Cindy and Evan would go down to the little room at the end of the hall, where the television was hooked up, and attend class. Hilary taught their science. We had to send her photographs of her students to use as she was teaching. She used them, I think, to get a feel for her students all over the west.

Herr Wohlert taught German. Evan opted for German over Japanese or Spanish when he had the choice because I'd taken German in college those many years earlier. I found that I could sometimes be helpful and that it was fun to refresh and relearn the language. The last year I was at the school, German by satellite expanded to half-hour lessons for the elementary students, thanks, I believe, to Herr Wohlert's wife, Frau Wohlert.

I enjoyed these satellite classes as they made me feel as if I was on a staff, working with other teachers, which I was in a way. However, I had to do no planning, just provide the time and the television for the students to get their lectures. Every now and then, though, the television didn't work. That was when we had one of our minus tides at the same time as their classes were scheduled. Then the hill behind camp blocked the reception from the satellite, much as it had blocked the sun in the winter. We were fortunate, though, that Sheri, at the other end of camp where the hill sloped down, still had reception, and either she would tape the lessons, or Evan would stay at home to view them. They rarely missed a class.

Those older kids also had the opportunity to travel in the spring. Evan, two years running, won the district's Geography Bee, earning a trip for his mom and himself to Anchorage. Another year, he also went to Washington, DC, with a group of students from another school in the district and their teacher. All three older students, Evan, Cindy, and Melissa, at different times traveled to Juneau for two weeks to participate in a program abbreviated R.S.V.P. (Rural Students Vocational Program), usually in the fields they requested. Melissa worked in a bilingual classroom in one of the elementary schools, while Cindy worked in a veterinarian's office. Evan came back with a meter reader after doing so well at an electrician's establishment.

One year, the school district gathered all the secondary students and their teachers in Thorne Bay, a large logging community on the east side of Prince of Wales. It had an impressive school with a full-sized gym and many teachers. Each of us from the smaller schools was asked to teach something to the group. I chose art; another teacher chose dancing, and I don't remember the rest. It was fun, though, to be a part of that large group and to watch the kids mingle with strangers, eat in a cafeteria, stay up late for a dance, and drag themselves in to breakfast the next day. This get-together happened only once, although I thought it was to be the first in a series of district-wide gatherings.

Another trip on which I accompanied them was our field trip to Sitka. Cindy's mom, Maggie, also came, so she and I were the chaperones for Melissa, Evan, Cindy, and Lacey. Lacey had moved up after Christmas with her mom, dad, and two sisters, and not only did she get to go with us to Thorne Bay, but she also arrived in time for the Sitka trip.

Every time I fly into Sitka, I am amazed at its beauty. Sitting on the side of the sea, the city is surrounded by walls of nature—on one side, a rugged peak; on another, a vast bay where humpback whales play; and on yet another, a dormant volcano dome, rising high above the water. If the sun is setting, and I am gifted with pinks and lavenders in the sky, then the beauty is magnified with the makeup that the sun applies. It is also a city filled with history.

I was told that its cultural offerings highlighted the Pacific coast, long before the cities of San Francisco, Los Angeles, and Seattle became noted. It was the Russian capital of Alaska, and the Russians brought their musicians and dancers to perform for the governors. Its influence is still felt, alongside the earlier contributions of the Tlingit tribes, making Sitka a wonderful place to visit.

Don and I had brought the students from another camp to Sitka several years before, so planning the trip was not difficult. We were going to many of the same places I'd visited, and I knew they were going to enjoy the trip.

We stayed at Sheldon Jackson College. Now closed, it was a school founded by a Presbyterian minister who wanted to help the native population. At the time we were there, an old dormitory was not being used, and we were assigned rooms for a modest cost. That cost also included breakfast every morning.

Being the teacher, I was given a suite with its own living room and bathroom. The bathroom held a claw-footed bathtub with a two-foot hose attached to the spigot with a shower nozzle at its end. It wasn't long enough to stand and pretend it was a shower, and the tub was so dirty that I didn't want to sit in it, so my cleanliness during the trip was created by "spit baths," which used very little water.

We met in the living room every night to eat what we called supper, having purchased chips and dips and fruits and vegetables from various grocery stores, write in our journals about what we'd seen, and discuss the next day's adventures. It was a comfortable way to debrief and find out how each student was faring.

The rest of our group lived dormitory style, sharing one communal bathroom. Cindy and Maggie shared a room, as did Melissa and Lacey, while Evan had a room to himself. The communal bathroom door held a sign with "women" on one side and "men" on the other, and whenever they used it, they had to flip the sign to the correct side. Maggie made another sign to flip saying "occupied" and "unoccupied" so nobody would walk in on anybody by mistake. Evan managed well, being the only male in the group, and became good at reading footsteps in the morning and evening, recognizing the females as they trooped to the bathroom and back, thus allowing himself the best chance to find it unoccupied.

In the mornings, we all trouped over to the cafeteria in another building to start our day with the breakfast it offered.

Then we were ready for our busy days. We visited the places of interest on the Sheldon Jackson campus. It provided a museum and a fish hatchery. We visited places of Russian history: the Russian Orthodox Church, the Russian Bishop's house, Castle Hill, the site of the Russian Governor Baranof's palace, and Sitka National Historical Park, where the Russians battled the native inhabitants and won. We visited the police department, the fire department, the newspaper, the grocery store, the hospital, the Coast Guard base, and many, many other places. I insisted we eat one lunch at a more formal dining room, part of a hotel complex, and of course, as soon as the kids noticed the McDonald's, I had to promise we'd eat there as well. Although we had a van to get from place to place, we did a lot of walking, too.

I was surprised when, during one of our evening sessions, the students complained, "Mrs. Robbins, you're wearing us out!"

"Yes," another agreed. "We're tired."

With only a day left of our four-day trip, I allowed them to go to bed early and sleep a bit later that last morning.

When we returned to camp and the photographs I took had been developed, I assigned them to write about our trip. Not-so-cleverly titled "Our Field Trip," this booklet chronicled our journey. Most of the entries were written factually, as I'd asked them to pretend they were news reporters, but an occasional insight or two was provided the reader.

Lacey began the commentaries with a page about our actual getting to Sitka. We boarded a floatplane, a de Havilland Beaver, to get to Ketchikan where we waited in the airport for the jet that would take us to Sitka, with two intermediary stops. Lacey wrote:

> *At the airport, we calmly waited for our jet. Lacey had just had her first floatplane ride and was about to have her first jet ride. Melissa had fun doing the two things she does best: shopping and talking on the phone. Maggie and Melissa got off at Wrangell to look around. Since the airport at Petersburg didn't look much bigger, they stayed on at the second stop. As we finished our flight, we ate our almonds and brazil nuts and drank our orange juice.*

It was always fun to see what was important to students. Obviously, flying and eating were important to Lacey. I think she enjoyed being included in the group with the older kids, especially with Melissa. They made good roommates, Melissa surprising me yet again with her patience and teaching. Although Lacey was a good student, she was naïve in many ways, and Melissa quietly and unobtrusively helped her become older and more mature.

From Melissa and the page titled "Public Safety Training Academy," we have:

> *While at the trooper academy we toured their classrooms and watched an interesting video about what it's like to attend the academy. We also watched a video that showed students getting sprayed in the face with a cayenne pepper spray that all troopers and public safety officers have to carry. The most exciting part of our tour was when we got to play with the f.a.t.s. machine. It holographed a scenario on a wall and you played the part of the police officer. Do you shoot? If so a laser sensitive panel picks up where and when your shots were fired. Both Evan and Melissa killed a perpetrator.*

Evan and Melissa were the fearless ones, the first to try new things. Whether it was a new food, a new pathway, or a new activity, such as shooting at a holograph, they led the way.

Cindy wrote about the grocery store, Sea Mart:

> *While in Sitka we got a tour of Sea Mart. It was fun to see where they keep all of their chill and freezer foods. Mickey Sarver, the one who showed us around, was very nice. After the tour she gave us a box of cookies (which Lacey especially enjoyed).*

Lacey, the youngest, quiet, newly arrived-to-camp girl, surprised us daily with the amount of food she packed away. Having a body frame that appeared slight, she always ate more than we expected she would.

Cindy also wrote about shopping.

> *We went shopping about three times while in Sitka. We were all busy looking for Mother's Day presents. Some of us decided flowers would be the perfect gift. Some of us also shopped for clothes while in Sitka. We all enjoyed playing with the stuffed animals at the different stores. The monkey at Sea Mart was great!*

Living out at a logging camp on a remote island didn't offer many opportunities for hands-on shopping, but I was surprised to see how they fondled and also goofed off with the stuffed animals.

Evan was the most factual writer of the group. He also wrote fewer entries than the others. About the police station he said:

> *Sgt. Ray Majeski showed us around the police department. First he showed us the computer they use to check people's records and the machine they used to record phone calls and radio transmissions. Maggie and Mrs. Robbins had the radio operator bring up their names on the computer. Then he showed us his office and the jail cells. The cells were just a concrete room with a toilet, a sink, and one or two beds. Melissa tried out the bed.*

His few entries could have been because he didn't like to write; it certainly wasn't because he couldn't write.

Even I contributed some pages to this booklet. I wrote about our evenings of entertainment: swimming, hiking, and bowling. It's most fun to remember bowling:

> *Children learn a safety rule very early: STOP, DROP, AND ROLL. Although it's meant for fires, Lacey used it for bowling. She would take her ball and run to the foul line, where she would STOP, DROP her ball, and it would often ROLL into the gutter. Melissa showed Lacey the spider technique, but Lacey preferred to STOP, DROP, and ROLL. We all had our problems. Maggie had to walk with "duck feet," Melissa and Mrs. R. had to concentrate through the shouts of encouragement and laughter, and Cindy and Evan learned how to score.*

Our time in Sitka drew to an end, and Melissa remembered our departure for home:

> *The time to leave Sitka came too soon. Yes, we were exhausted, but we weren't ready to go back to school. Before we left the Sitka airport, Mrs. Robbins, Evan, Cindy, and Maggie all bought pies from the Nugget Restaurant to take home. We put the pies and our Mother's Day flowers in plastic bags to carry on the plane. When we got back to camp, we gave Sheri the prism that we bought her in Sitka. Over half of the camp was waiting for us on the airplane dock. Mrs. Robbins said, "I would take these kids anywhere." Next year, how about the Bahamas??*

Although Polk Inlet School had a few more field trips, none seemed as special as that one. Reading the booklet's pages, I was surprised to remember that Lacey was only in sixth grade at the time, and Cindy and Evan were in eighth. Melissa, the eldest, was finishing eleventh grade, and they all got along so very well. I wish we could have gone to the Bahamas.

A week later I brought the primary children to Ketchikan for their day-long field trip. One sunny day, Telitha, Bret, and Lacey's younger sister, Katie, flew with me in a Beaver from camp across Clarence Strait into Ketchikan. We borrowed a van from the school district and began our tour. I don't have their words to describe our trip because I didn't make them write a book. However, photographs are good reminders of what we did.

We did visit the fire station where the kids got to sit in the fire trucks, watch a fireman slide down the brass fire pole, and meet a fireman all dressed up for a fire. That was important, explained the man, in case somebody who looked like an alien ever needed to rescue them from a fire. They should not be afraid.

We visited Ketchikan General Hospital, the place that people from camp went to when they were seriously ill. The staff showed us how they took blood, what some of the lab tests were, and how some of the physical therapy equipment was used, especially the big body balls. They allowed the kids to play for awhile on them.

From there, we went to the *Ketchikan Daily News*. Reporter Nikki Jones gave us our tour. We saw the computers that set up the stories and the wax machine that prepared the paper to print, and finally we were allowed into the room where the big rolls of papers were fed into the printing presses. It was unfortunate, according to the kids, that we were only told how the presses worked, as it was the wrong time of the day for them to be operating.

Telitha, Bret, and Katie were getting hungry, and I had set up a tour of McDonald's for them. When we arrived, we were shown the big freezer. It was really cold, we found out, as we were allowed inside it for a while. We also saw what was stocked in the huge refrigerator before we went back to where the rest of the customers were. We got in line and ordered our Big Macs, fries, and Cokes, the kids licking their lips at the tastes of such seldom-eaten treats.

Next, we drove to the native village of Saxman, just south of Ketchikan, which contains a totem park. We wandered in the sunshine among the totem poles, each student picking out a favorite as we talked about the symbols as we passed. In the middle of the park was a clan house, but it was locked this time, and we couldn't get in.

During a future field trip, our students were invited inside and allowed to accompany the cruise-ship passengers who had paid for a tour of the park. Inside the Beaver Clan House, we watched the native dancers perform in their button blankets. These were Tlingits whose families had lived here for generations, people of the Beaver Clan, dancing for different reasons. One dance that I remember was to welcome visitors, and we did feel welcome there.

We were tired and ready to return home when we waited for our plane at Taquan Air Service. Our visit to Ketchikan was an enjoyable trip.

When we weren't traveling, we were busy in camp, too. Spring was the time for another Spirit Week. Whenever the itinerants were visiting and we played our games and dressed funny, they participated as well. One particular spring, when school held only seven students, it was especially nice when an adult could make the teams even.

One time, Don Alderman was in camp the day of our Jell-O slurp. This was one of the kids' favorite games, causing lots of noise and giggles. Somebody volunteered to make two pans of red Jell-O, and somebody else brought straws. People were divided into two teams, and the pans of Jell-O were placed at the end of the hall.

Just as we were getting ready to start the game, the school plane flew in, bringing with it Evvy Fernald, the special ed. teacher, who was going to stay the night and planning to take away Mr. Alderman for his next school. But he wouldn't leave until he'd slurped with the kids. So the classroom filled with people who were on the plane that day: the pilot, Evvy, the assistant superintendent, and another traveling teacher.

They walked into the building just as the teams lined up at the other end of the school, and when Sheri said, "Go," the first of each team ran to the Jell-O, got on hands and knees, and began to slurp it from the pans.

"Stop." The slurpers pulled away, stood up, and ran back to their team, the next person going quickly to the pans and repeating the slurping process. While Sheri kept track of the time, thirty seconds per run, I ran the video recorder, enjoying the kids' efforts of trying to suck that stuff up with a straw and giggling at the sounds they were making, mostly like farting. The others all laughed too.

After about ten minutes, when neither team had finished its Jell-O, we decided it was time for a "group slurp," and then Sheri moved the pans of Jell-O from the hall to the classroom where there was room to spread out. The teams lay on the floor, on their stomachs, heads bunched together around their pan and straws inserted. Sheri's "Go" started the groups' slurping, and the fart-sounds increased with their combined sucking.

Don Alderman had joined in the relay portion, taking his turn with Bret, Cindy, and Lacey, running down to the bowls in the hall when it was time, slurping for his thirty seconds, and running back to his team. Obviously, he was a good sport. Remember, he also taught the kids good music, and he taught it well. And … he often chewed gum when he worked.

He also got down on the floor with the others, his head between Cindy's and Lacey's, and group-slurped.

Suddenly, he pulled up. "I lost my gum," he said.

Cindy came up from the group so suddenly I wondered if something serious was wrong. But she was laughing hard, and with a mouthful of Jell-O, she was beginning to spit it out and wanted to get to a trash can so she really could take care of it.

"She grabbed my gum," Mr. Alderman complained, and while we all laughed, he looked into the now almost-empty Jell-O pan and said, "Oh, here it is." He pulled it out and popped it back into his mouth, began chewing it, and looked around with a huge and rather mischievous smile on his face.

Meanwhile, Bret and Lacey had continued slurping and had cleaned the pan, ignoring the commotion.

"I guess we know who can slurp Jell-O around here," was Sheri's remark as she declared Bret and Lacey's team the winners.

The next day, Evvy joined the kids as they passed a ball over and under and then back around to reverse the process. It was a confusing mess, and as students tried to follow Melissa's directions, one team did one thing, the other another, and in the five minutes of going to the head of the line, passing the ball under, disagreeing about who should start, where the ball should be passed and such, Melissa finally declared a winner and the game was over.

The third day of Spirit Week, the kids played the telephone game, one person whispering a message in the ear of the next in a line of people, seeing what mangled words the last person would hear. This time Sheri was on a team.

I held the camera, and I enjoyed that job. It was a teacher's perk.

As the years came and went, the Spirit Week of the fall and the spring were truly welcomed by all. Kids loved to plan the activities and chose which games they would plan for, bring equipment for, and lead. They also chose what the days would be—nerd day, bad-hair day, go-to-the-beach day, pajama day, or mismatch day. Sheri and I enjoyed watching their antics, getting along together in the spirit of friendly rivalry, wearing funny clothes in the spirit of school unity, and learning leadership skills in the spirit of helping others. It was always a week of good spirits.

Our spirits were raised, too, when the unexpected happened. Twice when I was in Dora Bay, we were invited to go aboard one of the huge log ships that had come from Japan or China to get the timber that was waiting in log rafts floating near the shore. Each ship anchored out in the bay, looking like a giant spider or perhaps Medusa's head with leggy-looking appendages moving from high on the deck down to pluck huge log bundles from the water. The tiny boom boat worked in tandem with the giant tentacles that came down from above.

The first time, we went out on one of the tugboats with Richard at the wheel, but the second time was Evan's senior year, and he was allowed to drive the crew boat. In fact, it was part of his job to chauffeur the men to and from work. Since the logging crew left much earlier than we held school, he was able to take us out to the *Rubin Bonanza*, a log ship built in Japan. Arranging for a morning tour, we found that we were visiting them on their maiden voyage.

We bundled into the noisy crew boat, its engines idling while we boarded. As soon as all twenty of us (a big school enrollment that year—it was the year of the new cook) were safe, Evan pulled the throttle, and we were off. Soon we tied up to that big ship. It was so tall, rising like a skyscraper, comparable to an oil tanker. We were able to enter from the water level, but then we had to climb stairs to get to the rooms that we were to be shown. One of the crew who spoke English led us around the ship. We saw where they slept and ate, where their electronic equipment was, and where the engine and generator purred. The engineers who worked with those machines kept the room spotless; I noticed they left their shoes in the doorway when they entered. We never were able to see the logs being loaded. It was too dangerous.

We had our photo taken above the name of the ship before getting back down to the crew boat. Most students felt it easier to go down than it had been coming up and waved goodbye to each of the crew as they smiled and waved back. Then we cruised back to camp and to the four walls of the school again.

It always amazes me to look at the long list of logs that were loaded onto the *Rubin Bonanza*—three million board feet of timber, headed to three different Japanese cities. And this was but one of many, many log ships that sat in Dora Bay waiting to be filled.

***

Spring left reluctantly, and summer's advent heralded the last few weeks of school and a flurry of activity. It seemed as if this was when unexpected people shared their talents with us. Perhaps it was that the weather made flying, thus getting to us, a little more predictable, or perhaps their commitments were fulfilled, and they had the time to do something not on their regular schedule.

One year Pat Chapman came, carrying Annie. Annie was the CPR rescue doll, and Pat taught us first aid and CPR. She came to school and worked with the young kids on their first aid—Bret, Telitha, and Katie bandaged and were bandaged. They breathed into Annie's mouth and pressed on her chest. I don't think they had enough air because, at our spring program, they were awarded only first-aid certificates. However, the older kids also earned CPR cards.

They practiced their skills on each other and on Annie during class. Pat showed a proper splint using Evan and then asked the students to follow her model. Evan managed a perfect one on Melissa, but Lacey splinted Cindy's arm with a tourniquet—at least according to Cindy; it was too tight.

Even I was drawn into their practice. I was the unconscious automobile accident victim, the one who had to be assumed severely injured and carried to a gurney without messing up my back. Those four students maneuvered themselves so they could put their arms and hands under my body and moved me without my even twitching a foot. They worked hard and learned what Pat came to teach.

Pat also taught a group of adults in the evening. All women, mostly moms—Sheri, Marilyn, Vernadell (Marilyn's mom), Lisa (Katie and Lacey's mom), Michelle, who was by now teaching kindergarten, and I made up the class that bandaged and splinted, breathed into and pressed onto Annie, lifted and carried, and earned our CPR cards, too.

We now knew whom to call when an accident happened. Thank goodness I was never called.

Another late visitor was Betsy, our school librarian and a part-time puppeteer. She brought with her the stage, the puppets, and the play, inviting Melissa to play the part of the paper bag, one of the major characters. I can't remember the plot, but I do remember the entire community of women and children, clustered around Betsy's little stage, watching in awe as she and Melissa moved those puppets around by their sticks. What a gift to bring us.

Another gift to the community was graduation. This celebration happened when there was a senior—not often, given our student population, and only twice in the six years I was there. The class of 1993 was Melissa, and her graduation was something special.

She, her Aunt Susan and Uncle Milo, and perhaps others had arranged the school so that a few chairs against the walls met at the far corner of the main classroom. They'd set other chairs in parallel rows with an aisle in-between so that the graduation speakers could walk from the bathroom hallway, down the aisle, and sit against the wall while the audience faced them. White plastic sheeting hung over those two walls, covering the blackboard and the window, providing a background that wouldn't interfere with the proceedings.

When the first strains of "Pomp and Circumstance" played from the boom box, I began the procession down the aisle, followed by Don Alderman. Behind him were others: Ernie Hansen, the district's

Melissa's Graduation

assistant superintendent, and then Evvy, Melissa's grandfather, Murray, his nephew and camp owner Keaton, and Sheri. At the end, suitably beaming and smiling from side to side as she strolled down the aisle, was Melissa. It was time for her pomp and her circumstance.

I voiced a welcome, Keaton offered a prayer, we said the Pledge of Allegiance, and then we sat down. Sheri introduced Don Alderman, and he gave the first speech. It was quite lengthy, beginning with introspection about where we'd been and where we might be going, and ending with the idea that people who love and concern us give us gifts, that we should keep looking for and giving gifts throughout our lives.

When he was finished, Melissa took a deep breath, stepped to the podium, and proceeded with her bequests. For each student, she had something to offer: her creative ability to Lacey, her aspirations for high school to Evan and Cindy. "Never underestimate your potential," she told them. She bequeathed her ability to accumulate to Telitha, her humility to Bret, her individuality to Katie, her love of books to Craig, and to Josh, the youngest there, her typing speed and accuracy. She looked directly at each child in the audience as she spoke to him or her.

Ernie stepped up next and presented Melissa her diploma. "You are not alone," he said. "You are among the nineteen graduates this year throughout Southeast Island School District." He said that she had completed all the state of Alaska requirements and gave her the diploma on its behalf and sat down.

Melissa, still standing, took a deep breath, faced directly to the audience, and began. "Thanks for being here … As I look at this room, I can't help but feel proud and privileged to be sharing this with so many wonderful people. You're my educators, my family, and my friends."

Here she paused for one of the emotional moments she had warned us about before she began her speech.

"My supporters, my confidants, and my …" Whatever she said was lost in a deep breath. "You're the ones who helped me, and I can't thank you enough. When I walked through those doors two years ago, I knew everything." She glanced back at Evvy and me.

We smiled, remembering just that.

"Now, two years later, I don't know half as much as I did then … This place, this floating city, has eternally changed me."

Another emotional moment caused her to turn her back to the audience, bow her head, and try to gain her composure as her mother stepped up from the front row and offered her a tissue. When she was ready, Melissa turned back.

She thanked her Aunt Susan and Uncle Milo and offered "immeasurable gratitude and love." She thanked her mother, and she thanked the rest of us as well. Then she ended her speech by telling us that she intended to go on to college, armed with the knowledge she had gained here.

She sat back down to heavy applause, and it was Evvy's turn to speak. Evvy had worked closely with Melissa, helping her to cram three years of high school requirements into two, and Melissa had asked her to be personal with her words. Evvy smiled as she recalled the first time they'd met, when she'd asked Melissa about her life plan. Evvy remembered Melissa had said, "Well, I plan to go to college, get two PhDs, get married, and have children. All before I'm old … over thirty!" Evvy laughed, as did many of the rest of us who had a different definition of old.

Evvy continued recalling a series of hellos and goodbyes with Melissa—hello when Evvy came to camp for her bi-weekly visits and goodbye when she left; hello when she met Melissa at the airport for one of her school trips and goodbye when Evvy put Melissa on a floatplane headed back for camp. Evvy ended with this graduation day's goodbye, looking ahead with joyful anticipation to another hello in the future.

Melissa had asked her Aunt Susan, an excellent vocalist, to sing a song about friends at this point. However, Susan had developed a serious case of laryngitis, and when she stood up, she apologized and said she'd give the song her best effort. Melissa wanted the words to be heard by everyone in the audience, for they conveyed her feelings at that time:

"I'll keep you close forever; it won't even seem I've gone … for a friend's a friend forever …"

As Susan closed the song and sat down, her father, Melissa's grandfather Murray, approached the podium.

"That's a hard act to follow. Don't know that I've heard finer words of wisdom in any hall than I heard right here in Polk Inlet. And we can be proud." He paused for a moment, collecting his thoughts before continuing, "All broke up hearing my own daughter, and I got a daughter grand cryin' over here."

He turned to Melissa. "Nothing to cry about."

Turning back to the audience, he said, "This little girl's been real special. Asked me to give a benediction."

We all bowed our heads as he began, "Thank you, Lord …"

When he said, "Amen," Don and Keaton approached Melissa. Don helped Melissa take off her black graduation robe while Keaton turned the tassel on her cap to the other side. The audience recognized this as a signal to get up and move forward to congratulate Melissa before finding the table holding the cake, punch, and coffee. That was the recessional.

However, the ceremony itself, combined with the crowd's obvious pride and love, made that first graduation at Polk Inlet School unforgettable.

Melissa was now finished with school, and I realized it would be hard for the rest of us to settle down to get through a few more days in the classroom. But we managed.

***

Usually, the last week of school coincided with a minus tide. This very low tide exposed an area usually hidden from us. We put away the books, put on our boots, and headed for the beach. The beaches we were near were not the gently sloping, sandy playgrounds that the word "beach" might engender, but rocky, sometimes precipitous hills leading to the ocean's edge. The large rocks cradled tidal pools, a microcosm of marine life, and were homes to shellfish of all kinds. The intertidal region was a place to be studied, and students had fun doing it.

One year, Telitha and Josh's Uncle Rocky was visiting camp about this time, and they asked to invite him. He was a teacher himself, I was told. Of course he was invited, as were all the parents that could join us. That year, almost every child had an adult walking alongside, which was a good thing. The rocky slope was so steep and required such careful footing that it was almost essential for the young ones to have somebody's hand to hold onto for balance.

When we reached the area we were going to study, students pulled out their clipboards. Sheri and I had stapled sheets of paper onto a piece of corrugated cardboard, and I began to ask questions. Several of the adults carried animal identification books, and students stared into tidepools to see what they could find. Whenever they were unsure, they'd ask somebody with a book to look it up. We were sometimes successful in finding the creature they asked about.

Students were diligent in their search. They lifted small rocks to find little pink crabs that scuttled away from the light. They watched small black fish dart back and forth and found starfish, pink and orange and purple, clinging to rocks. They found chitons, barnacles, Chinese hats, and mussels, along with clamshells, most of which had small round holes through them. Somebody told us that they had been eaten by a starfish, and it made the hole to get to the meat. Finally it was time for the hermit-crab race.

Reminded throughout this time of exploration to keep an eye out for these creatures that find empty shells to live in, the kids had already plucked hermit crabs from the water and kept them on their clipboards. I had the master clipboard, and four at a time, crabs were placed in its center and were expected to scuttle to the edge. Whichever was first was declared a winner. Then we ran a second heat, and a third if needed, before the winners were pitted against each other. There was no prize but a good feeling of friendly competition, and it signaled the end to our trip, and we slowly made our way back up the hill and down the road to camp.

***

The day the number line reached 180, we cleaned out our desks. At least the students did. We took the pictures off the wall and made folders in which to take work home. When the room was pretty stark and bare, we could play a few games as we waited for our four hours to pass. We sometimes brought sack lunches and used the last hour to picnic. If it was nice, we went outside on the playground; rain kept us on the classroom floor, eating our sandwiches and talking about the year that had passed, what students were planning to do in the summer, how they might spend their time, and, of course, suggestions of books they could read.

One June, Sheri and I cut out tagboard hands and pinned them on the students' backs. Then we lined up and wrote compliments to each child, having them write on each other's paper hands, too. It was our way of giving a final "pat on the back" and ending the school year remembering the good things that had happened, the growth that the children had shown.

During the final few days, Sheri helped me put all the books away while I made out report cards, noted where the children should begin again in the fall, and filled out the district's required end-of-year report. While we were preparing for the summer vacation, we were already talking about plans for the next school year. It was going to be even better than the last.

Living—Seasons within Community

When I went back to the camp after a summer vacation, I first brought my luggage into my trailer, carrying suitcases down the walkway while children and their parents who had noticed me arrive walked with me. If I was lucky, somebody would also pack the boxes of groceries I had brought.

"Hi, Mrs. Robbins," one would say. "How was your summer?"

"Much too short," I'd answer. "And what did you do while I was gone?"

Perhaps the student had taken a trip south, although this was unusual during the summertime when the logging operations were in full swing and dads could make lots of money to help tide their families over the winter months when there was no work.

Often, kids would have passed their swimming test. This was important for them to do and for me to know.

So vital was the wearing of life jackets that, if I saw somebody who hadn't yet passed his or her test without a life jacket, I was expected to send him or her home to get one. Coat hooks inside every home held personal flotation devices (PFDs) if it contained children who had not yet passed their swimming test. Because the water was so deep and it was hard work to pull yourself up back onto the float if you fell in the water, PFDs were the safety device the powers of camp required children to wear if they hadn't passed the swimming test. All children. Even if you were in junior high and moved in and couldn't pass, you had to wear a life jacket.

The test involved swimming from camp to shore and back and getting back up onto the float without any help. The summer months were ideal for trying this as the water warmed to a toasty forty degrees or so, but in the sunshine of seventy-five degrees, it didn't feel cold at all. When somebody swam the required length and pulled up to safety, he/she was given permission to wander around camp unfettered by a PFD. It became a rite of passage and an embarrassment to the older kids who couldn't swim.

It was always fun to hear when I asked how their summer had been: "I passed my swimming test." Kids would stand a little straighter, smile a little brighter, and made sure I wasn't meaning them when I next said, "Now be sure to get your life jackets," before we went anywhere.

I'm certainly glad camp powers didn't require such a test of adults living there. I'd not have passed.

After our welcoming exchanges, my company said goodbyes as I climbed up the stairs leading to my front door, put my cases down inside, thanked the people who deposited my boxes on the floor, and began to put things away. My cupboards and refrigerator full for now, I could live comfortably for a week or two. Then I would need to restock some of the items.

When the camp was nestled in Polk Inlet, we could drive to Craig where there were grocery stores, not an easy feat over twenty miles of single-lane logging ruts, which led to the Hydaburg Road. This was a two-lane gravel road that led between the ferry terminus at Hollis and a Native Haida village near the south end of the island, called Hydaburg. Another ten miles took us to the Hollis Road where we could drive fifteen more miles into Craig on a paved highway. Two grocery stores were there, and we could shop and bring our groceries back to camp. If we didn't want to drive, we sent away for them.

When I could, I drove. The white Chevy pickup—in my mind, still my husband's—was parked up the ramp from the camp with other families' vehicles, and on Saturday morning, I'd take off down that two-lane, rutted logging road for Craig. Some days, I would detour and stop in Hollis, checking to see if the teacher there might want to join me for a trip to town. Sometimes she would, and other times, we'd just have coffee and talk.

It was nice to go into the store and handpick the items on my list, to stroll down the aisles, not only of groceries but also of the gift items that the store carried. I impulse-shopped because I could and came home with much more than was on my list.

I was ready to head back to camp by early afternoon, the drive being fairly long and taking me, who didn't like to drive that pickup with the stick shift and the hard-to-reach clutch, a couple of hours. I also wanted to beat the rush.

Saturday was the day off for the loggers; the camp had a Seventh Day Adventist history, and their Sabbath was Saturday. However, not all stayed home to rest. They, like me, would drive into Craig to purchase what they needed. Craig also held a department store geared for fishermen and loggers; whatever they needed, they could find—new cork boots, jeans, suspenders, fishing gear, whatever. But many did more than shop—they visited the Hill Bar. Just across the street and up the hill from the department store, a bar beckoned to them, and they sat there, drinking their beer, telling stories, forgetting about their hard labor and their living conditions until they decided to head back to camp.

I liked to be ahead of them. Not only might I not trust their sobriety, or lack thereof, but I also wanted to be where somebody could come behind me and help me out, should I chance to have some car trouble.

When we moved from Polk Inlet to Dora Bay, the roads attached to camp no longer led to anywhere but the forest being logged, and so I sold my truck. I then ordered my groceries from Ketchikan once a week, and the order was filled and sent out to me via floatplane. I wrote a list of the groceries needed and mailed it to the grocery store. A clerk then selected items, giving substitutes if what was asked for wasn't available, boxed them up, and prepared them to be sent.

One needed good credit, or the order had to be prepaid. If the money ran out before the order was filled, that's where the groceries stopped. And the perishables, milk, fruits and vegetables, and frozen foods were always packed last, so they were the first to go if insufficient funds were sent. People needed to be warned about the high cost of shipping, too. Most of the air taxis charged thirty-five cents per pound at that time, and that really hiked the cost of each can of beans, corn, and soup, not to mention the other items.

At school, I was working ten to twelve hours a day. I didn't have time to sit down and take stock of groceries I had, plan a menu, and order groceries I'd need. I found a solution: Brenda at A&P Grocery in town packed a twenty- to thirty-pound box of fresh produce for me each Tuesday and sent it to Taquan, the air taxi company I used, which in turn got it out to me either on Tuesday or Wednesday. Figuring out how to use this box with the least amount of spoilage became an ongoing problem I tried to solve. But, I ate well and enjoyed probably the healthiest meals in my life.

I specifically ordered what I wanted for my salads. Romaine lettuce, Roma tomatoes, a cucumber, a green pepper, and a bunch of green onions made up my standing order. I mixed up tossed salads almost every night. When I found cucumbers and tomatoes sliming up in plastic bags, turning liquid before I could use them, I began eating tomato, lettuce, and cucumber sandwiches for lunch. When I didn't find them, they slimed into liquid and were pushed into the far corners of my fridge for Sheri to find and pull out whenever she thought of it.

Brenda sent me unusual produce to share with the children. Because I was a teacher and also because their parents wouldn't order some of the more exotic produce on a normal basis, I asked her to broaden all our educations. When little orange fruits showed up one Tuesday, we all hustled to the encyclopedia to see if we could identify them. They were kumquats, sour tasting and used mostly for making preserves. We learned about pomegranates, quinces, star fruits, uglies, and mangoes the same way. The students complained when we received a seedless watermelon—no seed-spitting contests that day. But a battle erupted when students spat the seeds of the yellow watermelon that came in the next week's box. My produce box became an item in our weekly conversation.

Brenda and I maintained contact about what were hits and what were not. My personal favorites were the "first" batch of the season:

asparagus, strawberries, corn, and squash. I enjoyed the treats in one dinner sitting.

Once, when camp was frozen up after a week-long cold spell, Brenda really surprised me. Located amidst all the produce, in the center of my box, sat a large heavy-duty cardboard cylinder—about six inches high and a foot in diameter—and a roll of toilet paper. I showed it to the students, asking them what they thought it was intended for. Of course, someone piped up with the suggestion to use the cylinder for a toilet seat out on the iced-up bay, a moveable toilet seat, and we all laughed, knowing there was more than a little merit in this idea.

When Sunday night rolled around, I'd look in my fridge and take out whatever veggies were left from that week's produce box. Heating a pot of beef or chicken stock on the stove, I'd wash, chop, and plop into the pot the remaining peppers, potatoes, Brussels sprouts, broccoli, or cabbage, making the soup I'd enjoy for the next few days and cleaning out my refrigerator in the process.

Then I'd be ready for the next box from Brenda.

I remember one October when a friend from "down south" was visiting me. Elaine and I had been roommates in college, and while I moved west to teach, she remained in Minnesota and eventually married a farmer. She came to stay for a week.

One afternoon while we were at camp, a floatplane approached, landed, and taxied to the airplane float. The pilot came out, secured the plane, and offloaded boxes. One was mine. The produce box from A&P, my weekly order. I hefted it up by the yellow plastic tapes and, grasping twenty to twenty-five pounds of fresh fruits and vegetables, lumbered down the walkway,

Climbing up the stairs to my front door, I set the box down and got scissors to cut the tapes. When I opened it, I found my expected lettuce, tomato, cucumber, onion, and green pepper. But there were also Brenda's surprises—a mango nestled in one corner while a cantaloupe rolled along the bottom of the box. My eyes caught a plastic bag containing three ears of fresh corn. In mid-October, that was a treat for me.

"Look, Elaine," I held up the bag. "Let's have it tonight for dinner." The health nurse had come for an overnight visit, so there'd be three places at the table. Perfect for three ears of corn.

The turkey breast was baking, and Elaine put some fresh cranberries in a pan with sugar and water while I filled my soup kettle with water. Adding some milk, I thought back to the days when Mom made this for our family, and I also added sugar, as I remembered she'd done. I shucked the green husks from the yellow knobby cylinders and carefully pulled all the pieces of silk from between the plump kernels. Well, several weren't plump, especially ones on the open end of the husk; those were a little withered and wrinkled. But my mind continued to water in anticipation of corn on the cob. I placed the ears in the liquid I'd prepared and put the kettle onto the flames of the burner.

Elaine and Colleen, the nurse, were setting the table, making the salad, folding the paper towels, our napkins. The cranberry sauce sat in a bowl on the table next to the carved turkey breast. I checked to make sure lots of butter was in the dish. Corn on the cob was delicious with melted butter!

Finally, the corn kettle contents began to boil, and after two minutes, I drained the liquid and set one ear of corn tenderly on each plate. We sat down, said a brief grace, and began to enjoy our meal.

I started the butter around the table, putting a large knifeful on my plate next to the corn. Soon the turkey reached me, and with a piece forked onto my plate, soon joined by a spoonful of steaming cranberry sauce, my plate was picture perfect. I grabbed the corn prongs and shoved one into each end before lathering butter on my ear of corn, making sure to cover its entire surface. Moving the dripping ear of corn to my mouth, I took my first bite on the bad end, the withered kernel end. I began working my way across the ear, three rows of kernels per bite, to the good end and returning, like a typewriter roller, to the beginning, where I turned the ear slightly and munched my way to the other end. My eyes closed as I savored each chew and swallow.

"Ahem."

I looked at Elaine when she cleared her throat. She was holding her ear of corn like a conductor's baton, slightly waving it at me, and her paper towel lay by her elbow, a crumpled container for her first nibble of corn.

"We wouldn't feed this corn to our pigs," she told me.

Ignoring her words and actions, I continued eating until all my kernels were gone. I looked at her and smiled, licking the buttery residue from my lips while thinking how fortunate I'd been to get fresh corn, even not-so-fresh corn, in October.

Elaine slowly shook her head. "You've been in Alaska too long."

No, she'd not been here long enough.

***

As the days again grew shorter, the salmon began their migration back to their spawning grounds. Around camp, several rivers were homes to spawning salmon, and we watched the fish swim upstream, battling currents, dying by the dozens, rotting and stinking up the places where the road crossed or paralleled such a stream.

Sheri and Marilyn habitually walked two or three miles every afternoon, and on their way out of camp, they'd poke their heads in the school.

"Hey, Biz, do you want to walk?" one would ask.

Depending on what I had left to do, I made my decision. Seldom was it no, for I so enjoyed the company of these women and the restoring energy I felt after walking down the roads in the forest. The three of us walked many afternoons after school, up one of the two logging roads that led out of camp. Often Tweekie, the Bonines' little, fierce-barking black dog of unknown parentage, and Roots (short for Ruthless), the Gildersleeves' older beagle, accompanied us.

We had two ways to go when we were in Dora Bay: up the ramp and to the right, which led past the sort yard and along a stream, a more gently sloping road than the other fork; or also up the ramp but to the left, which inclined steeply away from camp, above an estuary that held a grassy plain.

I remember one fall day when we headed up the ramp, deciding to take the road off to the right, the one that went by the beach and the beaver pond. Chattering away in our normal conversational after-school patter, none of us paid much attention to the scenery until we approached the beaver pond.

"Do you see the ducks?" Sheri inquired. A pair of ducks almost always could be seen around the beaver pond. Sometimes they swam in the middle of it, sometimes they nestled in the grasses by its edge, and other times they hid behind a huge rock that was close to the road.

"No," Marilyn replied. "But look behind the rock."

We did, and I could hardly believe what we saw. A black bear, no more than twelve feet from us, sat on the edge of the beaver pond. With its back leaning against the rock, it looked rather like an old man resting in the afternoon sun. However, it slowly turned its head toward us, glared at us with steely black eyes, and appeared to be conducting a staring contest. We decided to let it win.

As one, we pivoted and began walking in the other direction, the dogs following us, never realizing that we had avoided messing with a bear.

"Wow, that was close," Sheri said, and Marilyn, with her longer experience in the forests of the loggers, began to tell us her bear stories. Once, one popped up just a few feet in front of her when she was walking. Another time, she never noticed one under a bridge she crossed until she was on the other side and it moved. She had several run-ins with bears. The first one was the most memorable.

She was out for her daily walk, about half a mile from camp, when she noticed something out of the corner of her eye. A large black bear was in the ditch by the side of the road, eating skunk cabbage. He noticed her about the same time she saw him, she thought. Her husband had told her that if bears were going to charge, their ears would flatten back and they'd gnash their teeth. Marilyn didn't notice that as she was too busy trying to run away. In her fear and hurry, though, only one leg worked properly, and she sort of went in a circle.

So she faced the bear and held up her can of bear spray and waited.

Then the bear stood up on its hind legs, looked at her, and ran toward her. She froze. He ran right by her and into the woods.

Richard said later that the bear was probably trying to determine if her ears were laid back and she was gnashing her teeth.

She just stood there, and a truck she'd heard a bit earlier pulled alongside and stopped. "Was that a black bear running across the road?" the driver asked.

Marilyn nodded her head.

"Do you want a ride back to camp with me?"

"No, I'll be brave and continue my walk," she said. But she walked the direction the truck was going, and she never let that truck get out of her sight. In fact, the driver reported that she tried to pass him a couple of times before they reached camp.

This, my first close bear story, seemed rather tame by comparison.

Back to the fork where we could either hike up the other road or return to camp, we chose to continue hiking. After all, we had not gone half a mile before our bear encounter.

Soon we were walking quickly again, chattering about this and that, when Tweekie took off like a shot and Roots followed, barking excitedly. A bear ambled across the road in front of us, noted the dogs, and shot up the hill to the cover of the trees. The dogs followed, barking and scrambling out of sight. Soon they were out of sound, too.

"What do you think? Do we want to go on?" I asked.

"I think we've had enough walking for today," was the answer I received as we turned around and headed home.

As we came down the walkway from the shore, I asked if we should be concerned about the dogs, which had as yet not returned.

"I don't think so," Marilyn answered. "They'll be back when they lose the bear."

They were home in time for dinner.

As the bears began to fatten up for their hibernation during the winter, so did we begin to prepare for ours. The days grew colder, windier, and rainier, reminding us that we were not going to enjoy the outdoors as much as we had before.

Days covered by rain clouds never appeared light. From morning until night, we were shrouded in darkness. Water, sky, trees, buildings—all were a dismal gray.

Gales storming across the bay whipped the water into a white-capped frenzy, sometimes stirring up what I called water tornadoes, those spinning funnels of water that danced over the frothy waves. Winds prevented small air and watercraft from traveling.

People began to be stranded as the days that floatplanes wouldn't fly became more frequent.

The school nurse, Colleen, had been weathered-in the day after Elaine had arrived, making it possible for her to share a meal with us. In fact, the storm that had pushed across the inlet raged for two days. Deciding to cut her visit short, Elaine flew back to town with Colleen on the next plane that came in. She didn't want to be stranded at camp the day her jet left Ketchikan. We learned to plan ahead, sometimes *way* ahead.

The first thing I planned for was being stranded myself. I needed something to do those weekends when I couldn't get in to town or those days when I finished my schoolwork but couldn't go for walks. So I began collecting yarn, patterns, and needles. I stockpiled several projects that I could complete when I was stuck in the house. I knit gifts, mostly sweaters.

But I didn't knit in silence. I collected videos, movies that I could watch when I knit. I brought the ones I'd kept after Don had died: *The Sound of Music*, *Singing in the Rain*, and other musicals, *Star Wars*, *Indiana Jones*, and other adventure movies, having given away all his prized John Wayne westerns. I could watch these when there was nothing on the one TV channel we received—well, stole. There was originally one satellite dish in camp, and I think that was Richard's. His sister, Susan, was wired into whatever Richard's household watched, and when I gave her blank tapes, she would tape programs for me. I remember enjoying the Olympics one winter. Thanks to Richard, I had noise and pictures to go with my knitting.

To make sure I didn't starve when those floatplanes didn't fly, especially those carrying my groceries, I stocked my cupboards with popcorn and soup. Several cans of chicken noodle, tomato, and vegetable beef kept Jolly Time containers company on my shelves. Peanut butter and honey huddled in there too—and I made sure I had a jar of yeast in the fridge and lots of flour in the canister to make some bread. I wouldn't starve.

I learned to use paper plates. During the winter, the water often froze, and nobody wanted to spend water on washing dishes when there were bodies to keep clean. So I had piles of large and small plates, bowls, and even cups to use.

I remember Marilyn sharing a story about her daughter, Telitha. Logging camp managers often served lovely dinners to many guests, and evidently at Keaton's camp, things were done a bit differently. When the girls were about six, his daughter was spending the night with Telitha and at dinner asked if she could put out the silver. Telitha informed her that in their house they used Dixie.

Marilyn, and I, still use them almost every day. Obviously they're not strictly winter dishes.

Finally, I brought books, good mysteries for the cold evenings and lusty romance novels—trash, some would say—that my aunt gave me during my summer visit. She was a rampant reader, devouring books that her daughter gave her, and when she finished, she'd save them for me. I'd mail them home from my Minnesota holiday and haul them out to camp when I returned.

Even as I was preparing, so were the mice. Unbeknownst to me, these little furry critters were sneaking their way in from the outside, hoping to share warm winter housing with me. They weren't company I wanted, though.

One morning, I noticed little black pellets, flax-seed in appearance, on the counter by my bathroom sink. "Oh, oh," I thought. "Not good." When I wandered into the kitchen to make my pot of morning coffee, more pellets dotted the counter there.

"Oh, mice," I wailed out loud. "I don't want you here. You aren't invited. Please leave."

I didn't expect them to leave, but I wanted to give them a chance.

When I arrived at school, I explained my problem to Sheri, who wasn't surprised. "It happens every fall," she explained. "Do you have any steel wool?"

I hadn't any but was planning to go to town the following weekend. I told her I'd purchase some and bring it back with me.

"Bring a bit extra," she said.

When I got off the plane that Sunday, Sheri was waiting for me. After asking if I'd bought the steel wool and finding out that I had, she accompanied me down to my float.

"What are you going to do?" I asked.

"Just watch."

I gave her the package of steel wool and watched as she marched over to my kitchen sink, threw open the doors that hid all the bottles underneath, and pulled out the bleaches and soaps and cleansers that I kept there. She opened the package and pulled a tuft of steel wool from its casing and stuffed it into the small space between the drain pipe and the wall board. She did that with the water pipes, too. Then she moved to my bathrooms, stuffing spaces wherever she thought a critter might enter from outside. And into the wanigan she went, again looking around the sinks, kneeling, and steel-wooling any cracks that she found.

Finally she stood up, half a package of steel wool left in her hand. "There," she said. "That should do it."

She wanted the extra steel wool for others in camp who were having the same problem for, as she explained, "If you have mice, so do lots of other people."

Well, the mice must have been already camped out somewhere inside my trailer, for the next day there were new traces of the varmints. I even saw one scurry under my stove. I yelled at it and told it to find new quarters or I'd be after it. I hoped it understood, but I trudged down to the office anyway to see what else I could do.

It seemed the whole camp had become infested with mice because the boss provided d-Con to all homes. For free. I brought a few boxes home and set them out in the bathroom and kitchen, places where I'd seen the most trace.

The poison didn't work as planned. One night I kept hearing little feet pattering from the d-Con container in my bathroom to the back of my dresser. Then a snuffling, crumpling sound from my drawers emerged before the feet skittered back to the bathroom. Back and forth, all night long. When I got up the next morning and went to put on a clean pair of underwear, I found my panties stuffed with the little poisonous green pellets … the mouse had been having fun. When

I told that story to Sheri and she told it to her husband, the comment came back that "at least something's getting into her pants."

Obviously I needed a new plan, so I vowed to get mice the old-fashioned way. The next trip to town saw me scour the shelves for mouse traps.

"What do you use for bait?" I asked Michelle when I got back to camp; she was the custodian. When I went to school to work on my plans Sunday evening, she was washing down the boards. She and I had talked about mouse traps before I'd left camp.

"You can use cheese, but peanut butter works just as well."

So I unwrapped the four traps I'd bought, globbed a bit of peanut butter on the ends, pulled back the metal things and placed them where I thought they'd be most effective.

The next morning I checked them out. Two traps had worked, flattening the little mice's necks when the metal thing sprang back. "Ooh, ick! Now what?"

I went to school and asked Michelle what she did. She freed her dead mice from the traps so she could re-use them. After school, I came home and donned my yellow rubber gloves, gingerly picked up one of the traps and carried it outside. Standing on the edge of the float, I held the trap and mouse over the water and pulled the metal thing off its neck. The mouse dropped into the bay.

"Rest in peace," I whispered.

That's not so bad, I thought, and I went to get the other trap to repeat the process. Then I dotted them both with peanut butter, pulled back the metal things, and placed the traps, now set and ready to spring, where they'd been before.

I was no longer awakened by little mice footsteps climbing up and down my dresser and into my drawers. The traps worked so well that soon I was not bothered by mice at all.

Now with the bears in hibernation, the mice eliminated, and my cupboards stocked with food and projects, I was ready to greet winter.

One major impact of winter's arrival was the loss of running water. Whenever temperatures dipped below thirty degrees, water could freeze in our pipes, and we'd be without running water.

Unlike the pipes that run underground in most communities on land, ours ran above deck. At one time, they had been submerged, but with a couple of cases of hepatitis contracted within the camp, they were relocated in case their being underwater caused the disease. However, that change also meant the water could freeze faster without the ocean's insulating warmth.

When the temperatures began to slip, we were warned to fill containers with fresh water. Although we also were told to turn on the tap that was farthest from the water source during the those cold evenings, sometimes I didn't open it far enough, and my water froze. Sometimes the drain of every home running its water overnight was too much for the water tank, and it ran out. I went to bed many a chilly night not knowing whether I'd have running water in the morning.

I kept three thirty-gallon plastic garbage cans filled with water for when I needed fresh water during these times. Heating water on the stove for sponge baths, hair washes, cleaning dishes, and scrubbing floors was common. From my front door, it was only a ten-step jaunt to the edge of the float where I could dip a bucket into the salt water and haul it back into the house to use for flushing. I tried to keep a spare bucket filled, set in the bathtub, for those late-night visits to the bathroom.

I found one best way to use the first pan of water each morning. First I filled my largest cooking pan and heated it on the stove. Then I took it into the bathroom and set it in the sink. With soap and washcloth in hand, I'd take a sponge bath. After drying my body, I leaned over the sink, put my head close to the pan, and wet my hair. I shampooed and rinsed, using a cup to pour the now tepid water over the suds. After winding a towel around my head, I looked at the cooling and soapy water before taking the pot, aiming carefully, and pouring the water into the toilet for the first flush of the day. During those times, it was always wise to conserve water. One never knew how long the cold spell would last.

One treat at the beginning of a cold spell was that Darrel kept one water line open. Water filtered from the nearby creek or spring eventually led into a holding tank. There chlorine was injected to prevent outbreaks of giardia, or beaver fever, before being sent on to a big tank with its own float on the edge of camp. From there, water was pumped to individual buildings.

The line from the water tank to the far bunkhouse was shortest, and somehow, Darrel kept that line thawed so that the homeguard (those who stayed in camp throughout the winter) could sign up for shower times. I always asked for 5 a.m. so I could hurry over there, take my shower, and not be worried that somebody else would walk in on me when I was naked. It was cold, bundling up in jacket and boots, to walk on the crunchy snow across two floats to the bunkhouse, then disrobe and head into the shower. The bunkhouse itself felt cold. However, it didn't take long for hot water to warm the shower stall, and I enjoyed having the luxury of being clean and warm at the same time. It was still a cold walk back to my quarters, though, but I had a good start to my day. Others would use the facility in the same manner. This would continue until the weather got so cold that either Darrel could not keep the pipe open or the water source itself froze up and none ran into the tank.

It was then that I really appreciated the special invitation I'd receive from Sheri. Every so often (maybe when it was when she noticed my smell), she'd ask if I wanted a shower after school, and I'd walk across camp to her house to take one. There was a hook above their bathtub, and they'd purchased a huge bag, like those sold in outdoor catalogs for camping, that could be filled with water and used as a shower. Sheri would heat some water and fill the bag, hang it above her bathtub, and tell me to enjoy it. I would. What a gift—a hot shower!

Sometimes, during an extended cold spell, the bay itself froze. Then excrement and dirty water would be stuck in the pipes and, instead of spilling into the ocean below, pop up, usually after a toilet flush, in the bathtub.

Dirty water usually was sent to a treatment box located beside each building. Each box contained a septic tank and a macerator pump, which ground the sewage into little pieces before pumping it into a holding tank. The bark within the tank filtered the sewage before it was released underneath the float.

When the water froze, our pipes were disconnected from the treatment boxes, which had frozen too, and were dropping debris directly into the bay. When flushing became slow, we were instructed to flush with hot water, hoping anything frozen at the base would be dislodged. Eventually, this no longer worked; sewage would back up, and someone would crawl under the housing unit and kick, pry, or use whatever force was needed to separate the pipe from the frozen base. When we all needed to move our sewer pipes out of the sea and place them on the ice, the home-made deposits then piled up; the pipe was moved every time the pile became too high. Walking around camp during these times became a pretty smelly experience.

Rick was my treasure—he wrested his big body under my trailer and kicked my pipe loose when I began having toilet water coming up the drain into the bathtub, a stinky job requiring skills I just did not have. And my asking the men around camp showed just how many of them did not want to do it for me. Solving predicaments such as this was a great problem of my being a single woman, living alone, and not only in the winter. There were so many things that broke down, things I didn't know how to fix, and I had to ask for help. Thank goodness there were a few like Rick who said yes.

When there were no yeses, I adapted.

The propane-fired water heater was supposed to save fuel and be on demand, but it didn't work well. It would produce hot water for about a minute, and then the flame went out, and the water went cold. As a result, I learned to hop into the tub, turn on the shower, soap up both my body and my hair and rinse off. If I did this as fast as I could, I often finished the whole procedure before getting doused with cold water. Only occasionally was I shocked with the cold cold rinse, and I grew better and faster at bathing with practice.

I had complained about the water heater not working to Darrel, and he told me that it was the school district's problem. So I informed the school district, and they routed me back to the camp maintenance man, saying that the district rented my home from the logging camp and the camp should be responsible for repairs. I never got either to accept responsibility for maintaining my home. Until well into my tenure there, the water heater was never repaired, and I became adept at minute-or-less washes.

A similar problem occurred when the forced-air furnace quit working properly. When my trailer became cold, I'd push the reset button, and the furnace might kick on again. Or it might not. Again I presented my complaint to Darrel, who again sent me to the school district, which again sent me back to the camp. Nothing was done until Sheri figured out that it would work better if the thermostat was set at eighty degrees. So I spent my winters wasting fuel keeping my trailer warmer than I otherwise would have, but I quit complaining. Being quiet and complacent was acceptable to both the school district and the camp with these particular issues. I was told that about three years later, the second teacher who followed me threatened to move to Ketchikan until these housing problems were solved. He—yes, a male—got quick action.

Another challenge of the winter was the snow. Often the cold spells were interrupted by heavy snow, which would pile up on the floats. The weight would cause the floats to sink, and although eventually the salt water would melt the snow, most of us were not comfortable thinking of our homes sitting that deep in the water. So we shoveled. While the kids often helped keep the school float and my float buoyant, I had to get back and forth to school before they were up.

Whenever the morning brought a new falling of deep snow, I shoveled a path down my steps, across my float, up a set of steps to the "bridge," across the bridge, down the steps onto the school's playground, across the playground, and finally up the steps to the school. The school district had provided me with a very classy, efficient shovel, and if I had it on my float in the morning, this shoveling was easy. If not, then I needed to wade through the snow to the school float to retrieve it.

On the other hand, if it snowed a bunch during the school day, and I'd left the shovel on my front doorstep, then I'd need to creep home in my shoes after school, through the snow, getting cold and wet, when I'd rather have shoveled a path before me.

So I developed the habit of carrying the shovel with me to and from school; it became my constant companion. I took the shovel home with me at night. In the morning, if I didn't have to shovel a path to the school, I made two trips before I began my school day. The first was with the coffee and schoolwork, the second with the shovel. So if I was at school, the shovel was there, but if I was home, I had the security of the shovel on my front step. Always, I could shovel my way to or from the school, no matter when the snow piled up.

Of course, I never thought that the bunkhouse guys might borrow it. They went home during the winter—but sometimes a big snow came along before the logging shut down. The few times they did, they didn't return it. So there I was, thinking the darkest thoughts about the so-and-so who'd taken the shovel and not shoveled me a path, leaving me to plow through the snow without my shovel. However, the times were few, and most of the time, my system worked.

I think winter was a difficult time for many of the households; darkness came early and left late. Although many men spent time outdoors, perhaps trapping, they weren't working. With no logging to do, money was tight, and many of them spent the days at home with their wives. Sometimes the closeness got claustrophobic, and sometimes violent quarrels erupted. The kids, of course, came to school without their rest, with their worries, unable to concentrate, and we all looked for the skies to lighten. Which, in time, they did.

I remember once when men weren't working, hadn't worked for a long time, and the kids were scheduled to participate in a Jump Rope for Heart fundraiser. We had to cancel it; nobody had any money. The only people earning wages worked in the school.

We all looked forward to the snow receding up the mountainsides, the temperatures slowly climbing, and the planes flying on their appointed schedules. We awaited spring.

***

In 1993, the contract with the forest service at Polk Inlet expired, and the logging company negotiated another contract, this time with a native corporation that wanted to log near Dora Bay. One Friday, near the end of March, preparations were made to move.

Moving the entire camp from one location to another was no easy task. Camp was a series of rafts, joined together by cables in rows of twos or threes. Several rafts contained two trailers for families, another held a cookhouse, bunkhouses rested on several others, and at the far end, there was Richard's place. The families were situated at one end of the camp, and I at the other, right next to the school. It was an arrangement that worked.

To get a bit more technical, the floats were constructed using eighty-two-foot-long logs, usually spruce, laying them side by side until they formed a square. Then the cross log, or rider log, was lashed to the others with galvanized cable, one across each end. Boards were nailed in place over the rough logs, finishing the float and making it look like a raft. One smaller float was dedicated to the water tank, and another to the incinerator. The school and the cookhouse were on individual floats, sixty-five-feet square, different from the others, too. Several floats long and two floats wide, all lashed together, formed camp. Preparing to leave would require moving some of the floats around, making camp easier to tow.

We were immobilized with cables. We couldn't move until the cables that tied us to shore were loosened and coiled on various floats and the anchors that hooked to the ocean floor were raised. Guys on shore loosed the cables, and guys on different floats pulled them up and laid them down carefully. An A-frame hoisted the anchors, and then we were free. A line of logs, like giant tinker toys, had been chained around the camp to hold it together and to take the pressure from the pull of the tug when we were moving.

Saturday morning, the water lines had been severed, and Everett's float detached from the rest of the camp when one tugboat, the *Norton Bay*, hooked up to the front of the camp. The camp had been refigured for this move to make it easier to pull. Now my float was at the front with the incinerator float attached between it and the tug. Another tug was ready at the rear to react to any emergencies.

We began to move out of the inlet, and I looked back. Everett, whose job required him to stay behind, was standing out on his float for awhile, and then he disappeared. I walked over to the school and looked out the second-story windows where I could see past the roof of my trailer to the tug and to the scene ahead. I could also turn and see

Everett's float growing smaller and smaller as we moved toward the entrance to Clarence Strait. Finally it was out of sight.

Camp on the move
Photo courtesy of Telitha Gildersleeve

Then I focused on the scene around me. We had prayed for calm weather, and a beautiful sunshiny day had appeared. People were walking around the boardwalks and floats, visiting, noting the change in the coastline, savoring this unique experience. Sheri and Marilyn ambled to my float, and the three of us sat in the sunshine on my front porch, drinks in plastic cups, chatting, sunning, watching the trees and the rocks pass by, and joining the rest of the population in the enjoyment of the move.

Marilyn sipped on her beer and said, "You know, it's going to be a big mess around here tomorrow when the guys have to hook us back up again. There'll be a lot of noise and commotion."

She was the only one of us who'd witnessed a move before. We chatted a little more before they left me and walked back down toward the office, stopping every now and then to talk to folks they met along the way.

Other people enjoyed our move, too. Keaton, the camp's owner, was in one of several planes that flew above us, dipped, and gunned a greeting when we were underway. The few boats that we passed honked and waved as we went by. Even the fuel barge moved in and tied up alongside as we cruised along at a modest five knots or so.

Night came, and most of us went to bed even though we were in Clarence Strait where the water was bigger. Bigger waves and bigger swells. Wind and waves caused the floats to move and groan, bouncing against neighboring floats and straining back. It was a bumpier ride than in the more protected inlet that we'd left, and although people complained of their doors opening and slamming shut, their curtains swaying against the windows, and other noises that kept them awake, nothing broke loose.

Sunday morning, we were in view of Frog Mountain. It's a mountain that looks like a frog, sitting high, perhaps a monarch frog, ruling Dora Bay from a big throne. Its two bulging eyes looked down on us, hopefully in peaceful welcome. We nestled in the calm under that mountain, and we also pitched and rolled a bit in the winds that attacked the area during storms, but Frog Mountain became the landmark of our new home.

When Sheri, Marilyn, and I walked, we'd note Frog Mountain, and depending on the weather, its expression would change. We pictured a kindly despot when the sun shone but one of an angry king when the winds blew hard. We in the school had a view of Frog Mountain from the second floor and would often pause before coming down the stairs to note the sun on its slopes or the clouds above its rounded peak. And every time I flew back from a trip, I looked forward to rounding the bend in the channel to catching sight of the mountain. It was a welcoming feature to me. I lived under its shadow for three years.

Frog Mountain to the left

We were towed to the site that had been selected. It had met the three necessary conditions: the inlet was deep enough so the camp wouldn't be grounded during low tides, a freshwater source (creek, river, or spring) was nearby, and the bay offered some protection from storms. Southeasters were especially fierce, formed with hurricane-force winds, upwards of ninety miles per hour, and common during the winter. The cables were readied to be reattached.

About eight that morning, there was a knock on my door.

"Biz! Biz!" Sheri yelled into the living room. "There's a plane coming in for some camp business, and Marilyn, Maggie, and I are going to hop on it, go back with it to town. Do you want to come with us?"

I had only a few minutes to get ready. As I heard the floatplane approach, I grabbed my purse and headed down the boardwalk toward the airplane float. Sheri and Marilyn were already there when Richard and Sheri's husband, Eldon, walked by.

"Where are you going?" one of them asked.

"Town," Sheri replied. "Bye." She hadn't seen her husband since the decision had been made but didn't have time to explain as she suddenly turned away. Evan's boat had arrived, and we all clambered aboard. He would ferry the four of us out to where the Beaver was waiting.

"Bye," she yelled again as we sped away. We all waved at the two men who, standing on the dock, were probably wondering when they'd see their wives again.

We left the men to uncoiling the cables, positioning us where we'd be safe from the tides and the storms, and finding the way to run water to the camp's water tank. When we returned later that Sunday afternoon, we were again attached to land and had water running through the pipes. Home life settled back to normal.

The weather at this time of year was rather like a capricious child—never deciding exactly what it wanted. One day could be clear, sunny, and blue-skied, while the next, cloudy and stormy.

After some clear and sunny days, the nights were cold, and one had to be careful the next morning. I kept a Tupperware container of salt near my door, and when I realized the planks were covered with frost, I'd sprinkle the salt ahead of my path. Milo, having caught sight of me one morning, called me "Bird Lady" for a few days, thinking I was scattering seed.

I forgot once, though, and slipped and fell up the school steps. That was the same day that the school was icy cold, too. I reset the furnace, but nothing happened. Checking the fuel gauge, I discovered an empty tank. So I crossed camp to get Evan, who was then in charge of fueling, and he filled the tank. With the furnace finally going, I went back home to get a cup of coffee. As I was bringing it to school, I slipped and fell, spilling coffee all over myself and bruising my right side. I went back home, changed clothes, and brought an ice pack to soothe the bruises as I began to write assignments on the board.

When the weather decided to be summer-like, I was reminded of the grandeur the land provides. During sour weather, most of us hibernated, never pausing when we had to venture outdoors during the sideways rain or snow. But when the sun shone on the mountains, their majesty glowed. The clear sky created a beautiful blue sea in which many creatures played. I often stopped along my walk to watch the yellow eyes dive and pop back up, dive again, seeming to play, but actually hunting for food.

One morning, a seal, which had swum along the walkway for several days but always dived out of sight when I opened my door, stayed. He looked at me, sort of backstroking away, but remained above water, his eyes watching my progress. I was graced with his presence for only that one time before he disappeared.

***

Spring meant that those who liked to garden shopped the seed catalogs and often bought plants when they shopped in town.

I didn't particularly like to garden, but I had inherited a gardening tradition and dutifully tended to my claw-footed porcelain bathtub, filled and overflowing with strawberries. I watched as the blossoms turned to red juicy berries, sometimes before school was over. Then I ate a few, but I didn't mind when folks, kids and adults alike, strolled past and plucked a few tidbits from the tub.

I also had several boxes on my deck. These I sometimes used to plant vegetables—carrots, perhaps, and onions. During school time, my students oversaw my plants' progress in the spring as a science study in seed growth and, in the fall, as a sampling of good nutrition. But during the summer, Sheri was the gardener.

She also tended the greenhouse that was on my back deck. If I provided the raw materials, she did the hard work. She, with the help of her menfolk, built shelves and boxes, hauled dirt, and readied for planting. My contribution was that, as I made weekend trips into Ketchikan, I bought peppers, broccoli, zucchini, tomatoes, lettuce, and other plants to be put in the greenhouse. That way, Sheri weeded and watered all summer, mothering the vegetables, but I enjoyed sharing the produce with her when I returned in the fall.

Max, the school pilot, also stopped by the greenhouse, making a detour from the school to the cookhouse for cookies. He loved Sheri's tomatoes.

It was one of the best deals in camp, I thought, to buy a few plants in the spring and then to eat fresh and tasty veggies, reaping the harvest, without lifting one finger in between.

As spring worked its way into summer, I began preparations for leaving camp. I summered in Ketchikan and left most of my camp belongings at camp. However, I did need to make sure my garbage was taken care of.

The food garbage was no problem. Rotten tomatoes, banana peels, moldy refrigerated leftovers, and such could be thrown right into the bay. Something would eventually eat it or it would decompose. I disposed of this food garbage as soon as I either created or discovered it. However, I had to clean my home of the "burns" and "nonburns."

Back view of camp: Incinerator to the left; behind it water tank float, bunkhouse float, and in the back, my float.
Courtesy of Telitha Gildersleeve

The burns needed to be taken to the camp's incinerator. It was a recycled buoy, reclaimed from Southeast Alaska waters, somebody having torched a door out of the metal side and attached hinges and a lock, and it was attached to a float of its own. I never knew what I'd find when I opened that door. Maybe a bunkhouse guy had thrown away his Playboy magazines, and a scantily clad bevy of beauties would stare at me. Or perhaps somebody had cleaned out a mail-order collection, and stacks of catalogs would still be unburned after the previous night's fire.

My best surprise came one morning before school. Carrying my bag of burns in one hand, I opened the door with the other, only to find myself staring into two huge round eyes. A little feathery body attached to them told me it was an owl, a little one. Later research suggested an adult pygmy owl, but it could have been a very young owlet. Perhaps it had flown in during the night and couldn't get back out through the narrow chimney the buoy offered. At any rate, we looked at each other for a few precious seconds, and then it fluttered its wings and flew off, right in front of my face. What a treat!

The nonburns needed to be bagged and hauled up the ramp to a dumpster resting near the edge of the road. It would be transported to a landfill when it was full.

My kitchen had two lined trash barrels: one for paper and one for glass and metal. When the trash can for paper was full, I carried it to the camp's incinerator and threw it inside. Somebody with a match eventually came by and set all the burnables on fire.

Whenever I emptied a glass or metal container that I was going to throw away, I first rinsed it out before putting it in the trash can. This can filled up more slowly than the one for burn items, and I learned that rinsing helped me avoid mold buildup and stinky smells. When the garbage bag became full, or as full as I could carry, I toted it across camp and up the ramp to the dumpster.

Plastic posed a dilemma: it created acrid black smoke when it burned, but it didn't deteriorate very quickly for dumping in the landfill. Usually I put my plastic with the "burns." In this way, we got rid of our trash.

As I was preparing for the end of school and my vacation, I ran into a bit of a problem. Late one night, around nine, I made spaghetti sauce, knowing I was going to be busy bringing my primary students to Ketchikan the next day for a field trip and would arrive back too late to prepare a good meal. Busy in my kitchen, I mixed together tomato sauce, sautéed onions and hamburger, and added Italian spices, throwing the hamburger packaging into my burns and the onion peels into the bay. Because I had just emptied my nonburns and I knew I wouldn't fill up another garbage can before I left, I decided that just this once, although I knew I shouldn't, I would pitch the tomato-sauce can into the water.

So I went outside to toss it into the bay, but somebody had left a board across my path that I didn't notice, and I slipped. Trying to prevent myself from pitching forward into the water, I fell backwards and softened the impact with my left hand. I forgot I held the can lid in that hand. Its sharp edge cut deeply into my index finger, and I noticed the blood before I threw the can and its lid into the water. Back inside, I ran my finger under the faucet, changed into my pajamas, wound a paper towel around my injury, climbed into bed, and fell asleep with my left hand above my head.

The next morning, the bleeding had slowed to an ooze, and I dressed and prepared to take the kids to Ketchikan aboard a floatplane. When I wandered down to the floatplane dock, Darrel, who was also an EMT, noticed my finger and asked why I hadn't come to see him the previous night. I said it had been late and I hadn't wanted to bother him. He frowned and muttered and then walked off. When the plane and the students arrived, we climbed aboard and left.

We arrived in Ketchikan, deplaned, and walked up the ramp to shore. Don Alderman was there to meet us. He took one look at my injury and decided that I was to go to the emergency room while he took the primary students to the police department, the first stop on our busy day of field tripping.

I arrived in the emergency room, and the nurse soaked my finger in a disinfectant while I waited for a doctor to arrive. When he examined my injury, he noticed that a nerve had been severed and told me that it should be reattached because of the finger's importance.

What?

He told me to pretend I was holding an object in my left hand and had me note how my index finger would wind around it. Especially if it were a coffee cup, I would need feeling in my finger to determine how hot or cold it was. Okay, I said, when he said he could schedule me for surgery the following Friday.

My mind worked over the plans I'd need to make: lesson plans for Sheri and Marilyn to follow, a flight into Ketchikan, a hotel reservation, a few phone calls to friends who might drive me to the hospital. There was the thought, too, that I'd never had a surgery. Would I be scared? I wasn't then—just glad something was being done to my injury.

With my finger rebandaged, I left the hospital, rejoined my students and Mr. Alderman, and finished the day of seeing the sights in Ketchikan. We returned to camp, I made arrangements to be gone the following Friday, and I had the surgery as planned to reconnect the nerve I'd severed. I returned with my entire left hand swathed in a huge pink bandage.

That was the year that Melissa graduated, the first graduation at Polk Inlet School, and so it was an important occasion. Keaton Gildersleeve, the camp's owner, had come to help us celebrate and noticed my injured hand.

"What did you do, Biz?" he asked.

I told him the story, and his response was brief.

"It serves you right. You know you shouldn't have done that."

I never threw another can into the water.

Eventually all the field trips were taken, the paperwork for the school district completed, the garbage cleaned up, and I could pack my bags and ask Maggie to find me a seat on the next available floatplane.

As the plane would swoop into the bay, I'd carry my suitcase down the walkway, waving to those who might be outside. "See you in August," I'd say, "and please call me if you're ever in town."

Becoming—Seasons of Growth

That first year after my husband died, I spent a lot of time trying not to think of his death. I poured myself into my work at the school, spending twelve or more hours a day. But, night always came, and reflections on what was and what might have been seemed so unfair. Often I would sit in the wanigan, that added-on-to-the-double-wide-trailer room, and sip my wine, smoke my cigarette, and think. It was winter in my heart—discontent filled my thoughts. Why did Don have to die? What was I going to do next? Over the months, answers—and spring—would come in that room.

In the beginning, Don and I had sat here. We'd designated this our smoking room, far away from any of camp's prying eyes, and often discussed the day and his health here after dinner with a cigarette or two. It was a place I felt was very private. A simple room containing very little furniture, it was there that I could share what I really felt.

Many times when I was teaching, he'd be sitting in his bathrobe in one of the two simple lawn chairs, the folding green-and-white plastic over aluminum type, smoking. An ashtray, sitting on the old weathered wood bench next to the chair, filled as the day progressed. As the disease worsened, he'd given up dressing much of the time, and his blue terrycloth bathrobe was warm. So was the wanigan when the wood stove was working. A little red wood stove sat in one corner, and he liked to keep it stoked.

There was a step up to get back to the main trailer, and one day as he entered the trailer after enjoying a cigarette, he fell on that step. It may not have been the first time, but Don Alderman noticed it and told me, "Biz, he's falling. I think it's time." He meant the time had come for Don and me to go to town until he died. My husband said, "But I didn't get hurt, and I didn't stumble on my bathrobe."

However, we went to town after the district found a long-term sub for me. There at the doctor's office, Don was given morphine for the first time. He didn't adjust to it well, was hospitalized, and within a week was dead.

I took a couple of weeks off to handle things, and then I returned. That's when the wanigan became a classroom. I could move off memories I'd shared with Don and build new memories with my students.

When Evan and Caleb were in ninth grade and had a few electives in their schedule, they chose small-engine repair, and this came with dozens of video tapes, a player, and two small engines with all kinds of parts and tools.

The boys helped set up the wanigan as their classroom. They put the tape player in the middle of the long counter, their engines and parts in the closet next to the freezer, and the tapes in the cabinet under the counter. A couple of notebooks and pencils lay next to the tape player, and they were ready to begin. The school district sent us two bar stools for the boys to use.

Each day at their small-engine class period, they and I, for they couldn't be unsupervised, walked from the school over to the wanigan. The boys climbed onto the stools, grabbed their notebooks and pencils, and put the next lesson's tape into the machine.

I sat in a lawn chair and put my feet up on one of the benches. I watched and listened and rested.

"Get Part C and screw it into the camshaft here." The directions came both orally and in print on the screen. The boys pushed "pause" and proceeded to find the part and tool from the cupboard before they completed whatever they'd been instructed to do.

Occasionally, not very often, after they listened, they turned to me. "We don't understand. Can you help us?"

I'd ask them to replay the part and, although I seemed to be listening to a foreign language, I'd try to interpret what I'd heard.

Most often, though, Evan'd say, "Oh, I get it now. It means to do this," and he'd find the place on the engine that needed something done to it. Then he and Caleb pushed "play," and I returned to my seat, and class continued.

Of course, I left the windows open every morning and cleaned and hid the ashtray after breakfast so the smell of cigarette smoke would be gone when time for class came for even after Don's death, I continued to make this my smoking room.

After a long day at school and whatever dinner I'd eaten, I'd return to the wanigan to sip my wine and smoke a cigarette or two, to think about life and see if I was plotting a course.

I wasn't always alone, though. That wanigan was the scene of many evening conversations, especially when itinerants came to stay overnight. They provided me with solace, with probing questions, with what I needed to grieve and heal.

Ernie Hansen, the secondary supervisor, came one day to help Evan with his computerized architectural design, and after dinner, we went back to the wanigan and sat in the lawn chairs and put our glasses of wine on the benches. I lit a cigarette. Ernie didn't smoke.

"Well, Biz," he said, "how's it going?"

And I began to talk. I was worried about investing the money I'd received from selling Don's toys (his guns, our Bayliner, his Jet Ski, and the 1932 Model A Ford), and he suggested I talk to his friend Wayne the next time I was in Ketchikan. When the opportunity arose, I did, and my financial picture improved.

Visitors also used me for a sounding board. Ernie's wife was diagnosed with multiple sclerosis, and he was dealing with its impact. He shared his frustrations about his wife's ravaged body and the hopes of new treatments she was trying. That wanigan was a place of give and take.

Steve Dempsey, the school district's counselor and a fellow smoker, sat with me for hours back there. He helped me become comfortable with my aloneness, reassuring me I was on the right path.

"Biz, what have you been doing?" he'd ask.

"I've been writing angry notes to Don and to God on the computer, and I've been trying to get to Ketchikan twice a month."

"And …," he prodded.

"I don't think I'm drinking as much as I used to."

"What are you doing in town?"

"Calling my brother, cousins, relatives in Minnesota, going to functions with friends. And Evvy and I began to go to church." I told him, too, about hiking after school with Sheri and Marilyn and trying to eat good food.

"Well, Biz, it all sounds positive." And he'd give me a hug, and we'd turn out the lights and head into our respective bedrooms. He was a counselor who thought I was going through the right steps and one whose counsel I valued.

Evvy, the special ed. teacher, and I forged a special bond. While we talked about student progress and behavior modification, we'd sip our wine and compare notes.

Originally from Oregon, she had moved to Alaska with her husband, Kay, who was retired from the military. Evvy had taught in the small village of Metlakatla before moving to Ketchikan and working for Southeast Island School District. One day when she had flown to Anchorage, her husband was on the highway, waiting a few cars behind a bus preparing to turn left into Totem Bight, one of our tourist attractions, when his pickup was rear-ended by a vehicle traveling much too fast. His truck smashed into the car in front of him, and he was pinned in the wreckage. After he was transported to the hospital, he lived only a few hours while Evvy, having heard about his accident, was trying to fly back in time to see him before he died. She didn't make it. He died that day, just three months after my husband, Don.

We shared many discussions: "Is it better to know your husband will die or not?" I did not have the financial problems Evvy found. As Don knew his life was limited, he initiated procedures to put all our belongings into joint ownership. He made sure his will was written so no probate or other measures were needed, that everything would automatically become mine. Evvy was grappling with her husband's possessions and their ownership. On the other hand, Evvy did not have to watch her husband suffer through two years of chemotherapy. She did not have to maintain the continual cheerful optimism I felt forced to do. But then, Evvy did not have a chance to say goodbye. She was in Anchorage when the accident occurred. And they'd parted without loving goodbyes. I was able to hold Don's hand as his life slipped away. Then again … And so it went.

We never did decide which way was better for a husband to die. We were fortunate, however, to be able to develop into single people again with each other. In fact, we were terrific supports for each other as we found ourselves heading back toward the church.

One weekend when I was in Ketchikan, I called Evvy to see if we might do something together. She had talked with Martha and planned to attend church with her that Sunday morning at eight o'clock. She added that she'd felt an increasing need for spiritual connections since Kay had died, and when Martha invited her, she accepted.

"Isn't she Catholic?" I inquired. When I was told that indeed was true, I suggested the Lutheran church. I'd checked the newspaper and found the Lutheran service began at ten thirty. "Their service is later, and I would be more comfortable since I was raised Lutheran," I encouraged.

"I was raised Lutheran, too," Evvy said. So she agreed to pick me up on the way to the church service the next day.

She parked a short way from the church, and we began walking toward the beautiful but imposing white building on the corner. We had to cross the parking lot, and as we did, our steps slowed. Grasping hands, we practically tiptoed across the tarred surface, Evvy exclaiming, "I don't think I can go! It's communion Sunday." I tried to convince her that we'd be fine and we wouldn't have to partake in that particular rite if we weren't comfortable. Holding hands, we ventured from the parking lot onto the sidewalk and then up the stairs to the church itself.

We opened the doors and entered and then looked up to check if the roof was still there. "See, it didn't fall down," one of us muttered to the other.

We sat down in a wooden pew near the back of the church, and the lady in front of us turned around, smiled at us, and extended her hand. "Welcome to First Lutheran," she said.

We smiled back, relaxed, and began our relationship with First Lutheran Church. We eventually joined it together and became active in its programs. However, we still kept our conversations going in that wanigan as long as Evvy visited Polk Inlet School.

***

Don Alderman came out every two weeks. Originally from Texas, he had taught in Barrow, Alaska, before moving to Southeast Alaska. He was a stalwart ally and long-time friend. He had known my husband and was our music teacher when Don was alive and the three of us had taught together at a different float camp.

Don Alderman was a wonderful cook as well. Many times his Tex-Mex dinner was perfect after a long day at the office. His chicken enchiladas were so easy to make—just boil the chicken, mix it with a little chopped onion and cheese, and roll the mixture into tortilla shells. He poured enchilada sauce over the top, added a bit more cheese, and popped them into the oven until they were hot. He also brought out an apple and a can of tuna. That became lunch, as he'd chop up the apple and drain the tuna, mix them together with a little mayonnaise and spread it on a piece of bread. He might add a piece of lettuce, then top with another bread slice, and voila! A tuna sandwich that even the most reluctant kid would try. It was really good.

Walking into the wanigan after one of his wonderful Tex-Mex dinners, Don and I often sat in the lawn chairs with our glasses of wine and put up our feet, his long and covered by cowboy boots, mine usually shoeless. I'd light up a cigarette and offer him one. He never smoked until those nights—maybe I was a bad influence.

"Well, Biz, how've y'all done since I was here last?" he'd drawl as he exhaled.

I found myself talking, crying, explaining, and he'd reply, "That's all right. Don would've wanted you to …," and either he'd tell me what I wanted to hear, or he'd interpret some comment Don had made to him earlier and apply it to whatever I had mentioned. I always felt comforted when that big tall Texan and I talked. He filled the wanigan with compassion, understanding, and often good advice.

These friends and co-workers brought concern and sympathy, kindness and love, along with their lessons and special dinners. They warmed my life as the sun warms the earth, and the hurt in my heart began to ease.

And then there was Everett. Perhaps summer had arrived.

He was a logger with twinkling blue eyes, a winsome smile, and one of the smoothest male voices I'd heard. He had his own trailer, unusual for single men who worked at camp, and he became a good friend—and more.

After Don died, he was living and working at camp. Once, Everett helped me out—I don't remember what he did, maybe shoveling a path for me or bringing my mail. I do remember writing a thank-you note and taping it on his door. Perhaps he found it when he finished work that day. We started talking, and he wrote me notes. I wrote him back. We began to leave notes for one another as well as to talk to each other when we met on the walkways. Our relationship began to develop, and we dated. I would invite him to dinner, and he took me for walks.

I remember the first time, when Everett took me out to where the road ended. With only a little snow remaining on the road, I had worn my XtraTufs and brought my camera. We started walking over a muskeg area, I stepping carefully in his footprints, staring at the ground. We walked along natural paths—forgotten were words. We moved uphill, the snow covering more and more of the ground.

Every now and then, he'd mutter, "You still there?"

He stopped once to get his bearings, maybe to look for the easiest way to proceed. And I stopped too. My feet then shot out from under me, and I plopped down right into the snow, my legs sticking straight out ahead of me and between the two of his, my face looking at his butt.

"Excuse me," I reddened.

He turned and grinned. I think I was hooked then.

We kept walking, and every now and then, he'd point something out. "Look, there's camp."

"Do you see that tree? It's gonna die."

"Look, there's camp again," as we continued higher along the ridge.

Uphill we trod until finally he stopped again. So did I. He turned and looked at me with a wondering smile—quizzical. So I stopped and looked around, entranced. In front of me was a huge, brown, rocky mountain, majestically rising to a peak, covered with white snowy spots. How can I describe the silence, the reverence? My eyes teared up, and I looked at him without words, grateful for this beauty he'd brought me.

"You oughta look up more often," he said.

He took my picture there, at the foot of that mountain, and it was the first that I made into Christmas cards—letting those folks on my list know that I was alive and well, even without Don.

We moved on to find a snow-covered natural log bench, which he wiped off and covered with a silver plastic blanket. Gesturing for me to sit down, he dug deeper into his backpack and brought out some cold fried chicken wrapped in foil. He sat next to me and handed me a piece. We sat together, munching and swallowing, savoring the snack. It was a quiet companionable time.

Then we wandered down the hill a way, and he laid the blanket on the ground against a tree, and he plopped himself onto that blanket, halfway sitting up, and shut his eyes. I quietly retrieved the camera from my backpack and snapped his picture. I thought I'd caught him, but the photo shows him looking at me with one eye, eyebrow raised in question. It was always hard to sneak up on him, to surprise him. The woods had been a good teacher, I think, and many of its surprises were dangerous.

It felt good—the attention and gentle humor afforded me by this man. As our relationship deepened, and we spent more time together, a ritual developed. I would be working late at school, checking papers and planning for the next day, and I'd look across the float to my trailer and catch sight of smoke rising from the chimney. Everett had lit a fire in the wanigan's little red wood stove preparing for the evening's conversation. We'd share a meal and then retire to the two lawn chairs, wine glasses in hand, light up our after-dinner cigarettes, share a bench for a footstool, and talk.

A happy day climbing with Everett

Everett once recalled when he was winter watching for another logging camp in this very wanigan and became snowed in, how the little wood stove, constantly tended and stoked, kept him warm throughout the cold spell. He put a pot atop the stove—vegetables and meat—and, whenever he was hungry, would scoop out some of this hot stew. He really knew how to feed wood to that stove, to maintain both the fire and a constant temperature.

Those nights were cozy, comfortable, intimate. They happened quite often for a while.

We kept each other company for a couple of years until the camp and I moved, and he stayed behind. When we were underway, I watched his float become smaller and smaller, and I wondered when I'd see him again.

It was about a month later when I made a weekend trip back to Polk Inlet to visit. Everett had stayed behind to clean up the camp's leftovers. There were many—machines that didn't work, stored parts, and other throwaways that littered the landscape. It was a short trip by floatplane from Dora Bay, just over some mountains and down again into Polk Inlet. No need to follow the coast in the water the whole way as we'd done moving the camp.

We had a good time. The weather cooperated and allowed us outside. We walked to some beaver ponds, hoping to see waterfowl. All we did was scare some geese off their nest and had to listen to them honk and try to steer us away from their eggs. Everett knew the signs in the woods, and if there had been more, we would have seen more. However, we did find this family-to-be, and that was enough.

We ate well—Everett was a good cook. Probably we had steak and baked potatoes in the evening, one of his specialties, with a glass of wine from the bottle he'd ordered especially because I was coming. He always had a glass of wine for me. The next morning, he brought me a bowl of oatmeal filled with sweet and spicy apple chips. With whole milk, not skim, poured over it, it was a royal treat. I relished not having to make meals and was grateful and touched that he'd been so thoughtful.

And we talked.

He wasn't enjoying the job he'd been assigned, and he didn't know what he'd do after it was finished. Our conversations were interrupted by the generator breaking down, which he had to fix when it broke, an unexpected arrival of a tugboat that he had to attend to, and a couple of women visiting from another logging site. According to him, who was not a particularly trusting soul, the woman and her husband had come earlier, perhaps to "case the joint," and then when the wife returned that day with another woman in tow, he wondered if maybe she thought the "lonely old grouch who's watchguarding the place might like some company." He chuckled, watching for my reaction. He didn't get much.

Once again in the warm companionship we had shared in Polk Inlet, the two days passed quickly.

When the plane arrived, I left and again watched him grow smaller, standing on the float, waving at the plane. Then he turned and walked away.

Eventually, he quit working for the company, moved south, and our relationship ended.

Again, I was alone. I sought solitude in the wanigan where I could look out the window at the rocky shoreline, the trees and grasses meeting the high tide line, and wonder what I was doing. When the evenings grew light and I had no company, I'd often take my glass of wine into the wanigan, sit in a lawn chair, put my feet up on the old wooden bench, and light a cigarette. I'd think about my future, or maybe my past, and stare out the window.

I became friends with a blue heron that hunted from the rider log just beside my float. He walked so carefully with his ungainly stride, his head bobbing back and forth. His eyes never left the water beneath his path, so intent was he on finding his next meal. When suddenly his head flew down, I'd wait and watch to see what he'd grabbed. Often only water droplets fell from his beak, but every now and again, a small silvery fish dangled from his grip.

I wondered if he and I were alike. Was I making my ungainly way toward something that would sustain me? I hoped I was. How many times would I reach down to grasp a piece of life and come up empty-handed? Would the results be worth the effort? I believed so.

But then I grappled with another idea. The heron knew what gave him life—those creatures in the water he sought to find. How about me? Did I even know what it was I wanted? I wanted to do good. I wanted to be needed. I wanted to become someone I'd like without my husband. I needed to grow single, and I was on my way.

The Children and My Gifts

Teaching and living in this community of loggers provided what I needed. First came the children. My heart sang as I thought of my students. I loved working with them, the challenges they often presented, and the rewards they gave in unexpected ways. They were "my kids." And they made me proud.

Melissa was a sophomore/junior when she arrived in camp. Struggling with her parents in Washington State, soon to be assigned to foster care, she came to live with her Uncle Milo and Aunt Susan at her aunt's request. Melissa was uncertain and frightened, I'm sure. However, one would never know it for she arrived armed with a bravado that any actress would envy. She smiled, she condescended, she instructed, she acted every inch the queen of her realm, a bright and knowledgeable young woman with dark hair and flashing eyes, a quick grin, and an unending vocabulary. Since she was the oldest in the school, the subjects to be taught in the high school would be determined by what she needed.

Evan and Cindy were mere freshmen, and their list of graduation requirements had not yet been started. These three students made up the high school class, and although a few others entered and then left after a month or two of enrollment, Melissa, Cindy, and Evan learned English, American history, algebra, and biology together.

Sheri and me with our kids

These core classes I taught, spending my weekends reading their textbooks so I could be helpful to them during their weekly classes. Not only was Melissa the oldest student, but she was also the most demanding—of herself and, although tacitly, of me. It was a good thing that Evan and Cindy were also bright students, for we needed all the brainpower we could get.

Although I was well trained and intelligent, I was never an expert in any one academic field. I had to read and study as much as the high school students did. I was more confident when I taught subjects I had enjoyed in high school and taken in college, but even there, surprises occurred. Biology was a science I thought I could teach well, and I enjoyed ordering the cows' eyes, starfish, perch, and frogs to use for dissection. However, when I had learned concepts in biology, DNA had not yet been discovered. When we began reading about the double helix and the way DNA worked, Melissa (and Evan and Cindy) needed more clarification to understand it. I didn't understand it either, and although I tried to find somebody else within the district to help us,

I couldn't. After a couple of weeks, I told the students that we'd have to move on. But they did identify a lot of body parts and understood how they worked, even though the construction of the double helix remained a mystery.

They studied Shakespeare, read some British and American poetry, and learned about Revolutionary and Civil War history and whatever else their textbooks covered.

As the four of us sat on the beanbags in the upstairs room and tried to decipher the meaning of a poem or the context in which a war was begun, I became a student too, and they were very good teachers. The discourses we shared I still consider to be a great gift as we learned together, enriching our education in a way that I've encountered nowhere else.

That particular high school class was special, and Melissa was its leader. Having come from "down south" and having attended a "real" high school, she knew about extracurricular activities. "What do you do after school?" she'd ask. "Do you have a school newspaper? Do you have a student government?" We didn't. But we soon did.

She enlisted the support of Evan and Cindy, and the three of them coaxed Lacey, our seventh-grader, to also participate. They needed four officers for the government: president, vice president, secretary, and treasurer, and the four of them made up the junior-senior high school. I think Melissa was the president, although she may have talked Evan into it. She was always persuasive. The student government, as I recall, caused me to add two practices to the school undertakings. One was the bestowing of awards: at each seasonal program, students were awarded pins for perfect attendance and for other activities.

Many of these activities were created by the students, such as Spirit Week. In addition to the fun it generated during the day, it also created voting opportunities for the students. They offered suggestions and determined our dress and focus for each day during that week. However, each day also came with a special game to play.

It was as exciting to decide which games to play as it was to participate. The older kids were each assigned a day to plan the games, beginning with the oldest student and going down the line for the next four in order, and they decided what we'd play. The Jell-O Slurp was the favorite. The oldest student (once Melissa, another time Evan) always chose to be in charge of providing the Jell-O slurp materials. One day of every Spirit Week saw a student come to school with straws and two pans of Jell-O of an identical flavor. The first year we'd held the slurp, the losers complained that the green Jell-O was slower to slurp than the red of their opponents. Since then, both pans were always filled with red Jell-O. I remember Melissa's last Jell-O Slurp—her final comment after her team had won the race and she was gathering up the dirty straws and pans: "I won't have to slurp Jell-O anymore." I wonder if she ever misses it.

The other children could choose whatever group game they wanted to play on their assigned day. Other activities included musical chairs (no, the big kids didn't always win) and various relays. Some were old favorites, such as wheelbarrow races, "pass the orange under your chin," and "push the peanut with your nose." But some were new to me, and I was impressed with the organizer's creativity. My favorite was "put Vaseline on your nose, pick up some cotton balls from the floor, crawl to the line across the room, and shake your head to deposit the cotton balls and then run back and tag the next person in line."

Another student made triangular chips from orange paper and put them in a bowl. The relay teams, using straws, had to suck up a chip, transport it (still stuck to the straw) to another bowl, and then release the chip from their straw into the bowl. No hands could be used, so if a chip inadvertently fell, students bent over, sucked it back to their straws, and proceeded along. Considering the student in charge had to provide the materials needed, I gave some students extra special praise for a job well done. However, they all received my thanks for their hard work making sure their Spirit Week game was appreciated by their classmates.

Besides introducing us to Spirit Week and awards for extracurricular work, Melissa offered us a model for treating the younger students. She was always ready to hold a hand, to listen to a need, to bandage an "owie." I think the younger children benefit in many ways from a multigrade classroom, but often the older children tend to ignore them. Melissa didn't, and then neither did Evan or Cindy or Lacey. Melissa's imprint stayed with the school as long as I was there.

Personally, I found myself growing to admire Melissa more and more. She had taken a situation over which she had no control, being sent to a foreign outpost practically, and made the best of it. Indeed, she seemed to thrive there. She began to share in conversations some of her hopes and dreams, and we talked about the worlds she could inhabit with an education after high school. She worked hard and received her diploma after only two years at Polk Inlet School.

Melissa embodied the person I hoped to help most—that young woman with great potential who lived in a logging camp where most females earned money by cleaning, cooking, and mothering. I hoped to be an example of what a woman could become with education. Although I chose to be in the camp situation, I wanted the girls there to think of other worlds that could open to them if they went to school to gain the skills they'd need. I didn't want them to immediately settle down and raise a family.

Another young woman I reached out to was Cindy. Maggie's daughter and two years younger than Melissa, Cindy had been living in Polk Inlet since I had arrived, and so I sort of grew up with her. Except for one year when she attended school south, she was a student of mine. A beautiful yet modest girl, she was soft spoken when she answered questions in class. Speaking in her low and quiet voice during our programs, though, she was often difficult to understand. When she walked out on stage, she'd ruffle her paper, look down at the words, take a quick peek at the audience, and then begin to read. Fast and soft. A poem nobody could understand—but one she wanted badly to share. This shortcoming was almost unnoticeable among her many talents, but I tried to help.

With a quick wit, she often found connections to subject matter that made us all laugh. And she wrote—poetry and stories, her mind was never idle. She loved drawing, too, and created some beautiful masterpieces. I do believe she was one of the most creative people in that school. And I wasn't the only one who appreciated her. Evan did, too.

Evan had come to camp from Oregon when he (and Cindy) was in sixth grade, and I got to watch him grow. An almost chubby, freckle-faced kid on his arrival, he reached well over six feet tall when he graduated. Always polite and gentle, he was a good role model for the rest of the school. And he was ever so helpful to me. If we needed a Christmas tree, we asked Evan to get one. If we needed help with some mechanical problem, Evan usually knew how to fix it. He was smart—not only with practical knowledge but also academically.

These three students comprised an intelligent and lively high school student body, and as I've noted before, my teaching methods reflected the respect I held for their ideas. I was so grateful that the students were understanding, self-motivated, and intelligent. We had no drug problems, no discipline problems, no major problems to speak of, but something did happen that surprised me, something I wasn't sure how to handle.

After Melissa had graduated and Cindy and Evan became seniors, I watched them fall in love. They were innocent and naïve. I felt as if I were interrupting something when I'd come across them looking out the window between classes, Evan's arm around Cindy's waist, or when one of the computer keyboarding programs died and I found Evan fixing it, but his arm also was across her legs. Was this inappropriate behavior? I wondered.

I finally said something one day when they were watching their German from Oklahoma, first period in the morning. Usually I sat in with them to begin the class but would often leave them alone to continue watching the lesson while I went somewhere else within the school to prepare for the day with all the students or to talk to somebody who had unexpectedly arrived. On this particular day, I had left their German class for whatever reason, and when I returned Cindy had moved to nestle within the crook of Evan's arm, his hand reaching over her shoulder and playing with her hair. She was rubbing her hand along his thigh as I opened the door.

"What are you doing?" I asked.

They looked at me … quizzically.

This is not right, I explained to them. Since this was a public school room, they were creating a public display of affection. That was not acceptable in this building. Well, that didn't really solve the problem. Cindy and Evan had fallen in love, it was springtime, they were about to graduate, and it seemed their previously tractable selves had morphed into something else. With Sheri's help, and our constant nagging whenever we thought they were too close, we made it through that senior year, and Cindy and Evan finally graduated.

Those kids, all of them, created memories for me in their own ways. I think I grew along with the high school kids—I into a high school teacher and they into adulthood—and that's why I remember what we did with more clarity and such fondness. The elementary students were special, too, providing their wonder, trust, and efforts to succeed with what I asked them to do.

Rewarded daily by these students, I was being fulfilled as a teacher.

I received rewards in unexpected places, too. One gift was Katie's "logger."

Katie, a third grade student, was at my house one evening, sitting with me as I poured all the fabric scraps I'd brought to camp onto the table. Planning to teach an art lesson utilizing these scraps, I ensured I had what I needed.

She asked, "Can I make something?"

"Sure, go ahead," I said.

Her parents had recently divorced, her mom had moved to Wrangell with her two sisters, and Katie stayed in camp to live with her dad. I continued my sorting, thinking, jotting down ideas, stopping only when Katie asked for a marker. I found one and went back to my task.

The scissors clipped away, Katie having found several pieces of fabric she liked. She had taken the stapler off the nearby counter and worked on her project, eyes focused downward, tongue slightly stuck out between her closed lips, concentrating and intent.

All finished, she prepared to leave and stood up. "I made this for you." She handed me a delicate doll, stuffed with snipped fabric and stapled crudely together. His head and arms were fashioned out of white corduroy, his facial features and curly hair carefully marked with the skinny marker I'd given her. His brown boots, red plaid shirt, and blue pants completed his outfit.

"Oh, Katie, thank you so much." I smiled as I helped her into her coat and opened the door for her to leave.

I set the logger down on my coffee table and forgot about him.

A few days later, Linda Packet, the school speech therapist, flew in for a visit. She noticed the fragile figure and asked about it. When I told her the story, she, who knew Katie said, "Biz, this is a real keeper." And so I had it framed.

To this day, when I look at it on my wall, I remember Katie and our time together that evening and how important the activity was for this little girl going through a very difficult time.

It is next to another treasure, this one from Bret. When he was in second grade, he took up cross stitching at home and carefully stitched an apple and two hearts above the quotation, "Teachers Have Class." There's another apple under the quote as well.

Another gift came from Craig. It was a Saturday in camp, and that meant I'd cleaned the trailer in the morning and spent the afternoon at school. Late in the day, somebody knocked on my door. I set my wine down and shuffled to the front door. Opening it up, I was surprised to see Craig. Even more unexpected than his presence was what he held in his hand. Two fish. He extended them out to me.

"Darrel and I went fishing, and we got lots of trout. Darrel thought you might like some, so here." He pushed them in my direction. "Here," he repeated. He wore a half smile as I took them.

"Thank you." I closed the door, and he skipped off down the walkway.

I had a pretty special dinner that evening to go with my wine.

Telitha surprised me, too. Every November, I'd take out the projects I'd purchased the previous spring to give to the children for their arts-and-crafts time, projects they could give away to parents or grandparents for Christmas gifts. This year's napkin-holder project was fairly big (at least expense-wise when it was purchased) for it called for three cut pieces of plywood (a base, a strip, and a bear's head), two dowels, and paint. The students painted features on the bear's head and then glued it to the strip of wood. Two dowels were inserted into the base, and holes on the ends of the strip made a cross piece, between which napkins could sit. The one she made, Telitha gave to me.

As the itinerant teachers had brought me spring, these children were bringing me summer. I found that they could pour sunshine into my life, just by doing what they did.

Homemade valentines often tugged at my heart. Every year, we made valentines. We also made envelopes from two nine-by-twelve-inch pieces of construction paper and taped them to our desks so that the valentines could be delivered. Whenever coursework was complete those first weeks of February, children carefully cut and pasted hearts and flowers onto mostly red, white, and pink construction-paper cards. On Valentine's Day, then, we'd open our cards and feel loved and appreciated. At least I did.

From Cindy: "Some people ask for smart biology teachers, or quick algebra teachers. Or perhaps a witty music teacher, but with you I've got all of them and more."

Wow! She captured what I tried to be, and I was thankful that at least, in her eyes, I was successful. Cindy knew how hard I worked and that I expected them to work hard as well. More than once, she thanked me. Once she wrote, "Thanks for always pushing us that little bit to get us to do our best." By telling me that, she pushed me further, too, so that she received my very best.

From Melissa in calligraphy, the outside of the card said, "Thank you for helping to lovingly heal my ..." and inside, "broken heart."

I can't remember from which relationship she healed, for she was bright and beautiful, and the young loggers in camp found her attractive. I think she had two or three special attractions while she was there, and I was privileged and honored to hear about them. Melissa and I shared a lot of our thoughts and feelings.

From Sheri's older son, Evan: "Happy Valentines Day." The cover of the card said way more to me than the sentiment inside for Evan knew one of my favorite flowers was the lily of the valley, and the artwork he did showed it. White bell-shaped flowers graced the center while many thin, green, carefully cut and cleanly pasted leaves framed the dainty petals. Evan always preferred working with his hands to wording with his head. (A card a couple of years earlier said, "Roses are red, violets are blue, I'm no poet, and I think you noet.") He was one really neat young man.

From Lacey:

There are red hearts,
White hearts,
Pink hearts,
Sparkly hearts.
But none of the hearts
Are as nice as your heart.

Lacey was the quiet oldest sister in Katie's family. Conscientious in her work habits and barely able to be heard when she had something to say, Lacey grew in confidence during her stay in camp. When she was recruited by Melissa, Evan, and Cindy to be part of their secondary social club, she appreciated the company, and it gave her self-confidence. I remember one snowy afternoon when she stopped by the school and I was working. "Do you want to go for a walk?" she asked. Of course I did, and it was another gift—time with Lacey to listen, to actually hear what she was saying because she was speaking loudly and with assertion, and to respond. It was fun watching her grow.

From third-grade Crystal:

Roses are red
Violets are blue
You are sweet
Stay that way too.

I didn't know Crystal as well as some of the other kids for Sheri taught most of her classes and our paths didn't cross for much more than a year. However, I did know that she was an optimistic, smiling little girl, quick to try to please. Her good nature and kind words were trademarks that I remember.

From Bret:

Mountains are tall, hills are small,

I couldn't put down on this Valentine,
Half of what you taught me at all.

Bret, Evan's younger brother, took to learning in that multigrade setting like nobody I'd seen. Even as a second grader, he'd work to get his own assignments completed during class, but his ears were always attuned to the lessons going on with the older students, and one just knew that he was filing the information away. He was a good reader, an exceptional math student, and he also was good to his classmates, helping them when they needed it and mostly ignoring the behavior that wasn't appropriate. He had a streak of playfulness, though, and sometimes would pipe up with comments that would crack us all up. Then Sheri would give her young son an evil eye, and he'd look suitably abashed, but we all knew he would rise to the next occasion that demanded his wit. He knew that a lot of learning took place in Polk Inlet School.

From Bri:

Bee my valentine. You are a very good teacher.

Bri wrote this on a nine-by-twelve piece of pink paper on which a large doily was glued. In the middle of the doily, a large bumble bee was surrounded by grape clusters, carefully colored and thoughtfully done. Little "buzz" words in the corners remind me of Bri's attention to detail. She worked hard, being in the same grade as Bret and not being as mathematically inclined. A good student and a beautiful girl, she and her sister were either helicoptered or boated from about a mile away on the other side of Dora Bay. Bri was a hit when she arrived in fifth grade, especially amidst the adolescent boys. It was fun to watch Ron, Nate, Bret, and Craig vie for her attention. She was good at smiling, bestowing good wishes on all of them equally, and I admired her calm manner and casual acceptance of her popularity. She and I grew closer as the years followed.

Craig, who had a dog named Toby and of course knew about Bret's dog, Tweekie, wrote:

Toby is black
Tweekie is too
I bet you like
Venison stew.
Happy Valentine's Day.

Craig, Cindy's dark-haired, sparkly eyed little brother, found it difficult to sit still. He had a quick mind, but his body seemed to need to move all the time, interrupting his concentration. He had a hard time working in class and completing his assignments and usually took homework with him every evening. This rhyme is special because not only did he take the time to think of it, but it's also neatly penned beside a carefully sketched pot of stew inside a purple card. I know this was hard for Craig to do.

From Michael, written in beautiful cursive:

Mrs. Robbins I like you.
Love Michael Olson

A red heart with a fun face, big eyes, little nose, and big smiley mouth filled with teeth is glued in the middle of a white doily on this card from one of the most accomplished students in the class. When Michael arrived to Polk Inlet School, he was of fourth-grade age but didn't have any of the academic or social skills of kids his age. He didn't have many skills at all. So we all worked with him. Evvy, Sheri, and I got together to determine a program for him and went right to work with it. We talked with the kids about how they could help Michael, and they did. I was so proud of them all for, rather than make fun of him and his outbursts and his lack of knowledge, they helped him. They offered to work with him. They ignored his bad behavior and complimented his good. Together, we all helped Michael make progress. When he wrote this valentine, he had been with us since the previous September. What fun to watch his growth.

He lived about five miles away with his grandparents, and his older brother, Ron, who was then in eighth grade, brought them both to school every day. Ron drove a beautifully made wood skiff, and Michael sat in the bow, both boys dressed in their Helly Hansen raingear and life jackets. When we gave our programs, Michael's father, who was a fisherman, and grandparents (Granddad was a boatbuilder) attended. Afterward, after Michael had played his recorder solo, had read his poem, and had acted in the play, his grandmother would tell me: "You don't know how bad my ears hurt when I listened to him practice." But listen and encourage she did. And Michael became a star.

From Telitha:

Roses are red
Lemons are sour,
You smell like
A daisy flower.

This verse on a small yellow heart with holes punched around the side show Telitha's creative bent. She wove lilac yarn into the holes along the side, framing the verse with a neat border. Marilyn's and Richard's oldest, Telitha grew into accepting the restraint she needed to work within the school setting. She shone when asked to do some creative writing and when playing her recorder. Her musical abilities had her playing with a trio of older students toward the end of my tenure, and they appreciated her talents.

From Telitha's brother Josh:

Happy Valentines Day
Mice eat rice,
I eat meat,
But your pretty neat.

This verse, carefully written in the middle of a yellow circle, is like the sunshine the card is supposed to represent. Spokes out from the circle highlight the name "Josh" as it is written on each one. A perfectionist, Josh worked hard to get his schoolwork done right and on time. However, one of my strongest memories of this little boy was watching each morning to see what he'd find on his way to school. He looked for small squid that had either jumped onto the boardwalk or were within easy reach alongside, and he'd pick one or two up, bring them to school, and set them on the window ledge of the coatroom, taking them home with him at lunch. "Good bait," he told me when I asked. He was going to follow in his father's fishing footsteps.

Those valentines, as well as ones I haven't shared, combined not only sentiment but also the effort of making rhymes and the cards themselves. They were some of the most thoughtful gifts my students gave me, and they reminded me that I was special. I didn't need a husband or anybody else in their eyes to merit the lovely wishes I received.

Adults, like me, who worked in the schools were expected to make cards for the kids, but they also gifted me.

From Maggie:

Teachers are neat
Teachers are cool
Just think of all the friends you meet
Because of school.

Maggie, Cindy and Craig's mom, taught kindergarten the last year I was there. She found out how rewarding it is to work within the framework of a place that wanted students to succeed and help them to do it.

From Marilyn:

Roses are Red,
Violets are Blue,
It is truly Wonderful,
To have a friend like you.

This, written in slanted calligraphy, reminded me of all the times Marilyn (Josh and Telitha's mom) and I were together. It may have begun with the calligraphy class I taught. Among others, Marilyn came.

She often was called to substitute at the last minute. Whenever I was stranded in Ketchikan because of weather, Marilyn would cheerfully come to cover the classroom with Sheri. Of course, it helped that I had promised to bring them hazelnut lattes from the barista in the air taxi's waiting room.

She came to listen to the kids read, she supported the school in whatever ways we asked, and she had a quick wit besides. We always knew we were going to laugh when Marilyn was around. This was especially fun when she, Sheri, and I walked after school. On the first day, she told me how she was pigeon-toed and seemed always to walk to the left, so she needed the right side of the trail. When we turned around, she needed to get on the other side so she wouldn't walk herself off the trail and down the mountain. We also talked about many of the adult problems that we faced and what we could do about them. Her remarks were witty and wise, and I felt wonderful having a friend like her.

From Sheri:

Dear Biz,
I've run out of rhymes and all the fun things to say.
So I guess I'll just wish you the very Happiest Valentines Day.

Outgoing and optimistic, Sheri was my right- and left-hand man at camp. She supported me at school by doing everything I'd planned for her to do, by asking questions when she didn't understand the content, by staying late and arriving early, by taking an active part, not only in her sons' education but also in the education of everyone else there. She helped me plan; she became the expert with the little kids as I learned the high school curriculum and taught the intermediate and junior high lessons. We grew into an excellent team. She even took a correspondence class with me when she learned that I needed somebody to discuss the concepts with. Never mind that the college offering the class wouldn't accept the comments of an aide, I was thankful to have Sheri with me, learning alongside, incorporating techniques we studied into our classroom.

She became my confidante, my first friend there. She happily took the reins whenever I was weathered in town; she even shooed me out of camp on occasion. "C'mon. You know you want to go to that concert (or play or program, or just get out). Leave!" I left, knowing all would be in good hands.

She tended to my needs at the homesite as well as the school. As the side rod's wife, she had access to his ear and his power, and she could usually get action whenever it was needed. In addition, her general friendliness toward everyone made people willing to do what she asked. As Evan's mom, she would get him to do things for me. More propane. Another light bulb. Reset the furnace. She was whom I went to after I learned that Darrel and the school district would give me the run around when mechanical things went wrong.

In a way, she was my husband's replacement. Whenever I ran into troubles, either at home or at school, Sheri found a way to make life better. I wonder today if that was why I fared so well there, that she actually provided a smooth path by riding interference. It probably was, but she was giving me summer, lessening the loss I'd had in this man's world of a logging camp.

She worked and played with me. I purchased two pairs of cross-country skis to use out there, thinking that Everett and I would use them. We never did, and when he left my life, they were still standing in a corner of the wanigan. One snowy day, I asked Sheri, "Do you want to go skiing?" She never had been cross-country skiing, either, so we were a perfectly matched set. Probably of idiots. We shouldered the skis and made our way up the ramp to the sorting yard. We thought a flat area would be a good place to start.

It was. We strapped the skis onto the boots and began poling our way in a big circle around the rim of the yard. Snowflakes, big and fluffy, filled the sky and covered the ground as we learned the feel of the skis to our bodies.

"This is fun," one of us shouted.

"Yes, but it's getting easy. Do you want to go up the hill?"

Our confident brave selves began to work our way up the logging road, trying to walk in that sort of ducky way that skiers use when they climb. Getting to the top of the first rise, we turned around, and Sheri headed down the hill. "Whee!" she cried as she surged forward and finally came to a stop on the landing. My turn came next.

Gingerly I pushed off, I who had never gone past the snowplow in my five years of downhill skiing, and began to speed into her ruts. I tried to slow down, putting my feet back into the snowplow formation that I remembered, and plop. I was down, and my skis didn't detach from the boots as I'd expected them to do. "Do you need help?" Sheri hollered from the bottom.

"I don't think so," I mumbled as I tried to get my pole into the uphill side of the snow and push myself upright. I tried and tried, but I just couldn't do it.

"I can't get up," I wailed down the hill, and Sheri moved to climb back up. She wiggled her way into position to give me a hand, praying that she wouldn't fall too, and managed to help me up. Slowly I headed down the hill, all tired out and not wanting a second try. Sheri agreed.

We undid the skis, walked back down to the camp, and put the skis and boots back into my wanigan. "I hope it snows again soon," Sheri commented. It never did that year. At least we never got the skis out again, and I was grateful she came with me that one time. It was a gift I still appreciate.

These gifts warmed my heart, especially when I realized I wasn't really expected to reciprocate. Folks were giving of themselves, freely providing me with love and warmth, spring and summer seasons to me.

Gifts of dinner out were appreciated, too. Some carry special memories.

Celebrating the first king salmon of the season was important to Richard. When he caught it, he stopped by the school to invite me to his home that evening, planning to grill the first catch of the kings. Marilyn prepared a Caesar salad and rhubarb-raspberry cobbler, the others who'd been invited were fun to be with, and I left not only full of food but also full of fellowship.

Richard and Marilyn didn't need a special occasion to arise before inviting me to their house for dinner. Their house was the restaurant at which I most often went out to eat—and the salmon, Caesar salad, and dessert were their specialty.

Sheri's "restaurant" was more like a pizza place. Occasionally, she'd invite me to her home on a Friday night and have her own special brand of pizza: home-made crust, lots of toppings, more cheese, a pizza so high it looked more like a casserole. Her husband and boys would sit with her and me at the table and "mmm" through each bite. The beer she gave me to accompany the pizza was something I didn't get every day, either. I relished those meals at the Bonines, but only once or twice returned the favor.

In fact, the people who most often ate at my table at camp were, apart from Everett, not from camp—Elaine and the itinerants. Eventually, though, I got to pay Sheri and Marilyn back when I moved to town.

***

As time passed and the pain of Don's death and my aloneness subsided, I found that I wanted more from life than teaching. At this camp, I was a teacher first, and then I was a friend and fellow citizen. I felt I was missing something.

I needed a place to find ways to develop my social and spiritual wellbeing, and Ketchikan was that place. Flying in every other weekend became a habit I enjoyed.

First of all, my condo in town had a dependable phone line. (I'd sold the dome two years after Don died because I didn't have the necessary maintenance skills and it was falling apart. Leaving it vacant in Ketchikan's weather while I taught caused leaks and rot that I couldn't repair myself.) Friday night, after I'd gone to the grocery store and settled myself in with a salad, I'd call relatives. Minnesota was three hours later, so the folks there were first. Then came the cousin in Colorado, only two hours later. Finally I could call my friends in Ketchikan to see if we could make plans to do something together Saturday night.

Saturday night in Ketchikan was a big event in my logging-camp lifestyle. Friends and I could attend the Monthly Grind (a local talent show offered once a month from September through May), a movie, a play, a concert, a high school basketball game, or a wrestling match.

If all else failed, eating out was a treat to me. (At camp, the closest one could get to the latter was to either be invited to someone's house to eat, thank you Sheri and Marilyn, or to knock on someone's door and see if they had anything that they were cooking to spare.) Various Ketchikan restaurants offered Mexican, Filipino, American, Italian, Chinese, and Thai food, and I tried every one. It was also a treat for me if, after dinner, all I did was sit in my living room to watch cable TV before going to bed.

After a good night's sleep, I'd rise to prepare for my spiritual growth. First Lutheran Church saw my smiling face every Sunday I was in Ketchikan. I stayed for the service and coffee hour and fellowship before hurrying home to call Taquan and check on my return flight.

If it was not raining, I'd walk the three miles to Taquan's office. If it was, a friend would take me down. Either way, once I boarded the plane and began my trip back across Clarence Strait, I gave thanks for once again participating in activities that allowed me to grow in spirit, to replenish the silent strength I needed to succeed during the next two weeks at camp.

I didn't realize it at the time, but I was building a support group for myself in Ketchikan. I think I knew in my heart long before I knew in my head that it was time for me to leave this protective setting that had been a safe haven for many years. All I knew was that the time I spent in town made me feel good, warm, and growing—as a spring and then a summer season might provide. Returning to camp began to feel like fall; perhaps everything I could offer there had been harvested.

After Melissa graduated and Cindy and Evan inched closer to the end of their high school years, I contemplated my future. What would life hold for me outside this camp? Was I brave enough to leave the place where people were so kind, where people treated me with respect and honesty, the last place I had lived with my husband and the first place without him? Would I find summer again? I didn't know, but I felt I had to try.

When Cindy and Evan became seniors, I gave serious thought to retirement. We had grown up together from sixth through twelfth grades, and so I figured we could graduate together. As they were planning for their guest speaker and decorations, I sorted through my household belongings and held a garage sale. They took their finals; I filled out paperwork for my state retirement income. We laughed and joked, worked and played; they, I think, were excited. I, I know, was scared.

How could I leave this place, this sanctuary of healing that I'd known after Don died? How could I not, though? I needed to try my wings, as Steve Dempsey's graduation speech for Cindy and Evan proclaimed. He said that they'd been provided roots in that very setting, and it was now their time to fly away. They were grounded in the goodness they'd known, and so was I. That thought was comforting.

So I did leave after graduation. Friends with a boat, called the *Bigenuff*, came to pack up what I didn't sell, and they brought it to Ketchikan and carted it up to my condo. When I arrived later, leaving camp on floatplane wings, I just had to unpack, settle in, and start my new life.

Epilogue - 2010

Once more I returned to Polk Inlet, this time with Sheri who had lived in the vibrant community with me. As we approached the inlet, Sheri began a commentary, as she and her husband had visited this spot a month earlier and figured out where things had been.

"The shop was here," Sheri noted as we drove by, "and here they dropped the logs into the water." She drove her pickup around a flat spot that bore traces of campers. A rock-bordered fire pit sat at the edge nearest the water, and a small stack of firewood was piled nearby.

"Here's where we parked our vehicles," she told me as we passed another flat area, this one thick with alders.

"What's that?" I asked as I noticed a white van parked across the road, a blue tarp serving as both a tent and an awning.

"That's Taquan's representative," Sheri told me. "The company offers the fish ladder here on its flight-seeing tours, and a plane brings the tourists, and they get off at the float. Then the guy in the van meets them and drives them to the viewing area."

"Viewing area?"

"Yes. There have been some changes since you were here last. We'll check them out on our way back to town," Sheri said.

Finally we reached the ramp leading down to the float. It was empty. As we walked down, she continued her memories.

"That little spit is where the brown trailer we lived in was. At low tide, I'd have sworn we'd hit the rocks, but we never did." I looked to my right and saw it there.

"Oh, and that grassy area to the left is where Everett's float was," she continued. "Do you remember how he fed that bear so he could watch it play in the grass?"

No, I didn't remember, but another thought rushed to mind. I smiled with its warmth. I had tiptoed over a float that separated Everett's from mine during our nighttime trysts.

We stopped, and as I snapped pictures, I again thought about the blessings I'd received from this community. "It was a good place to live," I commented.

"Yes, it was," Sheri agreed.

We left to visit Dog Salmon Creek and the fish ladder on our return to Craig where Sheri was now living. The road, now smooth and graveled, was used daily by the white van taking the tourists to visit. A graveled path led to some signs that illustrated the purpose of the ladder, as well as a fenced, flat wooden viewing area overlooking the structure. The ladder itself was the old structure, sort of concrete stairs to help the fish swim upstream, that I remembered.

Later that day, Sheri asked, "Why don't you write an epilogue?"

"Huh?"

"Yes, I've been thinking." She knew I was going to meet Bri and Evvy the next day in Ketchikan. "Your connection with these people didn't end when you left camp. In fact, many are still as important in your life as you are in theirs.

"Your readers might like to know what happened to them, too," she continued.

So …

Thanks to technology, cell phones, and the Internet with its email and social networks, and the fact that many of the camp people settled in or often visit Southeast Alaska, I have maintained contact.

Sheri now lives in Craig as she recently moved from Oregon to be with her husband. He logged in Southeast Alaska while she lived south, caring for other family members, until she had done all she could. They brought up a fifth wheel and reside in it, much like the trailer they lived in once at camp.

Her oldest son, Evan, married Cindy and began his own company. However, the economy forced the company to close, and he is now working at a logging camp further north, as a mechanic. Cindy and their two children live in Oregon and look forward to the times he comes home to visit.

The younger Bret is engaged to a lovely Irish lady with plans to marry in the near future. He's a technology wiz developing programs for a computer-security company.

Marilyn lives outside the town of Wrangell. The lovely cedar home that graced one end of the camp was moved onto land miles from the city's center, and Marilyn keeps the home fires burning. Richard has found work in the Gulf of Mexico, a tugboat captain, returning to Alaska every other month when he's off duty.

Telitha is married and lives in Idaho. She has two dogs, writes poetry, and has plans to return to school to finish an elementary education degree in the future.

Josh lives with his mom right now but had been a heavy-equipment operator in Massachusetts while his girlfriend attended school. When she finishes, the two of them will find somewhere in the Pacific Northwest to work and live. In the meantime, he works for an airline company, and whenever he can, he fishes, catching salmon, trout, halibut, and other bounty of the waters.

Evvy remarried, found jobs with the Ketchikan School District, retiring as its special ed. director. She and her husband now live in Denver, cheering for the Rockies, the Broncos, and the Avalanche. Sometimes she returns to Ketchikan to visit one of their girls who lives here.

Melissa is in California, newly married and happy. She carries a master's degree in some sort of social arena, and continues to be an outspoken proponent of equality—of the sexes, of race, of gender roles, of immigrants, of the weak and downtrodden and disenfranchised. Fighting social injustice, she seems fulfilled.

Bri lives in Anchorage after attending college in Ketchikan and Fairbanks. She is soon to graduate with a degree in natural resource management; she has worked several summers for Alaska Fish and Game in the Gulf of Alaska. Plans are for a New Year's Eve wedding with her geologist fiancé.

Bri and I met the day I returned from Prince of Wales Island. We talked in great seriousness about the sadness she once carried after leaving the logging camp, an overwhelming feeling that clouded everything she did. When she sought counseling, she learned she was grieving for her childhood; she, like me, had good memories of life on the water those many years ago. She told me she had to learn to let her childhood go.

I wondered then and am pondering now if I, too, have a grieving sadness that might color my present-day living, sadness for the disappearance of the time when I was younger, living in my safe, secure logging camp. I know that many who lived there remember with great fondness the good times, who long to go back to a simpler life, a younger self, "to a tiny little camp of the biggest people … resting in the palm of the Creator in some quiet bay or inlet … deep in memories and untouched by time." But we know that's not possible.

Perhaps writing this memoir is my way of letting go, releasing the sadness I feel for this now-lost way of life.

The walk to the school with Richard had filled me with a deep grief, but years later, my return with Sheri, stirred warm memories and an appreciation that we were allowed to share this experience with so many good people.

Many of them still remain in my life, and they have enriched, encouraged, enabled, and endured. I give thanks to my Creator for their presence.

Acknowledgements

The camp communities were such rich places to live. Communities became closely knit families, rejoicing in the good times and sorrowing in the bad, sharing what the fates bestowed. I was fortunate to experience the lifestyle when logging was still booming in Southeast Alaska. Thanks to all the kids, parents, teachers, and loggers who gave me their support and love when I most needed it.

My writers' group--such staunch encouragers and editors--Barbara Failing, Mike Harpold, Donna Hartley, Sharon Nobilio, Nicole Caple, and Sharon Monrean, helped me to persevere and to see this book to its conclusion. Thank you, guys.

What would I have done without the haranguing and help from Larry Luukkonen and Alvar Helmes? Thank you so much.

The perfect title came from Laurel Lindahl. Thank you for showing me how I used the float camp setting to survive and grow during this time of my life.

To Liz McKenzie, professor of English and teacher of the memoir-writing classes I took: thank you for offering them and for helping me find my voice.

The Book Publishers Network, especially Sheryn Hara and Julie Scandora, kept me on task with gentle persuasion and masterful leadership.

Finally, to all my family and friends who read this memoir in its various forms during the ten years of its development: thank you, thank you, thank you. You helped me craft and hone this piece that I have wanted to share for so long. I hope you delight in its final form.